Ritual and Religion among Muslims in India

Ritual and Religion among Muslims in India

Edited by
Imtiaz Ahmad

AAKAR

Ritual and Religion among Muslims in India
Edited by Imtiaz Ahmad

First Published 1981
First Aakar Edition 2019

ISBN 978-93-5002-601-4 (Hb)

Published by
AAKAR BOOKS
28 E Pocket IV, Mayur Vihar Phase I
Delhi 110 091, India
www.aakarbooks.com

Printed at
Sapra Brothers, Noida

In memory of
Professor Aziz Ahmad

Preface

This book is the third in a projected series of four volumes dealing with different aspects of Muslim social and cultural life in India. The first two volumes were concerned with a consideration of caste and social stratification, and family, kinship and marriage among Muslims in India. This volume is devoted to a study of ritual and religion among them.

Like their co-religionists elsewhere, the Muslims in India claim to be adherents of the Islamic faith. Islam is an extremely reified religious tradition, and its doctrines, precepts and practices are supposed to be universal. Even so, the corpus of the day-to-day beliefs and practices of the Muslims have been found to vary from place to place according to the circumstances in which they were converted to Islam, their pre-conversion orientations, and their historical experiences over time. Thus, while Muslims all over the world claim adherence to the principles and practices ordained by the scriptures, there is considerable divergence between the formal and the actual religious beliefs and practices of the Muslims in different parts of the world.

The essays presented in this volume explore the nature of the actual religious beliefs of the Muslims in India. Unlike Hinduism, Islam was intrusive in India. It arrived in the midst of an established civilization and gradually won over a large indigenous population to its fold. Because of its intrusive character and the recruitment to it of a large indigenous population which brought along previous religious beliefs and orientations into the faith upon conversion, the Islamic faith in India acquired a typically indigenous flavour. The essays in this volume explore this religious system typical of the Muslim communities in India.

The focus of these essays is on religion as it is practised

among Muslim communities rather than on the theological and philosophical principles and the accompanying social system as laid down by Islamic scriptures. Each paper presented here is based on data collected by the authors themselves through direct personal observations coupled with an analysis of existing source materials. Each paper is also concerned with the realities of religion and with actual religious behaviour rather than its ideology, its beliefs and hopes. The latter are dealt with only peripherally. It is hoped that these papers will contribute towards an understanding of the structure and processes of the religious beliefs and practices of the Muslims in India.

The procedure followed in putting togather this volume was the same as the one used for the previous volumes. Scholars who had worked on an aspect of religion from the viewpoint which inspires these papers were requested to contribute a paper based on their data. The choice of the aspect on which they were to write as well as the theoretical orientations were left to each contributor to decide. This flexibility with regard to the choice of theme, theoretical perspective, the methods of analysis, areas of emphasis and the nature and scope of data reported has turned out to be rewarding. It has allowed the contributors to capture the diversities that characterize ritual and religion among Muslims in India.

Five of the seven papers included in this volume were written specifically for this volume and are being published here for the first time. The papers by Professor Madan and Dr. Mines have appeared previously and are being reprinted here. Professor Madan's paper was originally published in *Contributions to Indian Sociology* (New Series). Dr. Mines' paper was presented at a workshop on Islam in Southern Asia at Heidelberg University and subsequently appeared in *Man*. I am grateful to Professor Madan and Dr. Mines and the editorial boards of *Contributions to Indian Sociology* (New Series) and *Man* for permission to reprint their papers in this volume.

This volume is once again an outcome of the cooperation and collaboration extended by the contributors. For their willing cooperation and sustained patience during the preparation of this volume for the press, I am deeply indebted to them.

I should add that whatever value this volume has is owed to them; at the same time, I must absolve them of any blame for its shortcomings which I reserve to myself alone.

Jawaharlal Nehru University Imtiaz Ahmad
New Delhi

Contents

The Contributors

IMTIAZ AHMAD received his training in anthropology and sociology at the Universities of Lucknow and Delhi. He was a Fulbright Fellow at the University of Chicago during 1967-68 and Visiting Assistant Professor in social anthropology at the University of Missouri during 1968-70. He is currently Associate Professor in sociology in the Centre for Political Studies at the Jawaharlal Nehru University, New Delhi. He has published papers in professional journals and symposia volomes and edited *Caste and Social Stratification among Muslims in India* and *Family, Kinship and Marriage among Muslims in India*.

LINA M. FRUZZETTI received her training in anthropology at the Universities of Chicago and Minnesota where she took her Ph.D. in 1975. She is currently Assistant Professor at Brown University. She has carried out extensive fieldwork among the Hindus and Muslims of rural Bengal. Dr. Fruzzetti's research interests include the study of kinship, rituals and religious symbolism. She has contributed papers to professional journals and symposia volumes.

KERRIN GRAEFIN V. SCHWERIN received her training in South Asian History at the University of Heidelberg, where she took her Ph.D. in 1971. She has held teaching assignments at the University of Heidelberg and Munich and currently teaches part-time at the South Asia Institute of the University of Heidelberg. She has carried out extended historical research in modern Indian History and the social and cultural life of Muslims during the modern period. Dr. Graeffin is the author of *Die Indischen Muslims and die Hindu-Urdu Kontroverse in der United Provinces* and has contributed papers to professional journals and symposia volumes.

PATRICIA JEFFERY received her training in social anthropology at the University of Bristol, where she took her Ph.D. in 1973. She is Research Fellow at the University of Edinburgh. Dr. Jeffery has carried out extensive fieldwork in India and Pakistan and among the Pakistani Muslim and Christian immigrants in the United Kingdom. She is the author of *Migrants and Refugees: Muslim and Christian Pakistani Families in Bristol* and *Frogs in a Well: Indian Women in Purdah* and contributed papers to professional journals and symposia volumes.

T.N. MADAN received his training in social anthropology at the University of Lucknow and the Australian National University where he took his Ph.D. in 1959. He has taught at several leading Indian, British and American universities and has been a Professor at the Institute of Economic Growth, New Delhi. He is currently Member-Secretary of the Indian Council of Social Science Resarch, New Delhi. He is the author of (with D.N. Majumdar) *An Introduction to Social Anthropology* and *Family and Kinship: A Study of the Pandits of Rural Kashmir* and has edited *Indian Anthropology* and (with Andre Beteille) *Encounter and Experience.*

BEATRIX PFLEIDERER received her training in anthropology at the Universities of Maryland (USA), Munich and Heidelberg where she obtained her Ph.D. in 1973. She was a Fellow of the Volkswagen Foundation at the South Asia Institute of the University of Heidelberg during 1973-76 and taught Ethnomedicine there during 1976-79. At present she is on a research grant of the German Research Association to carry out fieldwork in North India. Dr. Pfleiderer has carried out fieldwork in North Africa, among migrant workers in Germany, and in North India. Her major research interests are traditional healing and psychotherapy, culture-specific illness concepts and sickness behaviour. She is the author of *Socializations forschung in der Ethnologie, Tunesische Arbeitnehmer in Deutschland* and (with Bruni Ludwing) *Materialien zur Ethnomedizine* and has published papers in professional journals.

A. R. SAIYID received his training in sociology at the University of Bombay and at the University of Kentucky (USA), in der Ethiologic, Tunesische Arbeitnehmer in Deutschland where he took his Ph.D. in 1967. He has taught at Long Island University and is currently Reader in Sociology at the Jamia Milia Islamia, New Delhi. Dr. Saiyid's research interests are Muslim social structure, Islamic fundamentalism and religious change and modernization. He has contributed papers to academic journals and symposia valumes and is currently preparing a volume based on his research among Maharashtrian Muslims for publication.

Introduction

Imtiaz Ahmad

The study of Islam has traditionally been a province of the Islamicists and Muslim theologians. Sociologists and social anthropologists have paid comparatively little attention to its study. The reason for this academic division of labour is quite easily understandable. The fundamental theological and philosophical principles that can be said to constitute the core of the Islamic faith are enshrined in a single scriptural source[1] and are supposed to be universally adhered to by all those who call themselves Muslims. This reinforced the belief among the sociologists and social anthropologists that the Islamicists' understanding of the religious faith of the Muslims could be taken as wholly accurate and valid, especially as the sociologist or social anthropologist could in any case not match the Islamicists' expertize in handling textual materials.

No doubt the Islamicist's contribution to the study of Islam has been considerable. Through painstaking study of the textual sources and scriptural literature they have been successful in identifying and elucidating for us the fundamental Islamic precepts and rules which every Muslim is universally expected to adhere to. Unfortunately, however, the strictly and rigidly normative thrust of his approach has also prevented the appreciation of the bewildering diversity of beliefs, rituals and religious practices that underlies the faith in different parts of the world. It has also inhibited a satisfactory analysis of the response of

[1]It would be technical'y wrong to say that the Islamic *Shariah*, the Devine Law of Islam, is enshrined in a single scriptural source for the *Shariah* is in reality derived from four different sources and not just one single source. Even so, the Koran is the most basic of these sources.

the Islamic religious tradition[2] to different cultural situations and contexts and the adaptations and adjustments that it had to make in the course of its journey from its West Asian heartland to distant parts of the world.

Sociology and social anthropology are committed as academic disciplines to the empirical investigation of the social phenomenon. Where religion is concerned, they are concerned not so much with the theological and philosophical tenets of a particular religion but rather with the concrete form that those tenets take in the actual life of the people. Sociological or social anthropological analysis of religion thus takes the whole of a people's beliefs and practices towards the supernatural as well as the purposes to which they may put their faith in dealing with their daily worries and hopes (Mandelbaum, 1964: 5). Thus, the sociological or social anthropological understanding of religion is at once more comprehensive and more concrete.

This collection of papers on ritual and religion among Muslims in India was designed to bring together contributions by sociologists and social anthropologists so that we could form some idea of Islam in India as a practised faith rather than merely as a theological and philosophical system. Each contribution included here, except for the paper by Kerrin Graefin V. Schwerin which is based on historical source materials, is an outcome of fieldwork carried out by the authors themselves. Each contribution is also concerned with the realities of Islam as it is practised and with actual religious behaviour rather than with its theological and philosophical principles, though they have entered the analysis presented in some of the contributions. This makes them in a sense quite unique and distinct from the vast body of theological or historical literature available so for on Indian Islam.

It would be quite erroneous, and also absurd, to suggest

[2]One of the major short-comings of the work of the Islamicists was that it brought about what Srinivas et. ai. (1959) have in another context called a 'book view' of Muslim social structure and religion. A critique of this view as applicable to the work of the Sanskritists is contained in Srinivas et. al. (1959: 136). It has considerable relevance to an evaluation of the work of the Islamicists as well.

that the contributions presented here together provide anything close to a systematic or comprehensive coverage of Islam in India. We would require a far larger number of studies dealing with the different aspects of the ritual and religious life of the Muslims in different parts of the country than are included here before we can come anywhere close to a comprehensive and systematic coverage of all the facets of Islam in India. Even so, the contributions presented here do suggest certain broad conclusions and raise a number of questions for future research. Therefore, in this Introduction, I shall attempt to discuss some of those questions and summarize the generlizations which emerge from the contributions.

Let us, however, first take a brief look at the central concerns of the different contributions included in this volume. The papers by Madan and Mines are principally concerned with the role of religion as a basis of social identity in a religiously and culturally diverse situation as we encounter in India, although this question is also dealt with to some extent in the papers by Fruzzetti and Saiyid. Madan tries to demonstrate that religion is an important structural basis of identity articulation in the culturally plural social situation encountered in the Kashmir Valley. Hindus, represented by the single caste of Kashmiri Pandits, and Muslims, comprising a number of caste-like groupings, not only perpetually see themselves as members of distinct religious communities but also project their distinct social identities through a series of cultural symbols, including linguistic usage, dress, forms of salutation and other customs, etc. What Madan describes appears to me to be a specific feature of Hindu-Muslim interaction in the Kashmir Valley, owing itself perhaps to the absence of many Hindu castes in the region. If there existed many Hindu castes and Muslim social groupings, it it possible that the Muslims might perceive and interact with, as indeed they would have been seen and interacted with, by Hindu caste groups in terms of both their caste and religious identities. On some occasions, usually defined by context and situation, Hindus and Muslims might have seen each other as members of distinct communities and interacted with one another on that basis. On other occasions, they might see each other and interact in terms of caste identities. There is some indication that this might be so in the contributions by Fruzzetti and Saiyid as both of them show that in the rituals and festivals described by them the Muslims seek to assert their distinct religious identity and come together as members of a unified Muslim *umma*, but at other times they also operate as members of distinct Muslim castes or as members of distinct and separate Muslim neighbourhoods. Nevertheless, the significant point to which Madan's paper draws attention is really the practical utility and significance of religion and religious ideology as a basis of social identification and communal boundary maintenance.

Mines' paper carries this same theme to a more general level and focusses on the process whereby this identity articulation is achieved. Employing the concept of Islamization, Mines goes on to show how the Muslim Tamils residing in the urban centres of Tamilnadu have been trying to project an image of themselves as orthodox Muslims in the face of the culturally diffuse situation one is likely to encounter in an urban setting. A considerable body of recent literature has tried to present data on the operation of the same process in other parts of the country (see, for example, Misra, 1964; Aggarwal, 1966; Vreede de Steurs, 1968; Singh, 1973; and Faruqi, 1969). What is remarkable about Mines' discussion, however, is the point that he makes that the immediate motivation for the kind of Islamization that the Muslim Tamils are undergoing is not so much the urge to be truly orthodox Muslims or to adhere rigidly to Islamic tenets in order to be good Muslims in an abstract religious sense. Quite to the contrary, the immediate motivation is essentially local. Thus, the very people who have undertaken to Islamize themselves in the culturally diffuse situation of the urban environment relapse into their previous behaviour pattern which would be regarded as hetrodox by common fundamentalist standards when they visit the rural areas from which they had originally come. This is a perceptive distinction and suggests that discussions of the Islamization process that attribute the tendency toward adherence to what Islamic fundamentalists regard as religiously orthodox behaviour patterns as reflections of an individual's or group's urge to drop un-Islamic accretions due to religious motivations needs to be looked at more thoroughly and carefully and within the specific social context or sitution of the individual or the group concerned.

While religion is certainly a basis of identity articulation in a plural cultural situation, it also provides the individual with a plan for life from the daily ritual of worship, through the annual cycle of ceremonies, to the ritual observance of life cycle. Fruzzetti's paper focuses on this aspect and illustrates the significance of ritual observance of life cycle rites and public ceremonials through a study of birth rituals and Moharram in the West Bengal town of Bishnupur studied by her. Her argument is that the observance of life cycle rituals is a pragmatic response to the discomforting doubts and drifts of life and offers props and protection where one's own strength fails. It is a source of certainty and assurance where one's own wisdom is lacking. On the other hand, the observance of Moharram is a means of bolstering social cohesion in a situation where the Muslims live scattered in a number of separate neighbourhoods. Elucidating her argument through extremely rich ethnographic data, she also in the process touches upon the question of cultural syncreticism. She demonstrates that the Muslims of the township she has studied, and by extension we could argue the whole sub-continent, participate simultaneously into a local and an Islamic culture. Further, they do not see these as mutually antagonistic or exclusive but rather as complimentary, thereby allowing a greater degree of pluralism in respect of beliefs and ritual practices than would be possible within the framework of the formal principles enshrined in the scriptural literature.

More or less the same point is made by Saiyid in his contribution. Through a behavioural study of Moharram, he depicts the transformation, or metamorphosis as he calls it, that this annual ritual has undergone in the rural areas in several parts of the country. He shows that the occasion is regarded as a 'festival' where virtually everyone participates in performing the rituals in a spirit of gaiety and joyousness. Saiyid's explanation for this transformation is the psychic and social need for recreation, adventure and opportunity for attaining distinction and recognition in the otherwise monotonous life of a rural community. While this is certainly true, there can be little question that this joint action and participation also helps demonstrate and bolster the solidarity of the community. If this were not so, the lack of emphasis in this festival on kin solidarity and on the temporary suspension of social distinctions and sexual segregation would make little sense.

The remaining three contributions deal with the cult of shrines and what at least a few of the authors describe for want of a better term as saint worship. Graefin V. Schwerin's paper deals with the legend of Salar Masud Ghazi and the cult that has evolved around his shrine in Bahraich District in eastern Uttar Pradesh. Drawing upon a considerable body of historical and other secondary sources as well as her own casual observations, she demonstrates that both the legend of Salar Masud Ghazi and the cult associated with his shrine is heavily overlaid with Hindu influences. She also traces the Hindu roots of the legend and the cult and posits the possibility that the vast complex of rituals associated with the cult are actually Hindu in origin and have been integrated into what she calls Indian Islam.

Social solidarity, cohesion and unity generated by religion and ritual observances is a theme touched upon by several of the contributors to this volume. However, Jeffery shows that rituals are also vehicles of strife and social conflict. Using evidence drawn from a study of the public ceremonials held at the Nizamuddin shrine in Delhi, she shows how the performance of public rituals there is frequently marked by disruptions which are not just standardized ways of handling social conflicts within an unquestioned social order. Her argument is that the disruptions described by her cannot be understood within the ceremonial context alone but are merely masks hiding questions of geneological disputations, social and religious precedence and economic considerations.

Pfleiderer's account of the shrine of Mira Datar in the Gujarat State of Western India takes us to an entirely different aspect of the religious beliefs and practices: protection against disease and granting of special boons. Famous for curing of mental illness, the shrine draws pilgrims from distant places for the treatment of mental disorders. Her argument is that the indigenous or native concepts of disease and illness do not offer any explanation for the kind of psychological afflictions and diseases which most patients seem to suffer from. The shrine and the therapeutic cure offered there gives people a theory of illness which makes it possible for the patients to deal with, or to come to terms with, their illness. This facilitates their treatment and cure.

The evidence presented in the contributions included in this volume is clear that the Muslims in India, as indeed the Muslims elsewhere in the Islamic world, believe in and adhere to the cardinal pillars of the faith: the daily prayers, fasting during the month of Ramadan, pilgrimage to Mecca, and the giving of God's due (*zakat*), etc. This adherence to what is regarded as the universally ordained Divine Law, the *Shariah*, also gives the Muslims in India the unity and the sense of belonging to the universal brotherhood of thc Islamic faithfuls (the *umma*). At the same time, each of the papers included here also explicitly or implicitly draws attention to the fact that Islam as practised in India is heavily underlined by elements which are accretions drawn from the local environment and contradict the fundamentalist view of the beliefs and practices to which Muslims must adhere.

This is not by itself something new. Evidence of the persistence of what are usually described as popular Hindu influences in the ritual and religious life of the Muslims in India has existed for a long time. Sharif's *Qanun-i-Islam* (Sharif, 1921), compiled at the instance of G.A. Herklots, a surgeon in the Madras establishment, and Garcon de Tassey's *Memoir sur les Particularities des Islam du la Musalmans du l' Inde d'apress les Ouvrage Hindustanis* (Garcon de Tassey, 1869) had provided elaborate descriptions of the ritual practices and beliefs among Muslims which were quite unorthodox but enjoyed widespread public appeal. More recently, the evidence on the presence of such local and proximate as opposed to transcendental elements[3] validated by vernacular tales has also been adduced by some Islamicists. For example, Aziz Ahmad writes, 'At the popular level Indian Islam represents a mosaic of demotic supertitious and syncretic beliefs . . .' (1969: 44). The crucial question is

[3]Several different modes of expression have been used by scholars to characterize the theological and the folk and syncretic aspects of religious rituals and practices. The Islamicists themselves have tended to use the terms 'orthodox' and 'hetrodox' to refer to them. Mandelbum uses the terms 'transcendental' and 'pragmatic' to designate them (1964: 10). Redfinld (1955) refers to them as the Great and Little traditions.

whether the presence of folk-beliefs and syncretic elements as revealed by the sociological and social anthropological studies included in this volume should be treated as a part and parcel of Islam in India.

The attitude of the Islamicists to this crucial question has been characterized by a certain degree of ambivalence, though this ambivalence has taken two different forms. Some of them have been inclined to deny the presence of folk and syncretic elements in Islam in India altogether either by attributing them to the faulty methodology of the sociologists and social anthropologists which relies heavily upon the techniques of interview and participant observation or by relegating them to the level of a superficiality which has little to do with the essence of religion. Thus, Mushirul Haq notes:

> The social scientists in their research programme have generally been underrating the position of religion in the life of people who inspite of the possibility of their not knowing the intricate theological postulates of their religion are content with it, and find solace in it. To them religion is an ultimate solution of the problem of the meaning of life. Followers of any given religion may differ in their social practices and behaviour, but undeniable is the fact that they always regard their religion as the cementing force binding them with the world-body which their religion is supposed to create. *People intending to explain away in sociological terms the reality of religion have invariably taken, wrongly though, the outwardly socio-religious practices of a people as their religion* (1979; emphasis added).

Others, on the other hand, do not altogether deny the presence of folk and syncretic elements in Indian Islam, but are prone to regard them as a temporary anomaly susceptible of being eliminated or stamped out through the process of reform whereby the Muslims seek to 'recreate and reshape human attitudes' and 'revivify and revitilize human society by continuously infusing its structure with the principles of revelation which are providentially sent as its guide and which alone provide a criterion for its worth and value (Nasr, 1966: 96).

Aziz Ahmad's observations on the process of religious

change in the Indo-Pakistan subcontinent clearly illustrate how widespread is the view of the folk and syncretic elements in Indian Islam as a temporary anomaly susceptible of eventual elimination through reformist efforts. He writes:

> These folk-beliefs should be viewed in their proper perspective and should not be over-emphasized or over-rated. They are specific to microscopic Muslim communities and are generally the exception rather than the rule. They were challenged by the fundamentalist, orthodox and modernist movements alike in the nineteenth and twentieth centuries. They have completey ceased to exist in the Westernized upper class and nearly so in the orthodox lower middle classes. In the predominantly Muslim regions which now constitute West Pakistan their hold was not very strong even in the lower classes, and fundamentalism is now rooting them out. In the lower classes of East Pakistan, some folk-beliefs still persist despite the fundamentalist Faraidi movement's success in the nineteenth century, and the Jamait-i-Islami's growing influence on religious life today (1969: 51).

Aziz Ahmad expresses a sense of skepticism so far as the Indian situation is concerned, for he writes: 'In the Republic of India the situation is potentially different. Orthodoxy, in the form of the political influence of the ulema, is still powerful, but the extent of its infiuence is confined to economically retrogressive and numerically dwindling middle classes, which, in India, are no longer able to play the role of a creative minority by providing leadership for the vast masses of Indian Muslims. These masses, especially in the rural areas, are yielding to popular Hinduism's pull of absorption, largely through folk-beliefs and through participation in Hindu festivals' (1969: 51). However, Faruqi adduces recent sociological and anthropological evidence to show that even in India the process of religious reform has been bringing about greater purification of Islamic rituals and behaviour. Faruqi writes:

> Recent sociological and anthropological researches have endeavoured to bring out numerous traits of the culture of these regional communities to show that they are mutually

distinct and different in many respects. Conclusions on the basis of the data provided by these researches also show that Muslim communities belonging to the Little Tradition, with all their distinct cultural traits, have always aspired to relate their social and cultural values to those of the Islamic Great Tradition, thus asserting their identity, through a two-way process of Islamization, as an integral component of the identity of a larger and 'over-all religion-wide' Muslim community (1979;34).

The sociologists and social anthropologists who turned to the study of the religious life among Muslims in India in the fiftees and sixties accepted the basic premises of the Islamicists regarding the possibility of the eventual elimination of syncretic accretions from the rituals and behaviour of Muslims in India. Using the concept of Great and Little Tradition as propounded by Redfield (1955), they agreed that the theological and philosophical principles enshrined in the scriptural texts should be identified as the Orthodox or Great Tradition and the local, proximate religious elements traceable to the local environment should be characterized as the hetrodox or Little Tradition. Further, the sociologists and social anthropologists assumed that the process of Islamization, understood as a tendency involving a conscious rejection of syncretic elements that persist as remnants of pre-conversion orientations and ethos, would result in a gradual shrinkage of the hetrodox religious complex. 'The typical mode of Islamization', as Clifford Geertz had noted in the Indonesian context, was visualized as

> painfully gradual. First comes the Confession of faith, then the other pillars, then a certain degree of observance of the law, and finally, perhaps, especially as a scholarly tradition develops and takes hold, a certain amount of learning in the law and the Quran and Hadith upon which it rests. The intricate norms, doctrines, explications, and annotations that make up Islam, or at least Sunni Islam, can be apprehended only step by step, as one comes to control, to a greater or lesser degree, the scriptural sources upon which it rests. For most people, such control never goes beyond accepting, at second hand, the interpretations of those who control those

> sources directly. But that learning, however, crude, and access to scholarship, however shabby, are central to becoming a Muslim in anything more than a formal sense, is apparent everywhere in the Islamic world . . . . Islamic conversion is not, as a rule, a sudden, total overwhelming illumination but a slow turning toward a new light (1965: 96-7).

There is growing evidence in the literature which has been accumulating in recent years that the interaction between what we characterize as the philosophical or transcendental and the syncretic or pragmatic religious complexes in Islam in India is more complex and the transformative effects of Islamization are not quite as unilineal as was previously assumed. For one thing, Islamization has not always been found to result in the spread of orthodox Islamic beliefs and practices at the cost of what has been here called the hetrodox or syncretic complex. Aziz Ahmad, whom we quoted at length earlier regarding the transformative effect of fundamentalist and reformist movements in stamping out syncretic and folk beliefs, himself concedes this in another part of his work. 'Indian Islam', he writes, 'represents a mosaic of demotic, superstitious and syncretic beliefs, *which movements of mass reform like that of the Mujahidin in the nineteenth century have tried to erase, but not with complete success* (1969: 44; emphaiss added). Secondly, rather than totally displacing hetrodox religious beliefs and ritual observances, Islamization quite often results in the acceptance instead of a somewhat modified version of the religious complex which was originally prevalent. For instance, Lambat noted that 'Sunni Surati Vohras have been experiencing a struggle between custom and religion and in recent years this struggle has picked up great momentum . . . . However, the customary rites and ceremonies continue to enjoy a very strong hold on the group and have not been replaced by alternate religious practices. The religious leaders who raise hue and cry over un-Islamic customs have not been able to provide Islamic substitutes for them. For example, they have vehemently opposed the singing of *geet* by women, but they have not been able to raise their voices as strongly against the loudspeakers that blare out the latest film hits' (1976: 80). Finally, as Fruzzetti's paper in this volume so forcefully illustrates, the elements of the hetrodox religious complex persist side by side with the orthodox one without any apparent indications of conflict or contradiction.

This kind of evidence has led some sociologists and social anthropologists to reject the conceptualization of religious beliefs, values and practices in terms of a dichotomy of orthodoxy and hetrodoxy altogether and to treat them instead as part and parcel of a single common religious tradition. Thus, Satish C. Misra suggested some years ago that it was wrong to conceptualize the process of religious change in Indian Muslim society simply in terms of Islamization. He distinguished two processes that had been, according to him, operating throughout the Medieval period, and he called them indigenization and Islamization. He concluded:

> Indigenization denotes a process which in course of generations led to the adaptation of the mores of an immigrant people or community to the land where they came to settle. Certain mores were retained while others given up in place of those accepted. It was not usually a conscious process though, as in case of personal law, it could be and was legitimized. It also differed significantly from region to region: an Afghan indigenized in Rajasthan would develop different ways than another settled in Gujarat or Malwa or Bengal; the three of them would however have some culture traits which would identify them as Afghans (1973: 11).

More recently, Imtiaz Ahmad (1975) has presented a specific-level analysis of the religious system of Muslims in India. According to this mode of analysis, he argued that there exist several levels in the religious system of the Muslims in India, and the beliefs, values and ritual practices at each level enjoy a certain degree of autonomy, being relevant for presumbly differet purposes, yet at the same time remaining very much an integral part of Islam in India. At least three such levels were clearly recognizable according to him.

The first level within the Muslim religious system was identified by Imtiaz Ahmad as that of the beliefs and pratices that are traditionally described as belonging to formal or scriptural Islam. They are derived from the Islamic religious texts and command the awe that commonly attaches to sacred precepts.

Like Muslims elsewhere, Muslims in India also acknowledge them to be paramount and their observance is supposed to be on a higher plane than is true of the beliefs and rituals at lower levels. However, these beliefs and practices are essentially ideals enjoined on all Muslims. Correspondence between them and actual religious behaviour is a more open question.

The second level includes beliefs and values of a more limited spread. They are not derived from the Islamic scriptural literature, and it is not necessary that they must always accord with the beliefs and values enshrined in the Islamic scriptural texts. Sometimes they may even be opposed or antithetical to the latter. However, they are regarded by the Muslims who hold them as as much a part of their religious system as the values and beliefs of the level above. The essential characterstic of these beliefs is that they are pre-supposed by actual religious behaviour. Consequently, the correspondence between the actual beliefs and values and religious behaviour is much greater at this level. Fruzzetti's account of the life cycle rituals and Saiyid's account of the Moharram celebrations testify to the existence of this level.

The third level in the religious system of the Muslims in India comprises of the beliefs and behaviour patterns usually described by social anthropologists as pragmatic or practical religion. It contains a large number of non-philosophical elements such as supernatural theories of disease causation, propitiation of Muslim saints and, occasionally at least, deities of the Hindu pantheon, or other crude phenomenon such as spirit possession, evil eye, etc. Fruzzetti's account of the techniques of warding off evil spirits at the time of birth, Graefin V. Schwerin's treatment of the cult of Salar Masud Ghazi and Pfleiderer's excellent discription of trance and possession and exorcism practised by the *mujawars* at Mira Datar Dargah provide excellent illustrations of the presence of such beliefs and values in the religious system of the Muslims in India. Most of the elements of the religious system at this level are strongly antithetical to the beliefs and values prevalent at the other two levels and are so regarded by the Muslims. Presumably for this reason the rituals and behaviour that are characterstic of this level are observed secretly, often without the mediation of religious functionaries.

The contributions included in this volume provide adequate testimony that what Mandelbaum has called the transcendental and the pragmatic religious complexes are a part and parcel of an integrated and unified religious system even in Indian Islam[4] and it would be erroneous to think of them in terms of a dichotomy or to regard the pragmatic complex as eventually an eliminatable one. Fruzzetti asserts this clearly. 'The Muslims of Bishnupur,' she writes, 'have forged a unique culture by combining Islamic precepts with the experience of everyday life, its social contexts and the elements that come from a non-Islamic culture. There are points at which these two spheres overlap and, using this as a principle, the Muslims of the town see no contradiction between strictly Islamic and non-Islamic practices. In an abstract sense, they see both as having their concrete parallels in the world of action. . . .Whatever does not fit into the one fits into the other. Whatever is not in the Koran is *niom* (Bengali), complementing though never contradicting, the spirit of Muslim *dharam*, as the townsmen are aware of Koranic laws regarding the individual's actvities in all spheres of life. Local *achars* are also practised though they are understood within the local Bengali culture and not as part of Koranic laws. But this itself is an ideological question, for the boundaries of the two systems are ideally clear. However, on the level of experience, for the purpose of action, there is no need to distinguish them' (p. 111).

One does not have to go very far in order to understand why the Islamic theological and philosophical precepts and principles on the one hand and local, syncretic elements on the other should be encompassed integrally within Indian Islam. This is something that owes itself directly to the very dynamics of

[4]Mandelbaum perceptively makes this point in the context of the distinction between the transcendental and pragmatic complexes within Hinduism and Buddhism. 'The one aspect of religion', he writes, 'might more aptly be called the transcendental complex and the other the pragmatic complex. One is ultimate, supernal, derived from Sanskrit texts; the other is proximate, local, validated by vernacular tales. Whatever terms are chosen, the important fact is that both are used as part of the whole setting of religion in India, each is employed for generally differing (though frequently overlapping purposes) within the frame of religion and each is popularly considered to be complementary to the other' (1964: 10).

the spread of the faith in India. Unlike Hinduism in India or Islam in Arabia, Islam in India was intrusive in character. It came over an already established civilization and could establish itself only gradually and by slow degrees over the already deeply entrenched indigenous traditions. Already in the course of its journey through Persia and Turkestan, the Islamic faith had acquired certain accretions so that the version of Islam which had been introduced into India was quite different from what it had been in its original heartland. On arrival in India, it had been further diluted through conversion to its fold of large groups of local converts who were bound to bring their pre-conversion beliefs and practices into the faith. Thus, it was almost inevitable that the religious tradition of the Muslims in India should comprise two distinct elements : one ultimate and formal, derived from the Islamic texts; the other proximate and local, validated by custom.

The integration of the two elements to a point that they should come to co-exist as complementary and integral parts of a single common religious system was presumably conditioned by the constraints of Islam's own struggle for survival in an alien environment. As a distinct religious tradition characterized by a vigorous iconoclastic zeal on the part of those who were responsible for first introducing Islam into India, the intruding Islamic tradition would probably have liked to conquer the indigenous religious traditions wholesale. However, this could not be possible for Islam to achieve because the indigenous mores and traditions were already an integral part of the life of the people and their total displacement could be achieved only at the cost of Islam's own rejection.

It seems plausible that the resistance and resilience shown by the indigenous traditions encouraged Islam in India to accept and retain the local cultural traditions but adapt them to its own requirements and needs by putting an Islamic content into them. This seems to be the logical *modus operandi* whereby presumably Islam was eventually successful in establishing its integrity and at the same time stablilizing itself on the otherwise religiously clustered Indian scene. Fruzzetti's account of the rituals held in Muslim households on the sixth day after the birth of the child provides some indication of how this kind of a process might have operated. She shows that the ceremonies on the sixth day involve on the part of the members of the household of the visit of Angel Gabriel. According to her, this ritual has a striking similarity to the one among Hindus where the deity which is supposed to visit the house is called Bidata Prush. It is easy to see that this ritual had existed among the Muslims of West Bengal before their conversion to Islam. Upon conversion to Islam they could not have gone on observing this ritual without some of the formal Islamic principles coming into direct conflict with it. The possibility of such a conflict was suitably avoided by keeping the ritual intact but putting an Islamic content into it. Thus, Angel Gabriel came to replace Bidata Prush and the serving of a chicken came to be incorporated as part of the diet provided to the mother.

Perhaps the point indicated by the ceremony associated with birth rituals as described by Fruzzetti is even better illustrated by the institution of shrines and the various religious practices associated with what could actually be characterized as saint worship were the concept not antithetical to Islamic fundamentals. As far as historical evidence goes (see Bhardwaj, 1973), the institution of shrines was already prevalent among Hindus and was an important part of local religious traditions. Furthermore, pilgrimage to these shrine centres was always regarded as a sacred act within the indigenous traditions. Fundamentalist Islam could stamp out this widely prevalent belief complex for the pilgrimage to Mecca alone only at the cost of its own rejection. Consequently, what seems likely is that Indian Islam accepted the entire corpus of beliefs and practices associated wlth shrines and transformed the reverence for shrines within Hinduism into a typically Islamic institution by putting an Islamic content into it. Graefin V. Schwerin hints at this distinactive possibility : 'It is certain that in the course of the Muslim conquest of Indian regions, forced conversions occured on a large scale. But the majority of indigenous Indian Muslims were probably converted peacefully by wandering faqirs and Sufis. Indian temples and sacred places were taken over by Muslims who sometimes converted them into Islamic pilgrim centres. The local, not yet converted, inhabitants continued to visit these places or began to try their luck with newly founded *dargahs*, were consequently converted, or incorporated the Islamic cult into their system of beliefs by indentifying the Muslim saint with one of the gods already familiar to them' (p. 145).

Sufism, of course, played a vital part in the process of this adaptation and adjustment. Consider, for examples, the question of pilgrimage to shrines which, as the contributions to this volume so eloquently illustrate, occupies such an important place in the religious system of the Muslims in India. Pilgrimage to Mecca (*hajj*) has always occupied a very important place in the Islamic pillars. However, the performance of *hajj* has also been always beset with very considerable obstacles so much so that the prescription itself was often-times relaxed, as during the reign of Akbar when the *ulema* declared that the pilgrimage to Mecca was no longer obligatory for Indian Muslims (Shackle. 1965 : 159-60). Through its emphasis upon the spiritual interpretation of Islamic precepts, Sufism was able to convert the local shrines into a religious symbol of pilgrimage without belittling the importance of *hajj* among Muslims in India.[5]

According to Sufi doctrines, pilgrimages are of two kinds : (a) in absence (from God) and (b) in presence (of God). According to this doctrine, anyone who is absent from Mecca is in the same position as if he were absent from God in his own house, and anyone who is present with God in his own house is in the same position as if he were present with God at Mecca. Thus, the Sufi doctrine under-rated the fulfillment of pilgrimage in outward form. At the same time, the traditional Sufi doctrine enjoined reverence for one's spiritual guide and the practice of expressing one's devotion to him by going to his shrine became the concomitant of this philosophy. All in all, therefore, the classical Sufi teaching tended to devalue the performance of *hajj* and laid a corresponding emphasis upon the performance of local pilgrimages to the tombs of saints and local shrines. Since pilgrimages to local shrines could after all be capable of performance by most Muslims, like the observance of most other pillars, such local cults naturally involved what may be called the localization of Muslim spiritual geography to correspond broadly with the confines of

[5] I have benefited greatly from Shackle's excellent treatment of the Sufi view of pilgrimage in what follows (see Schackle, 1976).

their regions with some extension to the great all-India shrines. Thus, the shrines created, as Turner (1969) has indeed observed, a *communitas* for Muslims in a society which was not only culturally hetrogenous but also quite antihetical to the religious simplicity of Islam.

If what we have been arguing so far is correct, the implications of our argument for the understanding of Islam as a religious tradition in Indla are obvious enough, It is clear that as a practised faith Islam is far more pluralist in character than the extreme degree of reification commonly attributed to it by Islamicists and Muslim theologians would admit. While Muslims in India no doubt subscribe to the fundamental Islamic precepts, there is also no unified definition of what is truly orthodox or truly 'Islamic'. Each community carries its own social construct of what is orthodox and adheres to it. Mines indicates this clearly when he writes : 'Because they indentify themselves as Muslims, they want to be good Muslims. Accordingly, in Pallavaram . . . the leading Muslim Tamils attempt in their behaviour to set an example of austere orthodoxy which is generally accepted as a standard of behaviour . . . . It must be noted that what is considered orthodox by Pallavaram's Muslims is influenced by local beliefs' (p. 69). Thus, while Muslim fundamentalist may assert and maintain that there is one, and only one, version of what is orthodox from the Islamic point of view and whatever does not conform to it is to be dismissed as hetrodox, the peoples' own beliefs and behaviour admit of much greater variety in what they regard as truly 'Islamic'. Clearly, it seems to me that the Islamicists' vision has tended to obscure the inherent and underlying pluralism within Indian Islam as a practised religion.

There have recently been several attempts to criticize the sociologists and social anthropologists for laying too much emphasis upon the actual religious beliefs and behaviour of the people and for ignoring the Islamic principles enshrined in the secriptural texts (see, for example, Momin, 1977; and Talib, 1979). Some scholars (Momin, 1977) have even tried to outline alternative frameworks for avoiding the supposed pitfalls of the sociological and social anthropological frameworks. Unfortunately, the frameworks outlined by them do not appear to be very different from what most good sociological and social anthropological works have usually followed. Nonetheless, the essential point that needs to be made in this connection is that any attempt to draw rigid boundaries between the frameworks followed by the Islamicists and sociologists and socil anthropologists is bound to be both artificial and misleading. If the task is a comprehensive understanding of the religious life of Muslims in India, neither the Islamicists' nor the sociologists' or social anthropologists' approach is likely to be wholly adequate. Perhaps, as Saiyid indeed argues at the end of his paper, there is an undeniable need for the two kinds of specialists to come together to deal with the questions which are crucial to an understanding of the Islamic tradition in India.

Bibliography

Aggarwal, Partap C. (1966), 'A Muslim Sub-caste of North India: Problems of Cultural Integration', *Economic and Political Weekly*, 1, pp. 159-67.

Ahmad, Aziz (1969), *An Intellectual History of Islam in India*, Edinburgh, University of Edinburgh Press.

Ahmad, Imtiaz (1975), 'Unity and Variety in South Asian Islam', in Dietmar Rothermund (ed.), *Islam in Southern Asia*, Wiesbaden, Franz Steiner Verlag.

Bhardwaj, S.M. (1973), *Hindu Places of Pilgrimage in India*, Berkely, University of California Press

Faruqi, Ziaui Hasan (1979), 'Orthodoxy and Hetrodoxy in Indian Islam, *Islam and the Modern Age*, 32, pp. 9-36.

Garcon de Tassey, M. (1869), *Memoir sur les Particularties de la Religion Musalmans dans l' Inde d'apres les Ouvage Hindustanis*, Paris, Labitte.

Geertz, Califford (1965), 'Modernization in a Muslim Society; The Indonesian Case', in R. N. Bellah (ed.), *Religion and Progress in Modern Asia*, New York, The Free Press.

Haq, Mushirul (1979), 'A Note for the ICSSR Workshiop on Religion, Politics and Society', held on October 25, (Mimeo).

Lambat, Ismail A. (1976), 'Marriage among the Sunni Surati Vohras of South Gujarat', in Imtiaz Ahmad (ed.), *Family, Kinship and Marriage among Muslims in India*, Delhi, Manohar.

Leach, E. R. (1968), 'Introduction', in E. R. Leach (ed.), *Dialectic in Practicae Religion*, Cambridge Papers in Social Anthropology No. 5, Cambridge, Cambridge University Press.

Mandelbaum, David G. (1964), 'Introduction. Process and Structure in South Asian Religion', in Edward B. Harper (ed.), *Religion in South*

Asia, Seattle, Washington University Press.

Misra, Satish C. (1964), *Muslim Communities in Gujarat*, Bombay, Asia Publishing House.

——— (1973) 'Indigenization and Islamization in Indian History', Paper presented at the ICSSR Colloqiam on Problems of Muslims in India held at Hyderabad, November 5-8.

Momin A. R. (1977), 'The Indo-Islamic Tradition', *Sociological Bulletin*, 26, pp. 242-58.

Nasr, Seyyed Hossein (1966), *Ideals and Realities of Islam*, London, George Allen and Unwin Ltd.

Redfield, Robert (1955), 'The Social Organization of Tradition, *The Far Easrern Quarterly*, 15, pp. 13-22.

Shackle, C. (1976), 'The Pilgrimage and the Extension of Sacred Geography in the Poetry of Khawaja Ghulam Farid', in Attar Singh (ed.) *Socio-Cultural Inpact of Islam on India*, Chandigarh, Panjab University.

Sharif, Jafar (1921), *Islam in India or the Qanun-i-Islam. The Customs of the Musalmans of India*, (G. A. Herklots trans. and ed.), rearranged and edited witn additions by William Crooke, New Delhi, Oriental Books Reprint Corporation.

Singh, Yogendra (1973), *Modernization of Indian Tradition*, New Delhi, Thompson Press.

Srinivas, M. N. et. al. (1959), *Caste: A Trend Report and Bibliography*, Oxford, Basil Blackwell.

Talib, Mohd, (1979), 'The Social Context of the Contemperary Muslim Studies in the Sub-continent', Paper presented at the Seminar on Recent Trends in Muslim Studies held at Jamia Milia Islamia, New Delhi, March 28.

Turner, Victor W. (1969), *The Ritual Process: Structure and Anti. Structure*, Chicago, Aldine.

Vreede de Steurs, Cora (1968), *Parda: A Study of North Indian Muslim Women*, New York, Humanities Press,

1

Religious Ideology and Social Structure: The Muslims and Hindus of Kashmir

To me my religions; to you yours.
The Koran: Surah CIX : 6

T.N. Madan

In this paper I am concerned with defining the socio-cultural identity of the Muslims and Hindus of rural Kashmir. Such an exercise will have first to take note of those attributes that the two categories of people themselves judge to be of critical importance. I shall thus examine the images that Muslims and Hindus have both of themselves and of each other. Once the attributes have been defined, discussion will be focused on real life interaction observed in the course of fieldwork. To give historical depth to the materials obtained through interviews and observation, limited use has been made of selected published works. I have not burdened this essay with ethnographical and historical details, but have concentrated on exploring the general principles that may be shown to underlie what people believe in and what they do. In other words, an effort has been made to combine the views from *within* and *without*. Needless to emphasize, doing so is not an exercise in simple accumulation of points of view—the effort is to examine not the two views *per se* but the relation between them.

Situated in the Himalayas at an average altitude of 6,000 feet above sea level, Kashmir proper—not to be confused with the state of Jammu and Kashmir of which it is a part—is a basin, 85 miles long and 25 miles broad. It is located approximately between 33°—35° N and 74°—76° E, and has an area of 6,131 square miles. The people of Kashmir partake of the common cultural heritage of the subcontinent of India, Bangladesh and Pakistan. At the same time, they have their own distinctive cultural traits, social structures, and historical experience. In this respect, the Kashmiris are like any other regional community such as the Bengalis, Maharashtrians or Tamils; but the insights which our study of them is likely to offer would seem to be rare if not unique.

As a culture area, the Kashmir Valley is of crucial importance for our understanding of, for example, the synthesis of Muslim and Hindu world-views and such fundamental principles of social organization as caste. It has not, however, received from anthropologists and sociologists the kind of close attention that it richly deserves.[1]

Kashmir has a population of 2,435,701 of whom 832,280 live in the southern district of Anantnag. It is primarily from a village of this district that the ethnographical content of this paper is drawn. I have also visited a few other villages in this district and in the central district of Srinagar (population: 827,697). The rural areas of these two districts are generally believed by Kashmiris to be culturally similar. The northern district of Baramulla (population: 775,724) is, however, said to be culturally somewhat distinct in several respects. The present paper may be, therefore, said to be generally descripitive of the rural areas of the two districts of Anantnag and Srinagar. The rural population of Anantnag is 758,046, or 91 per cent of the total. The corresponding figure for Srinagar is 404,444, or 48 per cent (India, 1972a and 1972b).

[1] Literature of general interest on Kashmir, including travellers' accounts, is considerable; sociological studies of Kashmiris are few. Lawrence's book (1895; reprinted 1967) and gazetteer (1909) are invaluable sources of information. He toured the valley during the 1890s in his capacity as settlement commissioner. The only published major social anthropological study is Madan (1965). For a general introductory account and bibliographies see Crane (1956). Suggestions regarding future research are given in Madan (1969).

Muslims occupy a position of overwhelming importance in the population of Kashmir. They call themselves Musalman which is the Persian form of the word Muslim (see Hughes, 1935). They form 94 per cent of the total population in the three districts taken together—95 per cent in Anantnag, and 91 per cent in Srinagar. If we consider only the rural population of Anantnag, Muslims again account for over 95 per cent of it. The rest of the population consists almost exclusively of Hindus, though Sikhs also are present in a few villages. It must be noted here that there are no Hindus at all in about 56 per cent of the villages of the Anantnag and Srinagar districts (India, 1943). Village boundaries are not, however, impassable barriers, and exclusively Muslim settlements would often seem to have various kinds of relationship with Hindus in adjoining villages.

The native Hindus of Kashmir all belong to the Brahman *varna*, and are divided into two endogamous subcastes. The Kashmiri Brahmans call themselves Bhatta and are generally known in India as Kashmiri Pandits. 'Bhatta' is the Prakrit form of the Sanskrit *bhartri* which means 'scholar', 'doctor', or the same as the Sanskrit *pandit* (see Macdonell, 1924). Since I have elsewhere used the term Kashmiri Pandit (see, for example, Madan, 1965), I will continue to do so in this paper. How Kashmir came to have a single Hindu caste will be described later. I will first take up the problem of Muslim identity.

Muslim Identity: Muslim Representation

The problem of mutual identification among the Muslims of rural Kashmir does not arise very often. Within a village all adults know each other. The average population of a village in the district of Anantnag is 511 (India, 1966:5). When a person goes to another village, he stays with his relatives; the purpose of the visit most often is to renew contact with them. A Muslim tenant on a visit to his landowner in another village will stay with him and, if the latter also is a Muslim, eat with him. A Pandit landowner will supply uncooked victuals to the tenant, who will cook his own meal in the compound. Utensils for the purpose will be borrowed for him by the landowner's household from one of their Muslim neighbours. Mutual recognition in such situations is not problematic; but it is important, for Hindus and Muslims observe different degrees of mutual avoidance. More about this later.

Even when one encounters total strangers, there are several visible signs which identify them as one's co-religionists or otherwise. Thus, Muslims and Pandits do not dress identically: the differences may not appear striking to an outsider but a Kashmiri would never make a mistake in this regard. Besides differences of male and female dress—of headgear, gown, trousers, and sometimes even footwear—many Pandits wear *tyok* on their forehead: a mark of saffron or some other prescribed paste, oblong among men and round among women. Muslims wear beards more often than Pandits, and of a distinctive cut. There are differences of speech, mainly lexical (see Kachru, 1969:21-27). Though native Kashmiris look very much alike (see Raychaudhuri, 1961, and also Bhattacharya, 1966), two recent Muslims immigrant groups have distinctive features and speak a non-Kashmiri dialect called *Paryum* (literally, 'foreign', 'alien').

Identification of people in terms of the Muslim-Pandit dichotomy is thus not difficult in the rural areas, except perhaps when the stranger is from a town or is an urbanized villager, and thus likely to be without any of the above visible signs. Any purposive interaction with a stranger is dependent upon the initiation of a specific process of identity establishment. This process usually follows a predictable pattern.

The most crucial cue lies in the family name. Muslim personal names in rural Kashmir are identical with similar names anywhere in the world. Family names such as Baig, Sayyid, Mausodi, and Shaikh refer to the fact of descent: the Baig, Mausodi, and Sayyid are descended from early immigrant families, and the Shaikh, who constitute the overwhelming majority of the Muslims, from converts.[2] The immigrant families fall into

[2] Shaikh, an Arabic word (pl. *shuyukh*), literally means an old man or man of authority (Hughes, 1935). The term seems to be widely used

three categories: Arabs, Mughals, and Pathans. There is a fourth category of immigrant Muslims who entered the Valley late in the nineteenth century. They are called Gujar ('cowherd') and Bakarwal ('goatherd'), and constitute two somewhat distinctive groups. They are the Muslims who, as mentioned above, speak a non-Kashmiri dialect among themselves.

Not many Shaikhs use that appellation along with their names. It is more common to use other types of family name. One of the most widely prevalent of such names among Kashmiri Muslims is Bhat, which is, of course, the same as Bhatta, and obviously bears testimony of the fact of conversion. There are other examples of this kind of surname such as Pandit, Koul (Sanskrit *kaula*, originally the name of a Brahman sect), Naik and Ryosh (Sanskrit *rishi* or saintly, learned man). There is still another category of common family names which either directly refer to one's hereditary family occupation or indirectly through association. Thus, an Ali Khair is a blacksmith (*khar*) and a Rasul Navid is a barber (*navid*). A Samad Vagay will readily be recognized as a milkman, and even referred to as Samad Gur, for the Vagays are milkmen (*gur*).

All types of surname are called *zat*, and enquiries about them are made in the effort to obtain identity specification. The important question is what does *zat* denote? Apparently it points to birth, as does the well known word *jati* used elsewhere among Hindus. The Kashmiris, however, use the word *zat* in a broader sense to connote essence or inherent nature. *Bad-zat* is a term of abuse and is used to condemn an evil natured or mean person rather than to refer to lowly birth, which would seem to be the primary meaning of the term in the original Arabic-Persian (see Steingass, 1957). Similarly, Kashmiri Muslims refer to God as *Zat-i-pak*, the one whose nature is pure. *Zat* is also used in classifying breeds of cattle or varieties of

in South Asia to designate Muslims descended from Hindu converts (see Gait, 1911 and *Chambers Twentieth Century Dictionary*). In Kashmir: 'The census of 1891 does not show the divisions into which the Musalmans of the valley fall, but it may be stated that the great mass of the village people come under the head Shaikh, and are descendants of the original Hindus. . . .' (Lawrence, 1967:306). It is likely that some Shaikhs, particularly in urban areas, may be descended from immigrants.

inanimate object such as paddy or timber.[3]

When used as part of a person's name, *zat* has the narrower meaning of either birth (e.g., Sayyid, Shaikh) or hereditary occupation (e.g., Khar, Navid, Gur). It does not, however, necessarily indicate a person's actual source of livelihood: a family of any occupational category may have enough land not to want to exercise their traditional calling; or, a particular individual may choose to enter a new occupation. These facts are ascertained by inquiring about *kar*, a general term for work or occupation, or about *kasb*, skills.[4] It may be noted, however, that people rarely move from one skilled or specialist occupation to another, though agriculture is deemed to be open to all. Agriculturists are called *Zamindar* and non-agricultural artisan groups are designated *Nangar*, literally 'those in search of bread'.

At this stage it will be helpful to introduce some ethnographical details from a village.[5] Utrassu-Umanagri is situated 12

[3] Gould mentions a similar use of the term *jati* among villagers in eastern Uttar Pradesh: 'One also speaks of *jatis* of . . . animals . . . of botanical objects . . . (and even of) woven fabrics. . . . What we see operating here is *ethno-conceptualization*. In this instance Indians are manifesting a long established, culturally patterned tendency to regard endogamous, ritually and functionally differentiated social units *as if* they were natural species' (1969: 23). Marriott and Inden have been engaged in working out a general thesis regarding *jatis* as natural genera (see Marriott and Inden, 1974).

Eglar reports from the Punjab in Pakistan: 'When a mature person is asked about his zat, which means caste and also identity, he is most likely to answer: "What identity can a human being have? The only one who has an identity is the Almighty. I am a carpenter (or *zamindar*, or batter or this, that) by occupation"' (1960:29).

An interesting use of the word *zat* appears to have been made in Mughal administration. A *mansabdar*, or noble, was accorded a double rank. His so-called *zat* rank apparently gave recognition to his social status, and his salary was determined in terms of it; his *sawar* rank stipulated the number of troopers he was expected to maintain (see Gascoigne, 1971:105).

[4] Barth has recorded an identical use of these two terms among the Swat Pathans who, however, use *quom* for caste status (see Barth, 1960:118).

[5] My first period of fieldwork in Kashmir, the longest so far, was in

miles east of the town of Anantnag. It is a rather large, bi-nucleated—hence the hyphenated name—village of about 1,542 acres, inhabited by 2,644 persons (see Madan, 1965). Of these, 2,122 persons (80 per cent of the total population) are Muslims and the remaining 522 are Pandits. The Muslims are divided into two cultural subgroups; 1,352, or 64 per cent of all Muslims are natives and 770 relatively recent immigrants.

The natives engage in a variety of economic pursuits. Over half of them, totalling 121 Muslim households (728 persons), are agriculturists—peasant proprietors or proprietors-cum-tenants. Another 111 households (624 persons) fall in the traditional category of Nangar, though after the abolition of big landed estates in the State in 1950 (see Bamzai, 1962:716-18) there are no completely landless Muslim households in the village. Enquiries made by me in other villages indicate that the Nangar generally account for about one-third to one-half of all Muslim households. They never seem to outnumber the Zamindar. As will be pointed out below, several of the households of Utrassu-Umanagri that I have classified as Nangar in arriving at the above proportions are doubtful cases. But I will first give the distribution of the Muslim households in terms of occupation (see Table 1).

Besides the occupational categories listed in Table 1, I came across the following in other villages or in the town of Anantnag: (*i*) Aram (vegetable gardener); (*ii*) Band (minstrel); (*iii*) Barbuz (grain parcher); (*iv*) Gada Hainz (fisherman); (*v*) Hainz (boatman); (vi) Kawuj (attendant at Hindu cremation sites); (*vii*) Sangtarash (stone-cutter); (*viii*) Torkachhan (wood carver); (*ix*) Vonya (grocer).[6]

1957-58 when I was a scholar at the Australian National University. Since then I have returned to the area of original fieldwork for several short spells. I was there last in 1975. The tense employed in this essay is of the ethnographic present.

[6] Various census reports on Kashmir seem to have failed to distinguish between traditional roles and hereditary occupational groups. Thus, the 1931 report lists groups like Derwish (Muslim mendicant) and Jogi (ascetic) which are not such groups. Many other functional roles could be mentioned: e.g., *dandur* (vegetable dealer) *galadar* (grain dealer), *ghasi* (grasscutter), *hamami* (attendant at public baths), *varinya* (midwife) and *vaza* (cook). A hereditary group which I heard mentioned was that of the Galawan who reared and stole horses (see

TABLE 1
Native Muslim Households By Traditional Occupation

Occupational Category	*Number of Households*
1. Zamindar (landowner-cultivator, tenant)	121
2. Nangar	
(i) Dob (washerman)	2
(ii) Dosil-Chhan (builder-carpenter)	8
(iii) Domb (traditionally, messengers of revenue officials)	2
(iv) Dun (cotton carder)	6
(v) Gur (milkman, cowherd)	5
(vi) Hakim (physician)	2
(vii) Jalakhodoz (rug maker)	1
(viii) Kandur (baker)	2
(ix) Kanyul-Shakhsaar (basket weaver)	10
(x) Khar (blacksmith)	6
(xi) Kral (potter)	4
(xii) Navid (barber)	6
(xiii) Puj (butcher)	3
(xiv) Sech (tailor)	6
(xv) Sonur (silversmith)	1
(xvi) Tabardar, Arikash (woodcutter, sawer)	10
(xvii) Teliwoni (oilpresser)	3
(xviii) Thonthur (coppersmith)	2
(xix) Vatul (cobbler)	3
(xx) Wovur (weaver)	19
(xxi) Mallah (religious functionary)	10
Total	232

The Muslim Zamindar households of Utrassu-Umanagri may be deemed to be those who have no source of income other than cultivation of land, whether self-owned or leased in, or of both types.[7] There are no landless labourers in the

Lawrence, 1967:311). The 1941 census report lists Potters, Blacksmiths, Carpenters and Oilpressers, and groups all the rest together as Shaikh unless they happen to be Sayyid, Mughal, Pathan or Rajput. (See India, 1943).

[7] There were only a handful of literate Muslims in Utrassu-Umanagri in 1958; the oldest of them was about 18. This fact ruled out government service as a major source of livelihood for them. The two *lambardar* (revenue collectors) of the village are, however, Muslims. A few more are employed as forest guards.

village though many agriculturists work on daily wages for other landowners during busy seasons. The Muslim Zamindar of the village are small landowners. The average size of the holding is just under an acre and three quarters, but this figure is somewhat misleading in respect of the Muslims since it is based on all holdings, including those of the Pandits. There are 636 landownership registrations among the native Muslims of the village, the basis of registration being the individual and not the household. Recalling that there are 1,352 native Muslims, it will be noticed that the registrations are indicative of the already mentioned fact of widespread ownership of land. Of these registrations, 139 are in respect of holdings of 1 to 3 acres, 27 in respect of holdings above 3 but below 6 acres, and only 2 in respect of holdings above 6 acres. All the rest are below one acre. The ceiling on agricultural land was fixed at 20 acres through legislation in 1950. No Muslim household lost any land at that time. Only one Muslim landowner had more than 12 acres and was thus affected by the tenancy reforms which fixed the share of the tenant at three-quarters of the produce in respect of such holdings. A large number of tenants, mostly Muslims, received small shares of about 170 acres of land that was compulsorily acquired from Pandit landowners and redistributed among the tillers by the Government.

Turning our attention to the Nangar, it may be noted that:

(*i*) All the names of such groups, except the Domb, are directly descriptive of skilled work of some kind or of non-skilled but specialized services. The Domb have a traditional calling but their name does not originate in it. They seem to be descendants of a low caste (see Lawrence, 1967:311), maybe of the Domba mentioned in early historical accounts of Kashmir (see Pandit, 1968).[8]

(*ii*) Whereas most of the Nangar in the village are stable groups following their respective hereditary occupations, some of them represent the arrival of relatively recent skills in

[8] 'Dom : A widespread caste of scavengers, musicians, and sometimes weavers, traders or even money-lenders; possibly representing an aboriginal tribe of some influence and power (Domra Dombu) (Hutton, 1951:279).

the village, or seem to be more open to recruitment than others. The Bakers, Rugmakers and Tailors of the village, though natives, have had no predecessors there. The Butchers and Weavers seem to be relatively open categories. Only one of the four Butcher households have a tradition of being meat dealers. Similarly, the Weavers seem to be an assorted category, only some of whom are Weavers by birth. Incidentally, most of the Weaver households have a secondary occupation—the breeding of silkworms. Sericulture and silk weaving have been carried on in Kashmir for several hundred years (see Bamzai, 1962:451).[9]

(*iii*) Some of the households following the above occupations own shops. The Butchers are a good example and so are the Tailors; but the former also sell meat at their homes and the latter divide work between home and shop. Shopkeeping is not treated as an occupation by any group in the village, but grocers in the nearby town of Anantnag have a long tradition of it. Generally speaking, shopkeeping in the rural areas is merely indicative of a group's or a household's mode of operation.

Finally, a few words about the Gujar and Bakərwal. As already stated, they number 770, and comprise 98 households. They live on the upper boundaries of Utrassu-Umanagri, along and deep inside the forests. Some of the Gujar—the group which came earlier than the Bakarwal—have taken to agriculture and sedentary life, and a few have even intermarried with native Muslims. There are 71 registrations of landownership in the names of the Gujar. However, most of them continue their traditional occupation, as do the Bakarwal: they graze their sheep and cattle, and those of other people in exchange for grain, and sell dairy products. Most of them leave the village during the winter months in search of warmth and pastures for their flocks. The Gujar and Bakarwal are an important element in the life of the village but they are not of it. They look different from native Muslims, speak their own dialect, live in distinctive huts, follow their own traditional pursuits and customs, and have a system of social control centred round the *jirga* or tribal council.

[9] See footnote 6 on p. 27.

Occupations such as the above are widespread and stable categories in rural Kashmir and, therefore, are employed by the people themselves as indicators of socio-cultural identity. In any particular village one encounters them as groups of households, usually but not necessarily related by ties of kinship and/or marriage. The Zamindar category is the melting pot, as it were, inasmuch as anybody might become a cultivator, even if he has no land of his own. The various Nangar groups, however, are characterized by a low degree of occupational mobility and a high incidence of endogamous marriages. Only 9 per cent of the adult Muslims of the village are in skilled or specialist occupations other than those indicated by their *zat*. A count of marriages among the Nangar, spread over two generations, revealed a little under two-thirds of them to be endogamous. (Here it may be noted that marriage between both parallel and cross cousins takes place among Kashmiri Muslims but is not prescriptive.)

When asked to explain these cultural regularities, my Muslim informants generally stressed three considerations: (*i*) The most specific of these is what may be called practical considerations. Since every Nangar is assured of a clientele for his goods or services, it is only reasonable that he should pursue his traditional occupation. His relations with his clients are generally on a hereditary and family-to-family basis; landowning households pay for goods and services in kind according to pre-determined scales, while the others pay in cash. Barter is rarely practised nowadays. The most practical as well as efficient way of learning a craft is to start when quite young, by helping the older members of one's household in their chores. One's son is one's natural apprentice as well as one's successor. (*ii*) Endogamous marriages are desirable for reasons of compatibility. There often are differences in the life-styles of different groups. Boatmen and Mallah are good examples. Moreover, women often help men in their chores; a Carpenter's daughter would obviously be of no help to a Potter, or a Barber's daughter to a Boatman. (*iii*) Both pursuit of hereditary occupation and endogamy are commendable as being inherently right. The word *zat* (in its adjectival form of *zati)* is employed in this context also.

It follows from the foregoing that we ask as to how does one acquire one's essential nature, one's true identity, or *zat*, in terms of which certain actions become inherently right or natural? This was not a question which my informants generally welcomed as they felt that they were being pushed against the wall. Several of them, however, interpreted the word *zati* as meaning 'at the root or base' which was further paraphrased as 'at or by birth'. One might translate this statement to mean that one's essential nature is endowed upon one by the circumstances of birth. The notion of *zat* is genealogical but stands for more than the fact of birth.

If the foregoing is a culturally valid position to adopt in respect of the self-ascription of Kashmiri Muslims, the most crucial question that arises is, who is a Muslim?

There seems to be general agreement among the Muslims of rural Kashmir that anyone who avows to be a Muslim is to be regarded as such. They maintain that this is what the Koran teaches. They further assert that a pious Muslim (*i*) believes in the oneness of God and in Muhammad as His prophet; (*ii*) offers prayers (*namaz*) at the appointed times; (*iii*) gives alms (*zakat*); (*iv*) keeps the prescribed hours of eating (*roza*) during the month of Ramadan; and (*v*) performs the pilgrimage to Mecca (*hajj*) when he has enough savings for the purpose. My informants pointed out that lack of means, poor health, and preoccupation with household responsibilities often prevent a person from offering prayers, giving alms, observing *roza* or performing *hajj*. Such unwilling transgressions of the desired conduct are to be forgiven a person if he reaffirms the most important tenet of Islam by solemnly reciting the *Kalimah* on being challenged: *La illah illallah Muhammadur Rasul Allah*, there is but one God and Muhammad is His prophet.[10]

[10] Whenever Kashmiri Muslim villagers have to cite the authority of religion, they invariably invoke the Koran. Being illiterate, they are unable to cite a specific text. Far from being a disadvantage, their illiteracy and ignorance have emerged as a source of strength inasmuch as doubt has been banished from their lives. Whatever the source of their beliefs, they attribute them to the unimpeachable authority of the

To deny such a person the status of Muslim is to turn against the will and voice of God and the prophet. The *accident* of birth is irrelevant in this regard. One of my educated urban informants, a Shaikh, stressed this point by asserting that he who embraces Islam out of conviction is a better Muslim than he who follows it as the religion of his parents. 'Such a man is deservedly called *shaikh*, the leader who points the path to others'.

In the course of my fieldwork I heard of about a dozen cases of recent conversion of Pandits to Islam. I was able to interview one of these converts and to discuss his case with a number of my informants, Pandits as well as Muslims. Since this case throws considerable light on the notion of *zat* in relation to religious identity, I will briefly discuss it here.

He told me that his name was Ghulam but that, before conversion to Islam, which took place about twenty years ago, he was known as Darshan Krad, and belonged to a Pandit family of Utrassu-Umanagri. His *gotra* name was Shandalya. He had been much persecuted by his cousins, particulary because he was a bachelor.[11] He had several Muslim friends in the village and they showed him greater sympathy and understanding than his own kin, who robbed him of his property and would have willingly starved him to death. His Muslim friends fed him and gave him shelter in their homes. Ultimately, he became a Muslim. He was, however, very badly treated by Muslims once he changed his religion. Though he is living with a Muslim household of the village, he is doubtful whether they will give him a decent burial. It is for this reason that he begs and not merely to keep himself alive. He is obviously saving for the rainy day and hopes to have enough money for a shroud for his dead body and for its burial. He lamented over his moral and physical condition and called his act of conversion 'a stupid act' (*budhi-vinash*) by which he became a 'breaker of *karma*' (*karma-khandit*). As he sees himself, he is a totally lost man.

holy book. Distinctions between the *sunnah*, *hadith*, and *iman* (see Hughes, 1935) are not generally made by common people; only the literate are aware of them. I have dealt with this phenomenon elsewhere (see Madan, n.d.).

[11] On the sad lot of bachelor among Kashmiri Pandits, see Madan (1965:101-02).

The Pandits, to whose homes he comes to beg, generally pity him but treat him as a fallen man who is of course no longer a Brahman, even though he had been born one. Small urchins ask him to sing Brahman devotional songs (*lila*) and promise him handfuls of rice. He often obliges them. My Pandit informants said that he had given me a fairly accurate account of what had happened, but that he had omitted to tell me that he had been promised a Muslim girl in marriage to make him give up his religion. This might in fact be true as Ghulam told me that Muslims often tempt Hindus by 'showing them birds' and by making false promises. He did not say, however, that this had been his own undoing too. The Pandits look at such cases as a kind of wicked game which some Muslims play at the former's cost. It was alleged that such Muslims derive mean satisfaction from a Pandit's fall.

When I discussed this pitiable man's case with some Muslim informants, they made two points. Firstly, they maintained, it was imperative that one should distinguish between a person who becomes a Muslim out of conviction and one who embraces Islam in the hope of material gain. To them Darshan's conversion was not a true conversion: he had not been impelled by the best of motives. Nevertheless, a Muslim household has given him shelter, though nobody gave him a wife. What more could he expect?

Secondly, my informants said, Ghulam is a bad Muslim. He does not observe the essential rules of behaviour. For example, he begs and eats at Pandit homes. No good Muslim eats food cooked by Pandits. 'The plain truth', as one informant put it, was that Darshan was born a Pandit and could not possibly be as good a Muslim as himself, i.e., the informant, who was a *zati* Muslim.

The conclusion that seems permissible on the basis of the foregoing discussion is that, the alleged teachings of the Koran notwithstanding, in actual practice the Muslims of rural Kashmir attach crucial importance to the fact of birth in the

[12] Though all believers are called brothers in the Koran (49, 10) and a *hadith* (saying attributed to the Prophet Muhammad) contends that genealogies count for nothing among Muslims (see Levy, 1962:56-57), it is well known that Islam was never able to eradicate earlier social inequalities among Arabs (see Smith, 1903:42-55 and Levy, 1962:

determination of a person's nature and his legitimate socio-cultural identity. Whether this is an Islamic notion or not, it certainly accords well with Hindu belief.[12]

Hindu Identity: Hindu Representation

One of the most striking characteristics of the social organization of native Hindus of Kashmir is that they comprise mainly of two Saraswat Brahman subcastes. There is also one Vaishya caste, but it is very small in numbers and is found only in some towns. To the best of my knowledge. this is a social situation unparalleled in any other cultural region of the subcontinent. It is almost like a deliberately set up laboratory situation, and a study of it should yield insights into the Hindu caste system unobtainable elsewhere. The first question that must be answered is, how has this peculiar situation arisen?

Fortunately we have a precious historical document to fall back upon: the twelfth century Sanskrit chronicle *Rajatarangini* by Kalhana.[13] A perusal of this work yields two relevant conclusions regarding the social structure of Kashmir before the arrival of Islam early in the fourteenth century. First, it is obvious that there were many castes among the Hindus. All the four *varna*—Brahman, Kshatriya, Vaishya, Shudra—are mentioned and, besides, we read of castes, sects and classes such as the Chandala, Damara, Domba, Kayastha, Kirata, Nishada and Tantrin. It is not always clear, however, which is which. Thus, the Damara and Kayastha, it seems, were classes of land-owners and civil servants respectively, rather than castes. Tribal groups of various kinds are also mentioned. Of these, the Ekanga and Lavanya seem to have been professional soldiers.

The second relevant conclusion is that the caste system in Kashmir between the seventh and fourteenth centuries does not seem to have been characterized by stringent exclusiveness in

53-90). Besides, 'Birth as a principle of status honour was considerably important in the early Muslim society in India' (Imtiaz Ahmad 1966: 270 also see Ashraf, 1959:61-63).

[13] Kalhana composed the *Rajataringini*, 'River of Kings', in eight cantos of Sanskrit verse in the middle of the twelfth century. Though he draws upon both legendary and historical materials, his work has been acclaimed as an historical text in the true sense of the term (see Pandit, 1968: xiii ff.).

the relations between social groups. We read in the *Rajataran-gini* of low caste Domba queens of Kshatriya kings and Kalhana particularly mentions a low caste *aramika* (vegetable grower) who had successfuly entered the ranks of the Kayastha. A probable reason for the relatively flexible social organization may well have been the influence of Buddhism, which was introduced in Kashmir during Ashoka's reign in the first quarter of the third century B.C. and dominated the cultural life of the Kashmiris for almost a millennium.

By the beginning of the eighth century Hinduism had reasserted itself in Kashmir—the Brahmans, who led the resistance to Buddhism, seem also to have spearheaded its revival. They continued to play a prominent role in the political and cultural life of the Kashmiris till the arrival of Islam in Kashmir. The presence of Muslim (Turkish) mercenaries in Kashmir during the eleventh century is noted by Kalhana. It was only a couple of hundred years later, however, that the Islamization of the Valley began, first through the peaceful persuasion of missionaries and then through the persecution of some of the early Muslim kings.[14] The most prominent of the early missionaries was Sayyid Bilal Shah of Turkistan, who was associated with the Suhrawardi school of Sufis (ses Hughes, 1935).

The Hindu dynasties had an inglorious end. External invasion, court intrigues and internal disorder resulted in the emergence of the first Muslim king of Kashmir, Rinchana (1320-23). He was a Buddhist prince, a refugee from Tibet at the court of the Hindu king. This combination of circumstances and Rinchana's personal valour led to his seizure of the kingdom. He beseeched the Brahmans to allow him to become a Hindu but they refused. He then turned to Bilal Shah who readily accepted him within the Muslim fold. Thereafter, the Sayyid's mission as a proselytiser seems to have met with success after success. Of later missionaries who peacefully carried Islam into the length and breadth of Kashmir mention may be made of the saintly Sufi scholar, Sayyid Ali of Hamadan, who paid several visits to the Valley beginning in 1327. Many Sayyids came to settle down in these parts around that time.

[14] The following account of the political history of Kashmir is based on Kak (1936).

The scholarship, saintliness and peaceful intention of the Sayyids found their counterpoint in the bigotry and fanaticism of some of the early Muslim kings. The most notorious of these was Sultan Sikandar (1389-1413), whom historians have given the name of *butshikan* (iconoclast). Not only did he destroy practically all the Hindu temples of Kashmir (see Kak, 1936, text and plates), he also compelled his Hindu subjects to choose between Islam, exile and death. Whereas some chose one of the latter two alternatives, the majority of those who had resisted the missionaries now accepted defeat. It was thus that the Hindus of Kashmir, along with whatever Buddhists had remained, were nearly wiped out and Islam established in Kashmir during the fourteenth century.[15] It seems that only a handful of Brahmans still survived in Kashmir at the time of Sikandar's death in 1414; tradition puts the number at eleven. It is from them that the Pandits of today are said to be descended.

The most celebrated of the Muslim kings of Kashmir is Zain-ul-Abidin, remembered to this day as the *budshah* ('great king'). His reign, spanning half a century (1420-70), reversed the policies of the preceding hundred years of Muslim rule by making it possible for Hindus and Buddhists to live in safety and with honour in their homeland. He abolished the *jizya*, a tax imposed on non-Muslims by his predecessors; called a halt to the destruction of non-Muslim places of worship; showed keen interest in Buddhist and Hindu philosophy and scholarship; and appointed the followers of these religions to high positions in his administration. In his magnanimous treatment of his non-Muslim subjects, he was the true precursor of Akbar, the Great Mughal, who followed a hundred years later.

Encouraged by the king, many Brahmans returned to

[15] The similarity between the Kashmir and Bangladesh situations is striking. 'Here (in Bengal), in the course of the thirteenth and fourteenth centuries, a whole countryside turned to Islam. It is thought that the decaying Buddhism of the Pala dynasty in Bengal had been superimposed upon their rustic animism, that the substitution of the Brahminical Sena Kings for Palas had meant a lowering of status and caste restriction, and that the Muslim conquests of Bengal with its casteless religion offered a welcome avenue of social escape' (Spear, 1967:34).

Kashmir. The descendants of those who stayed behind during the darkest days, and of those who went into exile to return later, maintain a distinction amongst themselves to this day: the former are called *malamasi* and the latter *bhanamasi*.[16] More significantly, the Brahman families acting together,[17] took the major decision to study Persian and thus laid the foundation of a changed social organization.

It is clear from Kalhana's account that the Kayastha category had traditionally been recruited mainly from among the Brahmans. They had for long been accustomed to playing an important role in religious, civic and administrative affairs. Zain-ul-Abidin, who had inherited an administration which was in a shambles, held forth to them the renewed possibility of a similar role. The language of the court and administration had meanwhile been changed from Sanskrit to Persian. The Brahmans' decision to acquire proficiency in the latter language indicated their earnestness to seize the newly offered opportunities and become *karkun* (the Persian word for civil servants, revenue collectors, etc.).

The Brahmans' decision raised a problem: what was to become of their traditional scholarship and philosophical heritage, and who was to ensure the proper performance of rituals so crucial to a Brahman's life? During the days of Hindu rule they had not faced such a problem, obviously because the Brahman and the king belonged to one and the same socio-religious system and used the same language—Sanskrit—in the performance of their respective roles. The problem that resulted from this separation of the socio-religious and politico-administrative spheres was resolved through a curious strategem: a daughter's son would study *bhasha* ('the language'), i.e., Sanskrit, and administer to the spiritual and ritual needs of his mother's natal family (see Kilam, 1955:53).[18] Designated

[16] I have been unable to establish the exact meaning of the two terms. The common suffix *masi* (probably derived from *mas*, month) suggests a calendarical connotation; the two groups do, in fact, observe the same important ritual occasions on different dates during the Hindu leap year.

[17] There is evidence in the *Rajatarangini* that Brahmans often acted as a corporate group to, for instance, effectively intervene in the affairs of the state.

[18] The choice of a daughter's or sister's son would seem to have been

Bhasha Bhatta, they were regarded as the privileged category compared to the Karkun; they were the Brahmans *par excellence*, in deed as well as in name. What began as an arrangement of convenience has since frozen into a rigid division into two endogamous subcastes. What is more, the Karkun have arrogated to themselves the higher status. The Bhasha Bhatta are now called Gor (derived from the Sanskrit *guru*, 'preceptor', 'teacher'), which term is unmistakably one of contempt.

Both the Karkun and Gor are divided into exogamous *gotra* categories. According to Lawrence (1967:304) there are 103 Karkun and 18 'Levite' *gotras* among the Pandits. Koul (1924) mentions 199 *gotras* and names 189.[19] Within each *gotra* there are families which are identified by surnames called *zat* or, relatively rarely, *kram*. The *zat* among Pandits are sectarian or family nick-names, the latter oftener than the former. These nick-names have their exact parallels among the Browns, Blacks, Longmans, Pidgeons, Swindlers and such other Anglo-Saxon surnames.[20] The Gor also have *zat* but they rarely use the surname. It is instead customary to use the suffix *boi* (brother) with the personal name of each male priest. I have already pointed out that *zat* has to do with the establishment of identity by birth among Kashmiri Muslims; the same applies to Pandits. It may be added here that *kram*, a word of Sanskrit origin, sometimes used as a synonym for *zat*, means a ranked category and suggests that internal ranking was, as it still is, a characteristic of the Brahmans of Kashmir. Whether the basis of ranking earlier was politico-economic as it is now, or involved other considerations also, is a subject on which I lack any data at present (see Madan, 1965:22-27).

made in view of the fact that, since agnates suffer pollution together, such a kinsman would be unable to help in the performance of purificatory rituals of his *yajaman*; non-agnatic kinsman would not be similar by handicapped except by rare coincidence. The practice seems to have been prevalent in the Punjab also and Hutton curiously considers it evidence for the fusion of matrilineal and patrilineal cultures (see Hutton, 1951:156-57).

[19] For a discussion of the nature of *gotra* among the Pandit see Madan (1962).

[20] For an account (partly fanciful perhaps) of Pandit family names, see Fauq (n.d.).

In none of the villages in the district of Anantnag which I visited did I encounter any other kind of Bhatta except the Gor and Karkun. All the 87 Pandit households of Utrassu-Umanagri are Karkun. The adjacent village of Kreri has 7 Karkun and 5 Gor households. Pandit informants drew my attention to the presence of a doubtful and small category of Bhatta, the Buher, who are to be found only in urban areas. (There is a ward in the city of Srinagar named after them.) The Buher (also called Bohra) are Khattris, probably of Punjabi origin (see Lawrence, 1967:302; 1909:40). Hutton (1951:282) describes the Khattri as a trading caste of the Punjab and north-west India. The Buher are an endogamous caste of grocers and *halwai* (makers of confectionery, cheese, yoghourt and fried savouries of various kinds). In fact, the word *buhur* (singular of buher) is used in Kashmir in the sense of a grocer. The Pandits do not interdine with the Buher, nor allow them entry into Pandit temples. The Gor do, however, perform priestly functions for them. The Buher have built a Vishnu temple of their own in Srinagar. On their part, the Buher have adopted the life-style of the Pandits and would obviously like to be called Buher Bhatta. Already there are signs that, barring intermarriage, the Karkun and Buher are coming closer to each other in urban areas. The problem does not exist in rural Kashmir.[21]

In Utrassu-Umanagri and surrounding villages the Karkun are served by a large number of occupational groups. The first of these are, of course, the Gor. Each Gor household has a clientele fixed on a hereditary basis, of both Karkun and Gor households. The latter are referred to as *yazaman* (derived from the Sanskrit *yajamana*). When a Gor household dies out, its clientele is usually inherited by the nearest agnatic kin. A Karkun household may employ the services of the most readily available priest for minor purposes—such as consecrating routine food offerings or determining auspicious dates for doing or buying some thing—but on all important occasions only the *kola-gor* (family priest) will do. If he is ill, in a state of

[21] There are a few Kashmiri speaking Hindu families in Srinagar called the Purib or Purbi. They are probably descended from an immigrant Brahman group. Some informants told me that the Purbi come to Kashmir from the Chambha valley in Punjab.

pollution, or otherwise unavailable, it is his duty to provide a substitute.

Formerly the Gor were also teachers, not only of priestly lore but also of astrology, Sanskrit and *shastra* (religious literature) in general. Nowadays, the only pupils they have are their own sons, though not even all of them are willing to follow their traditional calling. The performance of all but the most essential rituals is coming to be viewed as dispensable. The Karkun feel that they do not have the time or the resources for them. The Gor lament the decline of faith and they complain that even the essential rituals are sought to be abridged. Whatever the reasons, the Gor are beginning to turn away from priestcraft. One of the young Gor of Kreri is a school teacher; another has joined the State militia. I was informed that the process of occupational change among the Gor is more visible in urban areas.

The Karkun are of course dependent on the Gor for the performance of rituals. There can be no Pandits without the Gor. The latter's dependence on the Karkun is merely economic. It is not inconceivable that a small community of Gor could exist without the Karkun and draw their sustenance from land or service. The secularisation of Pandit society has gone so far, however, that the Karkun look down upon the Gor and even consider them inauspicious. Several times during my fieldwork I noticed how a Karkun would return home if he met a priest just after he had started on an errand. There is general denigration of the Gor on account of their style of life and their alleged greed and lack of learning. Their worst fault would seem to be that they accept food and other gifts offered to the dead.[22]

The Karkun-Gor relationship has always been hierarchical, being ordered in terms of religious values and moral judgements. The two groups seem to have changed places, however, since the emergence of the division between them about 500 years ago. Even so, as a category, the Gor are essentially pure,

[22] I was told that in Srinagar there is a special category of Gor called *Achor*, who alone accept such offerings. They collect the goods under cover of darkness, either from the home of the gift-givers or from the nearest bathing ghat. See Dumont (1970:58) on the 'Mahabrahman'.

irrespective of how particular Gor may be regarded by their Karkun patrons. In principle the Karkun and the Gor are one: they are Brahmans—they are the Pandits.

For all other services the Pandits are dependent upon Muslims. An examination of these services is of great importance from the point of view of this paper as it will enable us to grasp the definition of Muslim identity by Pandits.

Muslim Identity: Hindu Representation

As stated earlier, Utrassu-Umanagri is a bi-nucleated village. The settlement of Utrassu is older than anybody can remember. Umanagri is, however, quite recent: it was founded about 200 years ago. I have given the details elsewhere (see Madan, 1965: 38-40), and will here confine myself to pointing out that originally there were no Muslims in Umanagri. The Pandits found it impossible to carry on without the services of Muslim cultivators, artisans, village servants, and other specialist groups and therefore invited them to come from other villages and settle down in Umanagri. This historical fact only serves to underline what my fieldwork revealed.

Being Brahmans, the Pandits are traditionally debarred from a large number of occupational activities. Thus, they cannot engage in polluting activities such as barbering, washing clothes, obtaining oil from oilseeds, removing and skinning dead animals, making shoes, winnowing pans and drums, slaughtering goats and sheep,[23] and so on. There are so many other types of activities which are not polluting but which no Pandit would engage in because they involve manual labour, no matter how light. Some of the poorer Pandits in Utrassu-Umanagri do engage in cultivation or cooking—the former only in their own village and the latter only outside it—but at the cost of being treated socially as inferiors by the others.[24] Ownership of land,

[23] Kashmiri Pandits eat mutton, wild fowl and fish, but not domestic fowl or their eggs (see Madan, 1975).

[24] Things have begun to change since 1947 following upon the drastic political and economic changes that have taken place in the State. During 1957-58, nine Pandits of Utrassu-Umanagri were working as labourers in an Indian Army ammunition depot four miles from the village (see Madan, 1965:146-48).

service (public or private) and shopkeeping are the only sources of household income among the Pandits of Utrassu-Umanagri (see Madan, 1965:149-50).[25] In such a situation it is not at all surprising that the Pandits should regard Muslims as an essential component of their social system. In this connection it is worth mentioning that the 1941 census shows only two villages in the Srinagar-Anantnag districts inhabited by Pandits alone though, as stated earlier, 56 per cent of the villages are exclusively Muslim.

In the Pandits' conception of them, Kashmiri villages are characterized by the simiple but sharp distinction between themselves and the Muslims. The latter are regarded in principle as being ritually impure. They are referred to as *mlechchha* (of lowly birth, outsiders); theirs is the world of *tamas* (darkness, ignorance). Muslims are outside the pale of values by which a Pandit is expected, as a Hindu, to order his life. In practice, however, the Pandits consider some Muslims as less polluting than others.

In Utrassu-Umanagri no Pandit eats food cooked or even touched by a Muslim. There are no exceptions to this rule except the acceptance of clarified butter from Milkmen, Gujar and Bakarwal. (Some Pandits also accept yoghourt and cheese from these three groups but others disapprove of the practice, which seems to be recent.) If transgressions occur they are so secretive that no Pandit claimed having actually seen another Pandit eating with a Muslim. There seems to have been some kind of a sumptuary ban on the consumption of such forbidden food till about 1925, when Maharaja Pratap Singh, a very orthodox Hindu, died.

Pandits accept uncooked food from all but the lowliest of Muslims (namely, the Domb and Vatal). Grains, vegetables and fruits are included in this category. Uncooked meat also is generally accepted but may be refused for fear of its being beef. (Killing beef cattle is a penal offence in the State, but it would seem that Muslims do sometimes slaughter such animals.) Unboiled milk is freely accepted from Milkmen, Gujar, Bakarwal, and Zamindar but usually not from any other group. The

[25] The 1931 census report lists government service as the traditional occupation of the Pandits (see India, 1933).

Pandits are much more hesitant to accept water from Muslims. Some well-to-do households employ water carriers but invariably choose a Milkman or a Zamindar for the chore and provide him with a pitcher. A Pandit is not expected to drink even milk from a container belonging to a Muslim.

There is no sharing of the *hookah* between Pandits and Muslims. A Pandit does not touch any part of a Muslim's *hookah* — its vase of water, pipe or the *chillum* (tobacco-cum-fire bowl). A Muslim is allowed to smoke the *chillum* of a Pandit's *hookah* by holding it between his palms but is never allowed to use the pipe.

The Utrassu-Umanagri Pandits avoid any physical contact with the cobblers and winnowing-pan makers (Vatal), who skin dead animals and have traditionally been suspected by everybody of being carrion eaters. (I was informed that in urban areas, where there are two types of Vatal, namely, leather-workers and scavengers, the latter are treated with less repugnance than the former.) Pandits do, however, buy the articles these craftsmen make. The Domb are also regarded as being very polluting and physical contact with them is strenuously avoided. In relation to other Muslims in the village, the Pandits are less anxious to avoid total physical contact. The more fastidious among them will wash their hands after touching a Muslim. I once saw a Muslim servant (a Zamindar) press the feet and legs of his Pandit master but the latter did not wash afterwards. (Only half a dozen or so Pandit households in Utrassu-Umanagri employ Muslim servants; the latter are all Zamindar.) Muslim-Pandit marriages are, of course, ruled out. Illicit sexual intercourse does seem to occur once in a while. This is a subject on which one has no evidence more reliable than village gossip. Among all Muslims, it is the Barber (Navid) and the midwife with whom Pandit men and women, respectively, come in most intimate physical contact. The Barber's services are particularly noteworthy and may be elaborated upon.

The Navid renders routine and occasional services to his Pandit patrons. The routine services consist of shaving the face and the head or cutting the hair. Shaving is regarded as *varzit* (derived from the Sanskrit *varjit*, forbidden) on certain days of the week and on most occasions when one has to perform a ritual. The act of having one's beard or hair shaved on such days is inauspicious in itself, and does not seem to have anything to do with the desire to avoid contact with a Muslim. That this is so is indicated by the fact that the Barber is called in to render his services on four highly important occasions of ritual performance. Sanskritic rites are interrupted to have a boy's *zarakasai* (*zara*=baby hair, *kasai*=shaving, cutting) done; to have a neophyte's head shaved during *mekhla*: ("waist string"; the investiture ceremony also called *yagnopavit* or *upanayana*); and to shave the beard and hair of a mourner at the end of the period of pollution. These rituals would remain incomplete without the Barber's services. The Barber's touch is polluting, however, and the person who has been served by him on the special ritual occasions mentioned above must have a bath. On other occasions too having a bath is desirable, but washing of the face and head is all that may be done. The Barber also shaves and gives a hair-cut to a bridegroom before the latter leaves for the bride's home for the marriage ceremony. During the *lagan* (marriage ritual), one of the rites involves letting the bride and the bridegroom see each other's faces in a mirror. This mirror is customarily provided by the Barber of the bride's natal household.

For his routine services the Barber receives a number of measures of paddy from his patrons at harvest time. Several Pandit households of Utrassu-Umanagri buy grain so as to meet the requirements of such payments to the Barber and other specialists. Many families pay for them in cash. On all special occasions the Barber receives the clothes, at least some of them, which the individual recipient of the services has on him at that time. The Barber also receives other gifts. He is treated as a well-wisher by his patrons, with whom he has hereditary relations.

I have described the Barber's services at some length because of their value as a paradigm of the relations between the Pandit and Muslim occupational groups. The essential elements of the paradigm may be recapitulated:

1. the services are of routine and special kinds;
2. they have a ritual significance for the Pandit and this is

known to the Muslim specialist;
3. the specialist himself views them in economic terms, but recognizes their traditional character;
4. the threat to his state of ritual purity arising from contact with a Muslim is tolerated by the Pandit because he is otherwise even more seriously in danger of being unable to enter or re-enter such a state;
5. the relations between the patrons and the specialists are on a hereditary basis and are paid for in kind, if possible.

I will take another crucial example: that of the relations between the Muslim Potter (Kral) and his Pandit patrons. The Potter supplies pots and pans of various kinds which he makes both for everyday use and for special occasions. Storage jars for grains, pickles and water; utensils for cooking, storing and serving food; smoking bowls; toys; and many other types of pottery are supplied by him. He provides a wide range of utensils in large quantities at weddings. It is on the occasion of Herath (a feast in honour of Shiva), however, that he makes for his Pandit customers the most unusual of all pieces of pottery.

As I have described elsewhere (see Madan, 1961:129-39), Herath is celebrated over fifteen days during the dark fortnight of the month of Phagun (February-March). Each day has its appointed task; on the eleventh day the Potter carries a basket load of pottery to each patron household for use in its kitchen and in the climacteric rites during the last four days. The number of each type of the various pieces of pottery has to be just right. Shortages are regarded as bad omens and the Potter is rebuked for such lapses. Among the many objects he makes is the rather inconspicuous looking *sanipotul* (*sani*=worship, *potul*= idol), which is the *lingam*, to be installed as Shiva during the rites. It is obviously phallic in shape. (In fact, it is in the shape of *lingam* and *yoni in coitu*, but not even all Pandits seem to know this.)

Though the Potters whom I questioned at Utrassu-Umanagri do not exactly know what kind of an idol the *sanipotul* is, they are all aware that it is an object of worship for the Pandits. As

Muslims they have no use for such idols, and abhor idol worship, but as Potters they readily make the objects for the Pandits. They look upon the work they do in economic terms; but not so the Pandits, who view the Potter's services in their relation to such basic activities as the preparation of food and the performance of one of the most important domestic rituals of the year.

More examples of such relationships between Muslims and Pandits could be given, including that of the familiar Washerman and the unfamiliar (among Brahman communities) Butcher. The latter supplies the meat which the Pandit offers to some of his gods and goddesses; in fact, it is the Muslim Butcher who, standing shoulder to shoulder with the Brahman Gor, slaughters the sacrificial goat after the latter has ritually rendered it sacred. Further, it is worth mentioning that, since the Pandits are major consumers of meat in Utrassu-Umanagri, the Muslim Butchers keep track of the capricious Hindu lunar calendar and avoid slaughtering too many animals on days on which Pandits abstain from eating meat, such as the birthdays of vegetarian gods and goddesses.

Limitations of space prevent me from going into the details of more cases.[26] Suffice it to add that most of the services that Muslim specialist groups render to their Pandit clientele are ritual liturgies when viewed from the receiver's end; but they appear as economic transactions, sanctioned by village tradition, when judged from the perspective of the giver. What are legitimately seen as occupational groups from the Muslim angle are castes, 'caste analogues', or 'caste substitutes' when viewed in terms of the Hindu caste system which they, in fact, help to constitute in Kashmir.

We will be justified in speaking of the social organization of mixed Kashmiri villages as a regional variant of the caste system if the cardinal principle of hierarchy is found applicable. It is obvious from the foregoing discussion that this certainly is so in the Pandits' ideological reconstruction of empirical reality. Moreover, the Pandits do not normally render any services to

[26] The case of the Muslim *Kawuj*—attendants at Pandit cremation sites in Srinagar, and probably in other towns—requires close study; particularly their relations with other Muslims should be of interest. Kashmiri Muslims regard everything dead (except fish) as polluting.

the Muslims nor provide them with any goods. The only exceptions to this rule in Utrassu-Umanagri are a Pandit *hakim* (practitioner of Graeco-Arab medicine), and some money-lenders, and (if we may include them) shopkeepers. I encountered several instances of a Pandit astrologer being consulted by Muslims. It is clear that all these roles are prestigious. Their representation of village society is shown diagrammatically in Figure 1.

FIGURE 1

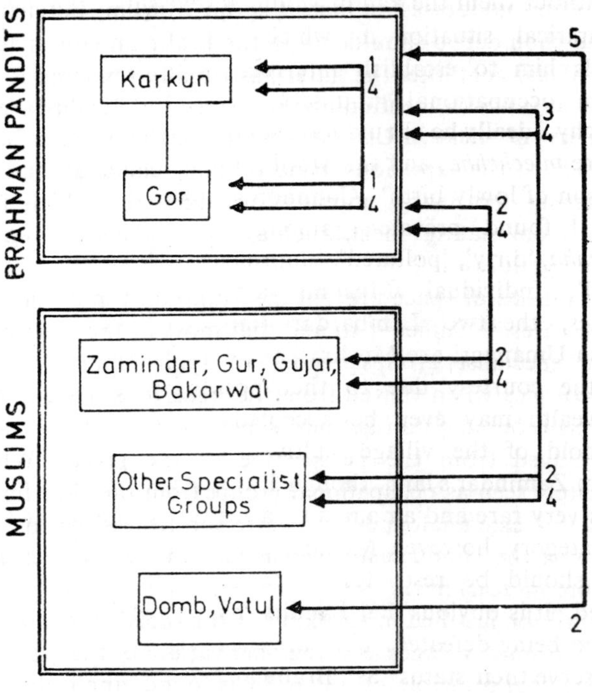

1—Acceptance of cooked and uncooked food.
2—Acceptance of uncooked food, milk, water.
3—Acceptance of uncooked food only.
4—Flow of goods and/or services without avoidance of physical contact.
5—Flow of goods and/or services with strict avoidance of physical contact.

It will be agreed that (*i*) the inferior status of Gor *vis-a-vis* Karkun, (*ii*) the inferior position of the Muslims *vis-a-vis* the Brahmans, and (*iii*) the division of Muslims into three ranked categories are all ultimately based on the same governing principle of superior dignity arising out of moral, i.e., religious considerations. As we move downwards from the Gor through the three rungs of Muslim occupational groups, the element of ritual impurity becomes increasingly salient.

The admission of Muslims into a common social fold is surreptitious, by the backdoor as it were: it cannot occur in terms of ideology but, paradoxically, is defended on the ground that without them the Pandit would lose caste. In other words, the empirical situation in which the Pandit finds himself compels him to establish interrelations of various kinds with Muslim occupational groups; he orders them in terms of hierarchy. Ideally he should have no relations with the Muslims: they are *mlechchha*, and this word means both 'an outsider' and 'a person of lowly birth'. Common stereotypes about Muslims which I found prevalent among Pandits included, besides *mlechchha*, 'dirty', 'polluted', 'unprincipled', 'omnivorous', and 'lustful'. Individual Muslims are respected for personal qualities; the two Lambardar (minor revenue official) of Utrassu-Umanagri are Muslims, and I saw Pandits treat them with the courtesy due to their position. Muslim households with wealth may even be accepted as patrons: one Pandit household of the village cultivates a portion of the biggest Muslim Zamindar's land, though I was told that such a relationship is very rare and amounts to a reversal of familiar roles. As a category, however, Muslims are polluting and contact with them should be restricted as far as possible if it cannot be avoided. It is obvious that Pandits have accepted compromise to avoid being defeated. They are faced with a moral dilemma: to preserve their status as Brahmans they need goods and services which only the Muslims provide, but the latter are themselves a source of pollution. Since the danger emanating from Muslims can be controlled and rectified, the Pandits' choice has its merits. A Pandit saying is apposite in this context: *Yath na push tath na dush* (whereof one is helpless, thereof one attaches no blame). This may be regarded as evidence of Pandit pragmatism; in Dumont's phrase, a concession to coexistence (see Dumont, 1970:206).

That this has not been an easy choice is illustrated by the manner in which Pandits switch codes when talking to Muslims. Though they all speak the same language, Koshur or Kashmiri, there are striking differences of lexical elements so that linguists have classified it into Sanskritized Kashmiri (SK) and Persianized Kashmiri (PK) (see Kachru, 1969:21-27). The speakers of PK are Muslims. I found in Utrassu-Umanagri that their use of PK words is consistent: they employ them with whomsoever they are speaking. The Pandits switch from SK to PK when certain crucial words have to be used in conversation with Muslims. A Pandit will generally stick to such SK words as *ponya* (water; PK equivalent, *ab*), *khovur* (left; PK, *khofur*), *shokrawar* (Friday; PK, *jummah*). He wavers when it comes to such words as God (SK, *Bhagwan*; PK, *Khoda*) and religion (SK, *dharma*; PK, *mazhab*) but generally uses the PK words when talking with a Muslim. I never found a Pandit use the SK greeting of *namaskar* when addressing a Muslim: there is no ambiguity at all on this point. A Muslim greets all, whether Muslim or Hindu, with *salam*; but a Pandit always says *salam* to a Muslim and *namaskar* to another Pandit. *Namaskar* is thus a marked term: when one hears it said, the only conclusion that may be drawn is that one Pandit has greeted another.

On being questioned, even the most intelligent of my Pandit informants would tell me no more by way of explanation than that it would be improper to say *namaskar* to a Muslim. 'Is that not obvious?', they asked me. It is apparent that saying *namaskar*, 'I bow to thee', to a Muslim is improper, for he is *mlechchha*, an outsider. He cannot be fully admitted into the Pandits' company. There must be no blurring of *zati* or natural distinctions, that is, of socio-cultural identities. Words like *Bhagwan*, *dharma* and, above all, *namaskar*, are signposts which the Pandits have set up as a boundary maintenance device. Those within are Brahmans; those outside, *mlechchha*. It is a kind of last ditch defence.

Hindu Identity: Muslim Representation

A question that arises from the foregoing discussion is, do Kashmiri Muslims also feel threatened by the Pandits? The answer, it seems to me, has to be in the negative, though Muslims do regard Pandits as being outsiders, non-Muslims. To understand this situation we shall now examine the Muslim representation of Pandit identity in relation to their own.

The Muslim's view of Pandits as non-Muslims has to be disentangled from his image of them as clients or patrons. Just as Pandits *qua* Hindus see themselves in opposition to the *mlechchha*, Kashmiri Muslims *qua* Muslims identify themselves with *umma*, the universal Muslim brotherhood, and regard Pandits as *kafir* ('misbelievers'), destined to go to hell. Internal divisions among the Pandits do not interest the Muslims in the least.

The relationship is hierarchical, based on Islamic values. The exclusion of Pandits stems from moral abhorrence but has nothing to do with ritual pollution. Earlier I mentioned Pandit stereotypes of Muslims; these may now be matched by Muslim stereotypes of Pandits, equally derogatory and expressive of the wish to exclude the other. 'Faithless', 'unfaithful', 'double-dealer', 'mean', 'cowardly', 'corrupt' and 'dirty' are some of the epithets I heard Muslim informants use for Pandits.[27]

Kashmiri Muslims countenance marriage with Pandits no more than the latter do. They have no objection, however,

[27] Probably the stereotype of Pandits most widely used by Kashmiri Muslims is *dali-Bhatta*, 'the *dal* or lentil curry Pandit'. *Dal* is considered the vegetarian dish *par excellence* and the very opposite of mutton curries; *dal* eaters are represented as cowardly and meat eaters as brave and courageous. Vegetarianism is actually no more than an occasional dietary restriction among the Pandits. Exceptions apart, I have encountered no vegetarian Pandit households in many years of contact with rural Kashmir, though there are vegetarian individuals. The Muslims also eat *dal* but never on festive occasions (see Madan, 1975). A well known Kashmiri saying is: *Bhattas phaka, Musalmans shraka, Shias baka*, the Pandits fast on important occasions, the Muslims wield the sword (to slaughter sheep and goats), and the Shiahs weep.

to physical contact with the Pandits. The latter have free access to all parts of a Muslim house though they themselves do not allow Muslims into their kitchens and into any room where a ritual is in progress or where rituals usually take place (see Madan, 1965:46-50). The Barber and the Butcher, whose role in Pandit religious ceremonies was discussed earlier, perform their assigned tasks just outside the ritually demarcated area. Similarly, the water carrier pours water into a vessel in the kitchen without stepping inside. Pandits are, however, debarred from entering mosques. Moreover, the Muslims of Utrassu-Umanagri do observe strict avoidance in respect of food cooked by Pandits. 'It is *haram* (forbidden)'—the Koran prohibits it--is the most general explanation given; when pressed to elaborate upon this cryptic remark, some informants used the word *napak* (impure) to describe Pandit food. (Several other less significant explanations were given, including the belief that Pandit food is injurious to health because their curries contain asafoetida, and is tasteless as it lacks onions and garlic.) A few Zamindar who have intimate relations with Pandit landowners were reported as given to eating food from their patrons' kitchens, but the number of such cases is negligible. Those who transgress this restriction are believed to be guilty of a moral lapse and therefore liable to suffer supernatural punishment. One of the villagers drew attention to his own brother, a sickly and poor Milkman, saying that the latter was an eater of Pandit food.[28]

[28] I discussed the Muslim attitude to Pandit food with *mufti* [a person 'learned in the Koran and Hadith and in the Muslim works of law' (Hughes, 1935)] of Srinagar, who is also a college professor. He disapproved of the villagers' attitude and maintained that they were acting out of ignorance and under the influence of long established habits. In this connexion it is worth noting here that a Muslim Washerman of Utrassu-Umanagri once told me of how he had fallen ill after he had eaten 'unusual meat' with some acquaintances in a neighbouring village. On my asking for clarification, he said he suspected that he had been served beef. I doubt if many Kashmiri Muslims would feel likewise about eating beef; what is remarkable is that even a few of them should. The influence of Pandit neighbours is an obvious but unsatisfactory explanation. I guess one has to fall back upon Dumont's other suggestion, 'psychological dispositions' (see Dumont, 1970: 211), preferably qualified as *residual.*

There is one more category of people whose cooking the Muslims of the village do not accept because it is considered impure. The people concerned are the Domb and Vatal. Whenever these families arrange a feast, they engage professional Muslim cooks who bring their own cooking and serving utensils. Other Muslims then readily join such feasts in the houses of these lowly groups, but do not otherwise eat with them. The Domb and Vatal get invited to the homes of other Muslims but they are excluded in a subtle manner. On such occasions four Muslims eat from a single plate. The Domb and Vatal will not be asked to share a plate with one another, or with any other Muslim, even if there are less than four of each of these groups present. Needless to add, the Domb and the Vatal are the two most strictly endogamous Muslim groups in the village.

Kashmiri Muslims clearly distinguish between dirty (*mokur*) and impure (*napak*). The two conditions may exist together as in the case of the legendary pig—the animal is non-existent in Kashmir—whose very sight is forbidden to the Muslim. The best example of the distinction between dirt and impurity was given to me by one of my informants when he expiained why Muslims are expected to dry the penis with clay after urination. 'I may have put on new or washed trousers, but if even a drop of urine falls on them, I cannot enter the mosque for prayers.' Muslim washing is quite an elaborate affair. However, their notion of pollution is in principle different from the Hindu notion inasmuch as they do not consider it permanent. I was told that if the Domb or the Vatal should give up their present occupations, they too would be accepted as equals by other Muslims. This is of course difficult to confirm, and though there has long been evidence of upward mobility among Muslim occupational groups, I doubt if the Domb and the Vatal could easily live down the stigma of their names, which proclaim their *zat*.[29] The Muslims point out that even a Pandit—any

[29] Lawrence calls the 'social system in Kashmir . . . delightfully plastic': . . . there is nothing to prevent Abdulla, the Dum, calling himself Abdulla Pandit if he chooses. At first the people would laugh, but after a time, if Abdulla Pandit prospered, his descendants would exhibit a lengthy pedigree table tracing their family back to one of the petty Rajas, lord of three villages and possessor of a fort, the ruins of

non-Muslim for that matter—can acquire true faith and become a believer (*mumin*). This is of course the ideological position, but we have already noted the case of the convert Ghulam alias Darshan and have discussed the significance of the circumstances of birth in the determination of *zat*.

Before we complete this discussion of the Muslim representation of Pandit identity, I would like to make a final comment on the notion of *zat* among Muslims. The status of Sayyids is the key to this problem. I have already pointed out that Kashmiri Muslims are not an undifferentiated category, and that they themselves acknowledge this fact. My informants in Utrassu-Umanagri spoke to me of the division between the Sunni and Shiah (see Hughes, 1935; Levy, 1962: *passim*), though there are no Shiah in the village.[30] They also mentioned Sayyids, Mughals and Pathans with a certain degree of deference. Muslims falling into these categories are to be found in the town of Anantnag.[31] The position of the Gujar and the Bakarwal has already been mentioned. I have also described how the native Muslims are comprised of many occupational groups including the Domb and the Vatal.

The Sayyids are the descendants of Ali and his wife Fatimah, daughter of the Prophet Muhammad. They are, therefore, entitled to respect. The Mughul and Pathan families are

which still stand in Abdulla Pandit's village . . .' (1967:307). Unless things have changed beyond recognition over the last 75 years, which I doubt, Lawrence's account seems rather exaggerated. I found no forts in ruins in the Kashmiri countryside and the people, Muslims and Pandits alike, take little interest in genealogies beyond half a dozen generations at best.

[30] 'At the census of 1890 no distinction was made between the Musalmans of the Sunni and Shiah persuasions, but it may be roughly said that the Shiahs form only about 5 per cent of the total Musalman. The Shiahs chiefly reside in Zadi Bal ward of Srinagar and in the Kamraj (Baramulla) district, though they are found in other parts of the valley' (Lawrence, 1967:284).

[31] According to the 1941 census the Sayyids formed 7 per cent of the Muslim population of Anantnag district, Pathans 3 per cent, Rajputs 2 per cent and Mughals 1 per cent.

also entitled to respect, but why? The Muslims of the village are dimly aware that these people were once the rulers of Kashmir. An equally important reason would seem to be that these groups have been Muslims longer than the others. The principle of proximity to the founder of Islam, which is apparent in view of the genealogical connexion in the case of the Sayyids, and acknowledged by the Muslims, is also applicable to the Mughals and the Pathans. In terms of this logic the Gujar and Bakarwal should also be accorded deference but they are not, though they themselves look down upon the natives. The empirical situation is, therefore, somewhat ambiguous; but the cardinal principle of genealogical relationship emerges clearly in the exalted position of the Sayyids. It is misleading to regard them as the Muslim equivalent of Brahman as some writers have done, because the criterion of ritual purity—or even of moral superiority—is not applicable.

All the above internal divisions among Muslims are ignored when Muslims are juxtaposed with Pandits. The situation then is dramatized by being reduced to stark opposition between the believer and the 'misbeliever', the Muslim and the non-Muslim. The Pandit lies completely outside the fold of Islam. His present status is inconsequential to the Muslim; his potential status as a convert, though significant in ideological terms, does not really excite the Muslim, given the latter's notion of *zat*. In any case, the convert is not a threat to the community of believers, which is open and to which he is in principle welcome. The contrast with the completely closed community of Pandits is too obvious to need further comment.

The answer to the question posed at the beginning of this section—namely why Muslims do not feel their identity threatened by interaction with Pandits—may now be given. As already explained, Kashmiri Muslims enter into relations with Pandits which they view as traditional economic transactions. The relationship is between a supplier of goods and services and his patron; religious differences are held in abeyance. It is a relationship of mutual dependence, but is asymmetrical. Whereas the Pandit cannot find substitutes or surrogates for Muslim occupational groups in his own community, Muslim specialists are free, at least in principle, to make their living by attending to the needs of their co-religionists alone. This is what happens in fact in many villages where there are no Pandits within the settlement or nearby. It is true that in mixed villages Pandit households have generally enjoyed enough economic power to make it worthwhile for the Muslims to serve them. The Pandits were favoured by and identified with the ruling class during the hundred years of Hindu rule between 1846 and 1947 (see Bamzai, 1962:553 ff.).[32] Economic need or advantage and political subordination of the Muslims do not, however, create among them a dependence on the Pandits in principle, which alone would be immutable; the existing dependence is purely empiric.

Dependence in deference to a principle characterizes the relationship of Pandits and Muslims. A Pandit cannot continue to retain his ritual status without the crucial services of at least some of the Muslim occupational groups. The dependence is absolute: in principle as well as in practice. To put it differently: the Pandit keeps Muslims out of the *sanctum sanctorum* of his cultural universe, but has to let them into his social world; hence the strain and anxiety that he experiences. A Muslim, on the other hand, considers Pandits as outsiders, both ideologically and empirically. He does not feel threatened on either plane. This sense of security has been considerably heightened since 1947 by the policies followed by a succession of democratically chosen governments of the State which have been dominated by Muslims.[33] The most noteworthy of the decisions taken have been in respect of land and tenancy reforms—the most radical in India—abolition or reduction of the debt burden of the peasantry, and provision of extensive education, health and transportation facilities in rural areas. Educationally, and perhaps economically, the Muslims of Utrassu-Umanagri are not yet the equals of their Pandit co-villagers, but politically they are on the right side of the fence. This would seem to be generally true of rural Kashmir.

[32] Lawrence notes that the Dogra rulers had vested revenue administration in the hands of the Pandits, who manned it from the lowest to the highest levels (see Lawrence, 1895:400-01). Also see footnote 25.

[33] Since 1948, the heads of government in the state of Jammu and Kashmir have all been Muslim: Shaikh Mohammad Abdullah. Bakshi Ghulam Mohammad, Shamass-u-din, Ghulam Mohammad Sadiq, Syed (Sayyid) Mir Qasim, and, currently Shaikh Abdullah again.

The Muslim representation of village society is shown in Figure 2. If we compare it with the Hindu representation of

FIGURE 2

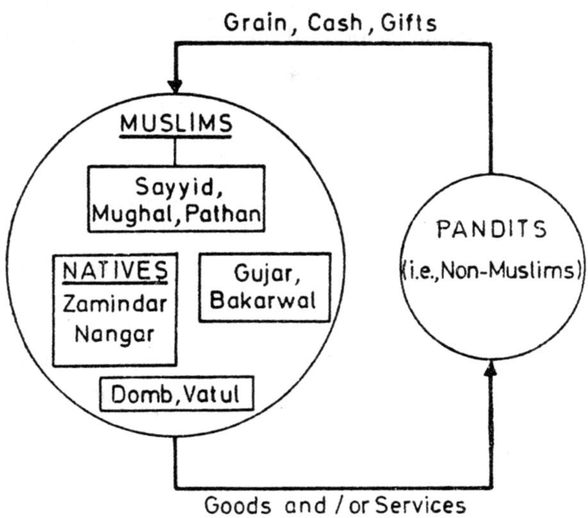

the same society presented in Figure 1, it becomes clear that we are faced with a situation of dual identities and of dual social orders. The only respect in which the two social orders appear identical is the position accorded to the Domb and the Vatal. In this parallelism between the two representations may be seen 'the exemplification of the Hindu Ethic *par excellence*' (Gould, 1962:194). What explains it? This is a difficult question to answer. With Dumont, we might attribute it to the permanence of 'psychological dispositions'(see Dumont, 1970:211). What I would like to stress, however, is the marginal nature of these two groups in both the versions of Kashmiri rural society.

Conclusion

It will be recalled that this examination of data, drawn primarily from a Kashmiri village, was undertaken with a two-fold purpose. It was hoped that it would, firstly, enable us to define the respective places of Muslims and Hindus in Kashmiri rural society and, secondly, provide some fresh insights into more general problems, such as the nature of Hindu-Muslim 'synthesis' and of caste society.

We have seen that the Muslims and the Hindus differ in the images that they have of themselves, of each other, and of Kashmiri rural society. This is a familiar situation in societies characterized by cultural pluralism, with each ethnic category being 'self-ascribed' as well as 'other-ascribed' (see, for example, Barth, 1970). The data from Utrassu-Umanagri reveal that each group has, in fact, two sets of representations, one stemming from ideological considerations and the other from the compulsions of living.

At the ideological level there is complete mutual exclusion. That this fundamental opposition between Hindus and Muslims exists throughout South Asia, is well known.[34] What is missed, however, is the very important though apparently paradoxical fact that both ideologies command identical behaviour towards non-believers—total exclusion— and are in that sense mutually reciprocal and reinforcing. In other words, Kashmiri rural society, when subjectively defined, comprises two social orders, not one.

At the empirical level we encounter another set of relations, those between the Muslim occupational groups and their Pandit clients or patrons. As we have already seen, the Muslims view

[34] There is widespread agreement on this point. See, for example (*i*) Aziz Ahmad (1964:73): 'As a religio-cultural force, Islam is in most respects the "very antithesis of Hinduism", (*ii*) Dumont (1970:211) '. . . Hindus and Muslims form two distinct societies from the point of view of ultimate values', (*iii*) A.K. Saran (gist of a statement made by him in the course of a conversation with me in 1970): 'When the Muslims came to India, the Hindus had only two valid courses of action open to them: a fight to the finish or conversion to Islam. Instead they made a soft choice: they swallowed the poison and pretended they had not died. But only the gods can perform such feats'.

these relationships in economic terms while the Pandits regard them as ritual liturgies with an economic content. This content is not to be equated with the value of goods or services transacted, for the Pandits' stakes are higher than can be measured by the economic yardstick. Thus, though the Muslims and the Pandits are mutually dependent, there is no reciprocity of perspective, if we take the surface level view of the situation. At the deeper level, however, there is agreement. The duality of the social orders is thus overcome. In the words of Levi-Strauss (used, of course, in another context), 'it is not the resemblances, but the differences, which resemble each other' (1962:77).

The relationship of the ideological and empirical situations may thus be seen as one of complementary opposition. The emic definition of the relationship would, however, seem to be as that of independence. Viewed in its own terms the empirical situation is of a piece; in ideological terms it is a compromise, a concession to the exigencies of co-existence (see Dumont, 1970:206). Compromise and concession spell ideological defeat; and it is as much in terms of it as of economic interdependence that, viewed from the outside, a synthesis may be seen to have been worked out by the peoples of Kashmir.

Turning to the problem of caste, we have seen that both Muslims and Pandits recognize the notion of *zat* as the crucial factor in identity specification and in determining an individual's natural or moral conduct. Further, Muslim specialist-Pandit patron relations were seen to be a close approximation to the familiar *jajmani* pattern. It was, in fact, argued that from the Pandit's point of view a caste system does exist in Kashmir. The significance of this situation lies in that it demonstrates more clearly than any other regional social framework that the castes of a 'Hindu' society, other than Brahmans, are not necessarily 'Hindu' by religion. The Kashmir data reveal how the Brahman will conjure up a system of caste substitutes even out of a non-Hindu environment. His capacity to do so is, of course, dependent both upon ideological compromise and upon politico-economic power. In the recent past—between 1846 and 1947—the Pandits had the monopoly of both political and economic power in rural Kashmir. In

1947 they lost the former. Though economically they are yet no worse off than they were earlier, their economic monopoly has certainly been broken and their association with land-ownership has been abolished. The future may yet hold an unprecedented challenge to the Pandits in the form of the withdrawal of cooperation from Muslim specialists. There have been a few straws in the wind to indicate that such an eventuality cannot be ruled out.[35] It remains to be seen what solution the proverbial Pandit ingenuity will find for such ritual lacunae.

The above considerations should not mislead us to conclude that the Kashmiri Muslim social order itself is a modified system of castes as might be suggested by the manner in which some scholars have dealt with so-called Muslim castes (see, for example, Dumont, 1970:210, Ansari, 1960; and Hutton, 1951:2). The temptation to do so is particularly strong in Kashmir where the bulk of the Muslim population is of Hindu ancestry (see Lawrence, 1967:286 but also 306). It is an easy way out but fails to attach sufficient importance to the Muslims' self-ascription today. I do not mean to suggest that the anthropologist should not venture beyond native models of social reality; he must not, however, ignore them.

Another pitfall would be the temptation to discuss Kashmiri rural society solely in terms of a system of economic classes based on occupation, on the ground that the caste model is totally inapplicable to Muslims in view of their ideology (see, for example, Saghir Ahmad, 1970). I trust this discussion has convincingly shown that our understanding of the peculiarities of rural social organization in Kashmir is dependent upon a prior knowledge of the Hindu caste system, which is not the same thing as saying that Muslim groups are modified castes.[36] The class model is an independent construct.

[35] Since 1947 some Muslim specialists of Utrassu-Umanagri have on two occasions threatened to deny their services to the Pandits: the Potters in around 1948 and the Barbers in 1967. Also see Madan (1966).

[36] Imtiaz Ahmad has, for several years now, been pleading for the study of the nature of interaction between Hindus and Muslims (see, for example, Imtiaz Ahmad, 1965, 1966). He believes that the Muslim

The inescapable conclusion—so it seems to me at least—is that, instead of trying to completely assimilate the Muslim and Pandit representations of Kashmiri rural society, we should acknowledge the existence of dual social orders, which are, however, accommodated within one overarching framework. The latter is defined partly in cultural terms (language, customs, etc.) and partly in terms of the politico-administrative set-up. Its members are not, as such, the Muslims and the Pandits, but rather people, *Kashir* (that is, Kashmiris), who either have the Muslim identity or the Pandit identity. Within this overall framework, the Pandits need the alternate Kashmiri identity to function, whilst the Muslims do not, but only use it conveniently because that is the framework within which they can, given the Pandit requirement, deal with their Hindu co-villagers. This is precisely what I mean when I claim that the Pandit identity is intrinsically a caste structured or related one, the Muslim is not so, and, again, the Kashmiri one is. Moreover, such a view of the relation between religious ideology and ethnic identity may turn out to be of value beyond Kashmir in helping us comprehend the sitaution not only of Muslims but also of other non-Hindu groups in South Asia and, *mutatis mutandis*, even of Hindus in such places as Sind in Pakistan or in Afghanistan.[37]

occupational groups of Uttar Pradesh whom he has studied are appropriately described as 'caste analogues' (see Imtiaz Ahmad, 1966) but does not clarify from whose point of view—the anthropologists', the Hindus', or the Muslims'.

[37] In the writing of this paper I have been greatly helped by the comments and criticisms of Kris Lehman, McKim Marriot, Jit Singh Uberoi, and Nur Yalman. Shernavaz Billimoria helped with the census reports and the dictionaries, and Mukul Dube with his editorial talent. I am grateful to all of them.

Bibliography

Ahmad, Imtiaz (1965), 'Social Stratification among Muslims', *The Economic Weekly*, 10, pp. 1093-96.

———(1966), 'The Ashraf-Ajlaf Dichotomy in Muslim Social Structure in India', *The Indian Economic and Social History Review*, 3, pp.268-78.

Ahmad, Saghir (1970), 'Social Stratification in a Punjabi Village', *Contributions to Indian Sociology*, New Series, 4, pp.105-25.

Ahmad, Aziz (1964), *Studies in Islamic Culture in the Indian Environment*, London, Oxford University Press.

Ansari, Ghaus (1960), *Muslim Caste in Uttar Pradesh*, Lucknow, The Ethnographic and Folk Culture Society.

Ashraf, K.M. (1959), *Life and Conditions of People of Hindustan*, Delhi, Jiwan Prakashan.

Bamzai, P.N.K. (1962), *A History of Kashmir*, Delhi, Metropolitan Books.

Barth, Fredrik (1960), 'The System of Social Stratification in Swat, North Pakistan', in E.R. Leach (ed.), *Aspects of Caste in South India, Ceylon and North-West Pakistan*, London, Cambridge University Press.

———(1970), *Ethnic Groups and Boundaries: The Social Organization of Cultural Differences*, Boston, Little, Brown and Co.

Bhattacharjee, P.N. (1966), 'Distribution of the Blood Groups and the Secretor Factor among the Muslims and the Pandits of Kashmir', *J. Mproh. Anthrop.*, 58, pp. 86-94

Chamber's Twentieth Century Dictionary (1959), London, W. & R. Chambers.

Crane, Robert I. (ed.) (1956), *Area Handbook on Jammu and Kashmir State*, Chicago, Chicago University Press for Human Relations Area Files Inc. (mimeo).

Dumont, Louis (1970), *Homo Hierarchicus: The Caste System and its Implications*, London, Weidenfeld and Nicolson.

Eglar, Zekiye (1960), *A Punjabi Village in Pakistan*, New York, Columbia University Press.

Fauq, M M. (n.d.), *Tarikh-i-Aquam-i-Kashmir* (in Urdu), 3 Vols., Lahore, Zafar Brothers.

Gait, E.A. (1911), 'Caste', in J. Hastings and J.A. Selbie (eds.), *Encyclopaedia of Religion and Ethics*, Edinburgh, T. & T. Clark.

Gascoigne, Bamber (1971), *The Great Moghuls*, New York, Harper and Row.

Gould, H.A. (1962), (Review of) *Caste Ranking and Community Structure in Five Regions of India and Pakistan* by McKim Marriott, *The Eastern Anthropologist*, 15, pp.73-103.

———(1969), 'Toward a "Jati Model" for Indian Politics', *Economic and Political Weekly*, 4, pp. 297-300.

Hughes, T.P. (1935), *A Dictionary of Islam*, London, Allen & Co.

Hutton, J.H. (1951), *Caste in India*, Bombay, Oxford University Press.

India, Government of (1933), *Census of India, 1931, Jammu and Kashmir*, Vol. 24, Part 2, Jammu, The Ranbir Government Press.

———(1943), *Census of India 1941, Jammu and Kashmir State*, Vol. 22, Part 3, Village Tables and Housing Statistics, Jammu, The Ranbir Government Press.

———(1966), *Census of India, 1961, Jammu and Kashmir, District Census Handbook, I, Anantnag District* by M.H. Kamili, Srinagar, Vishinath Printing Press.

———(1972a), *Census of India, 1971, Series I, Paper I, India, Final Population*, Faridabad, Government of India Press.

———(1972b), *Census of India 1971, Series I, Paper II, India, Religion*, Faridabad, Government of India Press.

Kachru, Braj B. (1969), *A Reference Grammar of Kashmiri*, Urbana, Department of Linguistics, University of Illinois (mimeo.).

Kak, R.C., (1936), *Ancient Monuments of Kashmir*, London, Royal Asiatic Society.

Kilam, Jai Lal (1955), *A History of Kashmiri Pandits*, Srinagar, G.M. College.

Koul, Anand (1924), *The Kashmiri Pandit*, Calcutta, Thacker, Spink & Co.

Lawrence, Walter (1967), *The Valley of Kashmir*, London, Oxford University Press, (1895), Reprinted, Srinagar, Kesar Publishers.

———(1909), *Imperial Gazetteer of India: Jammu and Kashmir*, Calcutta, Superintendent Government Printing.

Levi-Strauss, C. (1962), *Totemism*, London, Merlin Press.

Levy, Reuben (1962), *The Social Structure of Islam* London, Cambridge University Press.

Macdonell, A.A. (1924), *A Practical Sanskrit Dictionary*, London, Oxford University Press.

Madan, T.N. (1961), 'Herath: A Religious Ritual and its Secular Aspect', in L.P. Vidyarthi, (ed.), *Aspects of Religion in Indian Society*, Meerut, Kedar Nath.

———(1962), 'Is the Brahmanic Gotra a Grouping of Kin?' *Southwestern Journal of Anthropology*, 18, pp. 59-77.

———(1965), *Family and Kinship: A Study of the Pandits of Rural Kashmir*, Bombay, Asia Publishing House.

———(1966), 'Politico-economic Change and Organizational Adjustment in a Kashmiri Village', *Journal of Karnatak University: Social Sciences*, 2, pp. 20-34.

———(1969), 'Urgent Research in Social Anthropology in Kashmir', in B.L. Abbi and S. Saberwal (eds.), *Urgent Research in Social Anthropology*, Simla, Indian Institute of Advanced Study.

———(1975), 'The Gift of Food' in B.N. Nair (ed.), *Culture and Society, Festschrift for A. Aiyappan*, New Delhi, Thomson Press.

———(n.d.), 'Islam in the Everyday Life of Kashmiri Villagers', MS.

Marriott, McKim and Ronald B. Inden (1974), 'Caste Systems', *Encyclopaedia Britannica*, Vol. 3, pp. 982-91.

Pandit, R.S. (1968), *Kalhana's Rajatarangini: The Saga of the Kings of Kashmir*, New Delhi, Sahitya Akademy.

Raychaudhuri, T.C. (1961), 'The Pandit and Mohammedan of Kashmir: An Anthropometric Study', *The Eastern Anthropologist*, 14, 1961, pp. 84-93.

Smith, W. Robertson, (1903) *Kinship and Marriage in Early Arabia*, London, A & C Black.

Spear, Percival (1967), 'The Position of Muslims Before and After Partition', in Philip Mason (ed.), *India and Ceylon: Unity and Diversity*, London, Oxford University Press.

Steingass, F. (compiler) (1957), *Persian-English Dictionary*, London, Routledge and Kegan Paul.

2

Islamization and Muslim Ethnicity in South India[1]

Mattison Mines

The purpose of this article is to examine the structure of Muslim ethnicity in South India and to explain why the Muslims are undergoing a process of Islamization in Tamilnadu's northern cities despite their close identification with and integration into local society. I speak of the structure of ethnicity in order to emphasize that the components of Muslim identity form a framework which reflects the social order within which the Muslims live. Identity is not simply a name or a list of values and customs. A people's identity has a structure which sometimes involves a symbolic order and at times a corporate or social order. Thus, in India the identity of a caste group involves a symbolic structure associated with their caste including style of dress, caste speech dialect and caste specific ritualism as well as the social order of the caste structure.

It is also my purpose in this article to consider the generation of Muslim Tamil ethnicity, for the Muslim Tamils have

[1] Data on the Muslims of Tamilnadu State are based on research conducted between September 1967 and February 1969. I wish to express my appreciation to the Foreign Area Fellowship Programme which supported this research. In this article I restrict myself to a discussion of the Muslim Tamils all of whom belong to the Sunni sect of Islam(see Mines, 1972a; 1972b). The Sunnites form the vast majority of Tamilnadu's Muslim population.

emerged as converts from the Hindu Tamilian population with whom they share a common cultural heritage. While it is commonly felt that ethnicity is an adaptation to political and economic competition (see, for example, Barth, 1970; Bruner, 1974). Muslim ethnicity in Tamilnadu is not. It develops in response to other factors, particularly internal needs to acquire status and a sense of social position rather than in response to external relations. Like Deshen (1974), I find that ethnicity may find its basis in cultural considerations while political and economic considerations appear inconsequential. The implications for a theoretical understanding of ethnicity is clear. Ethnicity is more complex than generally recognized. In particular we need to know more about the way ethnic distinctions arise. The Tamil-speaking Muslims illustrate ethnic development where ethnic identity provides little political or economic advantage.

It has long been recognized that Muslim ritual and behaviour often owe as much to local custom as they do to Islamic tradition. Accordingly, it is not surprising to find Indian Muslims combining Indian and Islamic traditions. This is not to imply that Indian Muslims form a homogeneous population or that Islam is a monolithic religion: neither is true. Muslims in India are culturally, politically and linguistically highly diverse, and the character of Muslim identity and integration varies greatly. Thus, over much of northern India Muslims are characterized as reluctant acceptors of their minority status (see, for example, Spear, 1967:48). However, in Tamilnadu they are considered well integrated acceptors. While Muslim-Hindu antagonism is common in northern India, just the opposite characterizes such relations in Tamilnadu. As one might expect, the Tamil Muslims identify closely with their Hindu Tamilian neighbours. It comes as a surprise, therefore, to discover that in recent years in the city of Madras many Muslims have tried to purify their ritual behaviour and, through language and dress, to establish more clearly their distinct identity as Muslims. In so doing they have differentiated themselves from the Hindu population by Islamization.

Since they have lived in ast ate of harmonious syncretism with their Hindu neighbours for centuries, why should they seek to differentiate themselves? Why should they wish to Islamize?

Has a growth in religiosity caused the Islamization process and hence the differentiation of Muslim and Hindu? Or does Islamization bring political or economic advantages? Or is it the outgrowth of other forces, perhaps an undercurrent of anti-Muslim sentiment? This is the explanation Aggarwal (1966) gives for the Islamization process experienced by the Meos in Rajasthan and Haryana. However, this interpretation seems unlikely in Tamilnadu where the friendly nature of Muslim-Hindu relations is common knowledge. What, then, is the explanation?

The Tamil Muslims are the offspring of Arab traders and local converts. They are an autochthonous population which, it has often been remarked, bears the stamp of Tamil culture and the political heritage not of conquest and rule, but of mercantilism and integration (see D'Souza, 1955:43-6). As merchants the Muslims are known for their astuteness and honesty. And while trade took them abroad to Southeast Asia where, as in Malacca (see Ryan, 1967; Arasaratnam, 1970), they were for centuries an important economic and political force, India has always remained their home to which they have returned. As an integrated population the Muslims identify the bulk of their cultural traditions with those of the Tamil population. Thus, they claim Tamilian origin, speak the Tamil language as their language, in the countryside dress in much the same way as Hindu Tamilians, and even refer to Muslim contributions to Tamil literature, the *sine quo non* of the locals' view of Tamil culture. As a result, the extent to which the Muslims are distinct from their Hindu neighbours is the extent to which they have emerged as Muslims from the local population. An examination of urban Muslims in Pallavaram town reveals the extent to which this differentiation has taken place in the environs of Madras City, which is Tamilnadu's cultural and political centre.

The emergence of the Tamil Muslims as a distinct population separate from Tamil Hindus is particularly evident in Tamilnadu's northern cities. In this article I refer to these Muslims as Muslim Tamils in order to emphasize their orthodoxy in contrast to the Tamil Muslims who have not Islamized their customs. In the Madras metropolitan area, Muslim Tamils are readily distinguished from Hindus by their appearance and attitudes. In contrast to the Tamil Muslims, the majority wear clothes which distinguish them from the Hindu population. Men wear *lungis* (a sarong-like garment) and *topis* (distinctively Muslim hats), sometimes a shawl, and women wear brightly coloured *saris* of a kind Hindus do not wear. Frequently women observe some degree of purdah, which is a custom that has not reached Hindus in South India as it has in the north, and when in public wear a *burqa* or a white cloth to preserve their modesty. Muslim Tamils also distinguish themselves by language, because many do not share a loyalty to Tamil with the Hindus. Hindu Tamilians are zealous defenders of Tamil and its heritage, which they consider to be one of the world's great literary languages. In contrast many Muslim Tamils, especially those in the State's northern cities within the last three generations, have tried to replace Tamil with Urdu as their household language. They have done so under the misconception perpetrated at one time by Muslim League, that Urdu is *the* language of Indian Muslims. And they have wanted to be proper Muslims. It follows that the Muslim Tamils' loyalties lie not so much with their Tamil heritage, as popular knowledge would have us believe is true for all Tamil-speaking Muslims, as with what they think of as being Muslim. They see themselves as sharing and partaking in Tamilian culture, but also as separated from it by Muslim traditions and world view which they wish to emulate (Mines, 1972b; 1973b).

It is their vision of what a Muslim ought to be that lies at the base of their own conceptual separation of themselves from Hindus. Muslim Tamil world view and values emphasize equalitarianism, independence and a strong work ethic in contrast to the Hindu view which emphasizes social hierarchy, interdependence and status dependent on the ability to command others to work (Mines, 1972b; 1973b). While it is important to stress here that the contrast involves different perceptions of ideals, nevertheless Muslims are conscious of the distinctions, and their ideology does affect their behaviour even though it does not describe their behaviour. They are equally conscious that Muslims elsewhere do not fulfil their ideals, so they see themselves as standing between Tamil culture and their Muslim values which they strive to fulfil.

Because they identify themselves as Muslims, they want to be good Muslims. Accordingly, in Pallavaram, a suburb of Madras, the leading Muslim Tamils attempt in their behaviour to set an example of austere orthodoxy which is generally accepted as a standard for behaviour. As Sunnites of the Hanafi and Shafi schools, they attempt to follow closely the laws of Islam and their school's interpretation of the *hadiths*. They believe that minimally a Muslim should observe the *jummah namaz* (Friday prayer, the most important prayer of the week), although ideally the five daily prayers should be observed. They believe there is no mediator between the individual and God. And they believe that *Id* (festival) days should be observed with prayer, alms-giving and sacrifice, when requisite, and the appropriate feasting or fasting. It must be noted that what is considered orthodox by Pallavaram's Muslims is influenced by local beliefs. Among the community rituals they observe are *Moharram*, *Akhir-e-Chahar Shamba* (last Wednesday of Safar), *Milad-e-Nabi* (the Prophet's Birthday), *Laylatu-i-Miraj* (the day the Prophet was invited to heaven), *Shab-e-Barat* (a kind of All Souls Day), *Bakar-Id* (festival, commemorating Ibraham's faith), and *Ramazan* (the month of fasting) including *Idu-ul-Fitr*. Despite orthodoxy, Sufi-inspired saint worship forms an important popular undercurrent to the orthodox Islamic standards of the Muslim community's leadership, and certain saint's days (*urs*) are observed at various times during the year. The most important of these is the *Abdul Kadar Jilani Urs* commemorating the death of Mohaiyadeen Abdul Kadar Andakai Jilani (alternately: Pir-i-Dastgir, Ghaus-ul-A'zam Muhiy-ud-din), a Baghdad saint born in *Ano Hijra* 471. Throughout Tamilnadu, he is the most important saint, and his shrines (*dargahs*) are everywhere. Pallavaram has four *dargahs* dedicated to him under various names.

Pallavaram's Muslim Tamils disagree about the orthodoxy of all these ceremonials. For example, some think that celebrating the Last Wednesday of Safar is improper, since it is not in the *hadiths*, and accordingly argue that it should be ignored.

Similarly, the orthodox disapprove of certain activities associated with the Prophet's birthday (*Milad-e-Nabi*). Many Muslims in the vicinity of Madras City make the birthday an occasion for pilgrimage to the top of Pallavaram Mount where they view the Prophet's tunic (*jibbah*) enshrined there, pray for the Prophet's assistance in their affairs and offer special prayer (*fatihas*). Pallavaram's orthodox Muslim Tamils consider the pilgrimage reprehensible idol worship and make a point of saying that most of the pilgrims are not Muslim Tamils. The Muslim Tamils observe the birthday by attending speeches by *moulvis* (Koranic college degree holders), by listening to *moulut* (book commemorating the Prophet) readings in the mosque and to Tamil and Urdu speeches about the Prophet's life. A few consider even the *moulut* reading unorthodox. And so it goes; everyone is concerned with being a proper Muslim and follows practices which, according to his knoweldge, are orthodox. Each is perfectly aware that his behaviour is being judged by others and accepts the standards set by religious leaders in the community.

Sufi-inspired *urs* celebrations stand in contrast to the austerity of most Muslim Tamil festivals and respresent a different, more folksy focus. *Urs* festivals are pervaded by a holiday spirit and are much livelier, more joyous affairs than are the comparatively sombre, standard ceremonials such as *Bakr-Id*. Perhaps because of this they have a very wide appeal. The *urs* are in many ways reminiscent of Hindu festivals, since, in addition to detailing the wondrous feats of faqirs, they include processions and the sanctification of Muslim residential areas, much as Hindu cart festivals do. Nevertheless, in Pallavaram some effort is made to circumscribe *urs* festivals with orthodoxy, and saint worship represents a more popular undercurrent to the tenor of Islamic ritual than the dominant theme which orthodoxy represents. Thus the orthodox stress that saints are great men worthy of respect, but that prayers should never be offered to them, except, some argue, with the understanding that the saints will pass them on to Allah. Only Allah should be the recipient of prayers. Nevertheless, saints often become objects of worship and their worshippers become guilty of *shirk* (idolatry and establishing associates to God). As a result, most of Pallavaram's religious leaders stay away from *urs* celebrations, and argue that people should participate more for the fun than for the sake of worship. Nevertheless, almost everyone does worship on these occasions and all seem to enjoy *urs*.

Standards of orthodoxy set by religious leaders affect non-ritual behaviour too, and further differentiate the Muslims from Hindu Tamils. For example, Muslim men sit close together at feasts so that they touch and may pass delicacies from plate to plate, a practice which is radically contrary to Hindu behaviour. Hindus generally consider such acts ritually polluting, but Muslims encourage such practices as expressive of their equality. So, too, many Muslims have adopted Urdu as their household language, because they associate it with being Muslim. The orthodox also avoid a number of activities which many Hindus enjoy, including attending the theatre, playing cards, drinking alcohol, and using music for ceremonial purposes. Again, avoidance of these activities separates Muslims and Hindus. Quite clearly, the Muslim Tamils have a view of the ideal Muslim which is distinct from the Hindu ideal. This ideal creates a tension among Muslims which reflects their wish to be seen as orthodox by their fellows, that they be considered good Muslims even when it is not always clear what is orthodox. Viewed from the perspective of their social origins, Muslims are stressing their distinctiveness, not their similarities, with the majority population. Their social status as Muslims comes not from their relationship with Hindus but from how closely they fit the Muslim ideal: that they dress, speak and behave like Muslims.

Emerging from a common cultural matrix with the Hindu Tamilians, the emphasis on orthodoxy differentiates the Muslims and represents the formation of a separate Muslim Tamil ethnic identity. An ethnic community is a population which:

1. is largely biologically self-perpetuating,
2. shares fundamental cultural values;
3. makes up a field of communication and interaction; and
4. has a membership which identifies itself, and is identified by others, as constituting a category distinguishable from other categories of the same order (Barth, 1970:10-11, following Narroll, 1964).

An important aspect of the first criterion is community's sense of being biologically distinct—that their origins if not their race are unique. The Muslim Tamils are an ethnic community [2] which has emerged from a homogeneous cultural setting after the introduction of Islam. The definition obscures the obviously dynamic character of group boundary formation and maintenance. Further, it suggests nothing about how ethnicity becomes an important component of social identity.

It is easier to explain how Muslims maintain their ethnic identity than it is to explain their group boundary formation. Disregarding modern conversions to Islam, which are few, the Muslim Tamils are biologically self-perpetuating and consider themselves as different from other Muslims and from Tamil-speaking Hindus. They marry among themselves and only rarely marry Muslims from other groups. This is largely a result of the Tamilians' marriage preference for kinsmen rather than any restriction on establishing marriage ties with other Muslims. In any case, the pattern helps maintain the Tamilians' separate identity. Similarly, their sense of self-awareness is heightened by the central role of the mosque in their social and religious lives. Usually children learn about Islam in schools associated with mosques, and the management of mosque affairs provides a context for community leadership in much the same way that temple management does for Hindus. Through Urdu, the mosque, and Tamil newspapers (especially *Nuurul Islaam*, *Maru Malarsi*, and *Urimai Kurul*) oriented towards Muslims, a field of communication and interaction is created. Further, since Muslims have their own standards for determining prestige and status, they distinguish themselves from others on the basis of orthodoxy as well as distinctive dress and sometimes speech. In other words, newspapers, marriage ties, particularly Muslim standards for behaviour, Koranic schools and mosques contribute to the maintenance of Muslim identity. The Tabligh Movement (a reformist religious movement) and the Muslim League have also

[2] I purposely choose to use the term community instead of group in this context in order to avoid implying any group organization or corporateness.

contributed to this consciousness even though neither organization now draws much support from the Muslim Tamils. But why Muslims have consciously differentiated themselves from Hindus by language, dress and orthodoxy is less clear, especially given their comfortable integration into Hindu Tamil society, for, in many ways Muslims are integrated and think of themselves as an integral part of Tamil society. Is the answer to be found in political or economic considerations? Does orthodoxy lead to political or economic advantages?

In many spheres of urban life, Muslims and Hindus (as well as other minority communities) interact closely and share the same opportunities. Most significantly, a relatively large number of Muslims are prosperous, reflecting their success as businessmen throughout Tamilnadu. Their relative success adds to their sense of involvement in Tamil society, which is reflected in many of their activities. Muslims and Hindus of similar economic interests often interact cooperatively when they feel it is in their interest, and in Pallavaram they have jointly organized and now head a merchants' association for their mutual benefit. They do so because it is in their best economic and class interests to do so. Religious identity is not nearly as significant as these practical interests for determining interaction and cooperation among merchants. Mayer's (1970:19) study of Muslim political attitudes in the city of Trichchirapalli located just south of Madras arrives at a similar conclusion: class considerations are politically more significant than religious affiliation. A simple case in point is the cooperation merchants show in lending money to one another without charging interest when they are in a pinch (Mines, 1973b), or in their live-and-let-live attitude toward black-market activities, a potential sore point among competing businessmen. Cooperation arising from coincidentally shared economic interests results in a high level of Muslim-Hindu integration in the bazaar.

Similarly, Muslims and Hindus interact freely in politics, joining with others of similar persuasion regardless of religion in their support of various parties. The lack of political unity among Muslims reflects the absence of a perceived external threat which might otherwise unify them. Instead, Muslim political behaviour to some extent parallels that of the Hindus.

Very few of the Muslims are first and foremost supporters of the Muslim League, which we might take as a sign of their pursuit of religious separatism into the political sphere; and those that do are often regarded as fanatical even by Muslims. In contrast, they do support in large numbers Tamilnadu's ruling party, the DMK (Dravida Munnetra Kazhagam), just as Hindus do, and they have participated in its membership for years. Incidentally, the DMK espouses a strong separatist ideology for Tamilnadu, and Muslim support consequently is in line with their local identification as Tamilians. Muslim Tamils of different politicnl persuasion support Indira Gandhi's Congress. In Pallavaram, members of both religious communities hold local leadership roles in these parties. A Muslim is the head of the local DMK organization and has a large Hindu and Muslim clientele. Similarly, Muslims and Hindus participate jointly in the administration of Pallavaram (see Mines, 1972a:20). Muslims feel they have equal opportunities to achieve class status and prestige as well as leadership positions.

The Pallavaram Merchants' Association similarly demonstrates inter-community cooperation. It has members belonging to all the major religious communities—and of course without the help of its members, the Association could not exist. This association does little more than regulate shop hours and bazaar holidays during normal times, which is an important function in itself. But in times of crises and when problems of mutual concern arise, it provides the organization for taking quick and effective action concerning a wide range of activities. During the Indo-China altercation in 1962, for example, the Association donated Rs. 2,000 to the Indian effort. And in 1969, when Annadurai, the popular Chief Minister of Tamilnadu State, died, it organized a feast for the poor in his name. Muslim and Hindu merchants from both the main parties participated. The merchants cooperated because it was in their personal interest to do so. Annadurai was such a popular man, that merchants of different political persuasions had little choice but to agree to sponsor the feast. The Merchants' Association, therefore, cuts across ethnic and religious lines and in conjunction with the foregoing supports the contention that ethnicity provides little economic or political advantage to the Muslim community as a whole. I say little rather than no advantage, because economics and politics are far-reaching phenomena and it would be unrealistic to say that no such advantages occur. It is clear, however, that in Tamilnadu to consider these advantages as being primary would give the analyst little heuristic insight into the phenomenon of Muslim Tamil ethnicity.

Perhaps as good an indicator as any of the Muslims' relative position in Tamilnadu is the intensity of their expression of felt integration. Granting their minority status and the existence of inequality, Muslim Tamils in Madras City and Pallavaram consistently point to Hindu-Muslim sociability and are adamant about Hindu-Muslim good-neighbourliness. They get along and they are fond of pointing out how well they do so, well aware that elsewhere Hindu-Muslim relations are not so convivial. They attend one another's weddings; they have friendships with one another; and they even contribute to one another's shrines.

Muslim Tamil ethnicity provides no overt political or economic advantages. Except for the Mosque administrative organization which restricts itself almost entirely to mosque and inner-Muslim affairs, there are no exclusively Muslim voluntary associations in Pallavaram. I have already noted that the Muslim League has only a handful of supporters, so there are no corporate groups organized on the basis of ethnicity designed to advance or safeguard Muslim Tamil interests, even though other Muslim groups do have such organizations. For example, the Da'udi Bohras have the Anjuman-e-Burhani, a voluntary association designed to promote Bohra social and economic welfare. Consequently, the Muslim Tamils' concern with their ethnicity does not stem from economic or political considerations, but from some other basis. Economically and politically, they are an integrated population.

Clearly, Muslim Tamil integration in the cities involves the dichotomization of religious and secular activities. The Muslims seek to separate themselves as Muslims from Hindus, yet participate as an integrated population in other spheres of life. Hindu tolerance allows them the freedom of a strong religious identity separate from their relations with Hindus, while the lack of discrimination allows Muslims to pursue opportunities on a par with Hindus in areas of life not dominated by Islam. Yet the question of why they have sought to differentiate themselves ethnically through the process of Islamization remains unanswered. Clearly, Islamization is not a reaction to Hindu hostility. Nor does it provide political or economic advantages. To what is it then a reaction?

Is the nature of Muslim integration and identity uniform throughout Tamilnadu? Is there this same separation of religious identity and behaviour from secular behaviour, this same push to Islamize ? My observations in the village of Edaikottai, near Dindigal City in Madurai District, demonstrate that the answer to both questions is no. In Edaikottai village, Muslim Tamils do not maintain a separate ethnic identity. First of all there is not the uniformity of dress which distinguishes Muslims from Hindus in the city. Many Muslim men wear the *dhoti* in the same manner as non-Brahmin Hindus. Women, however, do observe purdah. Second, Tamil, the local language, is spoken both within the mosque and in the village, and Urdu is not considered the language of Muslims. Third, and most significantly, there is not as clear a separation between Muslims and Hindus during Muslim ritual activities as there is in the cities. Furthermore, an individual's Muslim identity and public status are not based on orthopraxy as they are in Pallavaram. On the contrary, class and caste-like interactions, not only among Muslims but also among village Hindus, are particularly important for determining status and prestige, while identity is determined by descent. A Muslim is born a Muslim just as a Hindu is born into his caste group. What makes the differences noted here all the more important is that the Muslims of Edaikottai do not live in the village all the year round. They are city-dwelling merchants who return to their native village annually in order to attend the festival (*urs*, known in Edaikottai as *kurs*) of the Baghdad saint, Abdul Kadar Jilani. During the year, most of them live in Madras City and its environs, including Pallavaram. In other words, they are the same Muslims described above as striving to Islamize. Accordingly, village behaviour provides a striking contrast to urban behaviour. In Pallavaram and Madras, saint worship occurs more as an undercurrent to the orthodox rituals of Sunni Islam, while in Edaikottai saint worship provides the focal ritual of the year. Furthermore, the village's saint worship is much more opulent and dramatic than is seen in either of the two northern cities. Clearly, social contexts determine the particulars of self-image and Muslim integration in the two different settings—one urban, the other rural. Since it is the same Muslims behaving differently, it is possible to isolate the factors which account for the differences between the two social contexts.

A short description of Edaikottai's *Kadar Jilani Kurs* serves to illustrate how different it is from the Muslim festivals observed in Pallavaram and Madras, and how different there the basis of Muslim identity is. The festival itself is influenced by Hindu custom, and is in fact reminiscent of Hindu annual cart festivals when village gods circumnavigate their villages on temple carts, sanctifying the villages and their inhabitants for the coming year. The *Kadar Jilani Kurs* lasts eight days, the last three involving nightly processions circumambulating the village. These processions are the most important part of the festival, and the Muslims of the village return from all over the State to attend them. The processions sanctify the participants and the village. Sandalwood paste, flowers and sugar which are carried in procession are distributed at the end of the eighth night and are believed to be a powerful prophylaxis against disease.

The processions are influenced by Hindu tradition. The image taken out on the sixth night is a floral and paper replica of the saint's grave (the image is called *vasaga malai*, garland of recitation, referring to the recitation of the saint's genealogy). The image carried on the seventh and eighth nights is a *kurs*, a towering cone of brightly coloured paper and lights, crowned by peacock feathers which are thought to have strong curative powers. The processions begin at midnight and last until dawn, beginning and ending with a *fatiha* (prayer). At each crossroad, the procession stops and the men of the street make floral offerings of jasmine. The processions stop every few yards.

The processions are preceded by neon lights and the roar of a generator. Immediately in front of the image walks a group of faqirs with tambourines, emitting a cacophony of sounds and calling the praise of the saint; then comes a *nagaswaram* (a double reed musical instrument which Hindus associate with joyous occasions) troupe, a three-piece western band, a group of Hindu drummer-dancers and a group of men demonstrating their skills at *lathi* (bamboo pole) fighting.

While the processions proceed at night, during the day the Muslims rest, talk, arrange marriages, feast the poor, renew old acquaintances and compete with one another in their efforts to demonstrate their business successes. In other words, the days are crowded with status competition, the formation of new alliances and the continuation of disputes. For the Muslims who live scattered throughout the state for the rest of the year, these nightly processions represent the symbolic unity of the village Muslims. In Victor Tuner's terms the ceremonial creates a feeling of *communitas* (Turner, 1969:96) when the unity of the village Muslims is felt and social differentiation is minimized. The daily activities represent the opposite: diversity and status differentiation. Anti-structure is sought at night and structure dominates the days.

There are several features about the *kurs* which are strikingly different from the festival occasions in Pallavaram and Madras. First, there is the use of music as an important aspect of the ritual occasion. Muslims do not use music in this manner in the cities. One has only to recall that many riots between Muslims and Hindus have been sparked by the music of Hindu processions to realize the significance of the Edaikottai Muslims' behaviour. Not only are the processions accompanied by music, but the Muslims are the same ones that in Pallavaram, Madras and other cities would be offended by such behaviour.

Second, the processions involve non-Muslims as well as Muslims interacting in relationships of inter-dependence. The *vasaga malai* and the *kurs* are carried on the shoulders of large numbers of Harijans, members of untouchable castes. The drummer-dancers are also Harijans. The relationship between the Harijans and Muslims is traditional, as is the grain and money payment the Harijans recieve. The musicians and faqirs are paid in a similar manner. This inter-dependence is contrary to Muslim ritual activities in Pallavaram and Madars, where Hindus of any caste, let alone Harijans, are not participants. In the cities, Muslim festivities are exclusive affairs. In Edaikottai, Muslim religious activities are not as clearly segregated. Muslim and Harijan inter-dependence in Edaikottai is hierarchical and the Muslims are in the superordinate position.

Third, the use of the *vasaga malai* and *kurs* images runs contrary to urban orthodoxy, where images are not carried even during *urs* ceremonies. The village practice smacks of idolatry and saint worship (*shirk*), which in the urban setting is rejected by Pallavaram's Muslims but which in their village they accept as appropriate behaviour. In Edaikottai the stress is not on Islamic orthodoxy but on pomp and wealth, and Sufi-inspired saint worship is the focus of religious activities. Identity is a product of birth. while prestige and status are achieved not by orthodoxy, but first and foremost by the Muslims' demonstrations of wealth and social super-ordinance.

How are the differences between the behaviour of these same Muslims in Pallavaram City and Edaikottai village to be explained? How is it that in Pallavaram religious behaviour stresses orthodoxy while the same Muslims in Edaikottai blatantly ignore their austere urban standards of orthodoxy in favour of music, saint worship, pomp and display? And what does the explanation tell us about Muslim identity and Islamization?

The answers are to be found in what the Muslims stress in their evaluations of themselves and others, and in the structural basis of their identity. Identity, status and prestige are all closely intertwined. In the northern cities of Madras and Pallavaram, a Muslim's identity is based on his group identity as a Muslim and on his personal prestige and status. But in no case is his identity a purely ascribed appellation; it is something which he establishes in his relationships with others and in the way that they perceive and evaluate him. Identity is something which is actively pursued and maintained. It is a plastic thing, so if he changes his behaviour in a significant way he also changes his identity. Thus, in terms of his personal prestige and status, a Muslim is judged on the basis of factors like class, political affiliations, wealth, power, education, intelligence, likeableness, as well as on the basis of what kind of a Muslim he is. Among urban Muslims, this latter factor is particularly important because it determines how they relate with one another. Since all the Muslim Tamils are Sunnites, in Pallavaram they evaluate one another in terms of their orthodoxy and perceived behaviour, the standards for which are set by the leaders of the Muslim community.

The two aspects of Muslim identity—religious identity and personal prestige and status—are not mutually exclusive. A wealthy man, for example, may be considered a low status Muslim. Muslim merchants who sell liquor often display wealth but are given a low status by their fellow Muslims. They find it difficult to arrange marriages for their children with families of similar wealth. Obversely, a person may have considerable status as a Muslim and yet be poor, as the case of Kabir illustrates. Kabir is a poor man, but he is one of the religious leaders of Pallavaram. His political influence among his followers is considerably greater than that of many wealthier men. His followers look to him for advice on all aspects of their lives, and I found that members of his community often took his word as final. Among Muslims, a wealthy, capable man, who is also considered orthodox, ranks high as an individual and as a Muslim. Few men hold high status in both identity spheres. Typically, the wealthier a man becomes, the harder he strives to establish an identity as an orthodox Muslim.

The appearance in Pallavaram of Muslim-Hindu integration stems from social contexts where Muslim identity is not socially relevant, but where Muslims and Hindus coincidentally share political, social, or economic interests. In these instances, Muslims and Hindus as individuals interact according to their interests. They join together to achieve common goals, to enforce bazaar rules which are beneficial to them, to support the political parties of their choice, to further their business interests or to maintain friendly relations with business associates.

To speak of the dominance of the majority group when discussing these relationships is misleading, because it suggests an actively subordinate position for the Muslim minority and an actively superordinate role for Hindus. Instead, both Muslim and Hindu individuals interact independently, coming together in joint efforts when they see the value of the other's support, both accepting the same standards of success. In this sense, Muslims are compliant with the interests of the majority population and are integrated (see Schermerhorn, 1970:6-7), as is also indicated by their contributions to the Indian war effort against China in 1962 and by their sponsorship of a feast along with Hindu merchants in 1969 to commemorate the death of Annadurai. In their pursuit of wealth and political power, Muslims are able to achieve success sharing the standards of the majority society. But their religious standards are different from the Hindus'; they cannot achieve status as a Muslim among Muslims except by pursuing their own standards. In order to establish their Muslim identity, they have 'Islamized' and segregated themselves from Hindus. Thus, urban Muslim Tamil ethnicity stems from an internal need among themselves to achieve status. It currently owes little to Hindu-Muslim relations. Yet it is possible that the rise of ethnic distinctions may open the door to subsequent discrimination in so far as it emphasizes the Muslim Tamils' visible distinctiveness. May not Hindus resent this 'clannishness'?

How do the Hindus view the Muslims? It is apparent that Muslims offer no social threat to them. Tamil Hindus do not fear Muslims, and, like the Tamil Muslims, they point to cooperation and to friendship between the communities. Thus a Muslim acquaintance of mine was invited by his Hindu friend to the latter's first viewing of his bride. Hindus recognize Muslim distinctiveness but are unconcerned about Muslim ethnicity. This nonchalance is possible because Muslim ethnicity is not an attempt to regulate external relations with Hindus and Hindus are not affected by it. Consequently, boundary maintenance, which Barth (1970) finds so important in contexts where ethnicity does define external relations, is not a source of political or economic tension among Muslim and Hindu Tamils. It is clear, therefore, that analytic approaches which consider ethnicity as a population's adaptation to political and/or economic competition are taking an unnecessarily limited view. Muslim Tamil ethnicity is for the internal consumption of Muslims and arises in response to the dictates of what is considered orthodox. This orthodoxy is non-Tamilian in nature, having a decidedly northern character involving as it does the acquiring of Urdu. This northern influence is also apparent in the hiring of *Hafizes* from the Daru-l-Ulum Deoband to recite the Koran during Ramadan in Pallavaram's mosques.

Status and identity in Edaikottai village appear in striking contrast to the urban situation. The dual aspects of identity found in the urban setting are still present, but, significantly, Muslims do not have to segregate themselves from Hindus in their religious activities. This is because their identity as Muslims is not something they must achieve; on the contrary it is ascribed by birth. In the village, therefore, little concern is paid to establishing an identity as a Muslim. Most are concerned about establishing their personal status and prestige. Within their own community this is done through personal displays of wealth and power. Hence, status-seeking explains several of the ceremony's characteristics. A *kurs* as elaborate and as opulent as that performed in Edaikottai involves a great deal of money in terms of the cost for decorations, feasts and fireworks, as well as for the performers, so it provides opportunities for individuals to display their wealth and successes through contributions to the festival as well as through public feasting. In addition, the *kurs* is a demonstration of the Muslim community's wealth, religiosity, and relationships to all others in the village. The *kurs*, therefore, combines ritual and secular features with status seeking. Muslim status is expressed through the medium of their ritual relationships and the grandness of their ceremony.

Edaikottai's *Kadar Jilani Kurs* begins to make sense. On the emotional level, it is a time of excitement and fun, a chance to get away from daily routines. It is also a ceremonial which acts as a prophylactic against disease and misfortune. At the more abstract level of social relations, its significance is threefold: First, the *kurs* is a ritual expression of the social unity of the Muslim village community. It is a joint endeavour and the circumambulation of the Muslim residential area sanctifies it and the residents. Second, the festival provides an arena of status competition among the Muslims while demonstrating the symbolic cohesiveness of the group. And, third, it is an expression of ritual status which indicates the relative hierarchical position of Muslims compared with other castes which form their audience in the village. At the highest level of abstraction, the *kurs* expresses the multiple relationships that exist among the Muslims, their village, and a supernatural, their village saint. It is the second level of meaning which is most pertinent to an understanding of Muslim identity and integration.

In the performance of the *kurs*, individual identity is of secondary importance compared to the demonstration of group unity and wealth expressed in a ritual milieu. Being a Muslim in the village means something different from what it does in the city. It is an identity determined not by religiosity but by birth. To be a Muslim is to be part of a group which holds a status *vis-a-vis* the other communities within the village. It is the Muslim community as a whole that sponsors the festival, and their status relative to other communities is determined by their combined demonstration of power and wealth. A corporate Muslim identity of this sort is absent in the city because the community is dispersed and is not a unit of social interaction as households and voluntary associations are. The *kurs*, therefore, provides a symbolic expression of Muslim status as a corporate group within the village, and in its use of music and in its stress on saint worship it is comparable to customary veneration of a village deity. It takes this form understandably because in effect the Muslims are playing to a village audience where such behaviour is traditional. Urban orthodoxy, in contrast, would be meaningful only to themselves and would not establish their position in village society as it does in the city. In other words, the village Muslims are completely integrated into the village society. They share not only the Hindus' standards of success, but also their standards of religiosity founded in group identity.

The Muslims say that at some time in the past they were converted from Hinduism. Conversion began a process of religious differentiation which still goes on. Partap Aggarwal has documented such a process among the Meos of Rajasthan and Haryana (1966). The Meos were originally nominal converts to Islam. They retained their Hindu names and continued after conversion to interact with the Hindu of their region as a dominant caste. This included maintaining ritual ties with caste Hindus. During the period leading up to and following the partition of India and Pakistan, the Meos underwent a process of Islamization. They changed their names to Muslim ones, they purified their religious practices and ended their ritual ties with caste Hindus. In other words, they moved from a state of complete integration to a state where at least in the religious sphere they were no longer integrated.

A similar process of Islamization is observed in Tamilnadu. The Edaikottai Muslims have emerged from their Hindu environment, have left the village for the city and there have Islamized themselves. But the process is not uni-directional; it is contextual and reversible. Why? Because urban Islamization is a response to differences in rural and urban social structure rather than to deep-lying social change such as the Meos have experienced which prevents reversibility. The Meos have lost their pre-partition social position as a result of radical political and economic change emanating from the division of India and Pakistan. But the Muslim Tamils have not experienced a similar change and are able to respond more flexibly to different social environments. There appears to be no pressure from the dominant Hindus forcing Tamilnadu's Muslims to Islamize. On the contrary, urban Muslims have consciously chosen to Islamize their customs. In the city, Muslims lack a corporate identity and religious identity is achieved, as are status and prestige. In order to establish and maintain their religious identity they have found it necessary to create a new group sense through Islamization. Muslim identity in the village, however, is corporate so that religious identity is ascribed, but social status and prestige are achieved.

The argument which grows out of the particular case of the Muslim Tamils is that social structure is the determinant of the structure of identity. Village social structure is characterized by hierarchy defined by interaction and closed corporate status defined by birth (see Marriott, 1968:105-07). Muslim identity structure is ascribed as is that of closed corporate groups which are ranked. Urban structure, in contrast, is relatively open. Status is defined by readily-apparent attributes and behaviour (Marriott, 1968b:103-05). Class is more significant than corporate rank (consider Mayer, 1970:19), and group identity is that of vaguely-ranked ethnic categories. The cultural content of identity is not determined by social structure, but it is influenced by it. In the village an identity based on orthodoxy would make only limited sense to fellow Muslims but contributes little to the Muslims' identity and status in the community. Descent, interaction and displays of wealth establish religious identity and status in the village. However, in the open urban context, group identity is vague. Identity in cities cannot be based on corporateness, because fellow villagers are dispersed. Identity as a Sunni Muslim is all that remains and orthodoxy helps to establish and maintain this identity.

In sum, when the structure of ociety is open, then Muslim identity will be based on attributes and the appropriate Islamic behaviour will be stressed. However, when the structure of society is closed and when identity is corporate, the Islamic content of behaviour need not be stressed, while local traditions for determining status will be, and they may contradict Islamic customs as they do in Edaikottai.

The implications of the rise of Muslim Tamil ethnicity are multiple. Barth (1970), Cohen (1974) and Bruner (1974) all see ethnicity heuristically as adaptations to political and economic niches where ethnic boundary maintenance and the regulation of external relations are important. Bruner, for example, shows how urban ethnicity operates in Indonesia to affect job hiring and to determine which ethnic groups will dictate standards of etiquette in different urban settings. In other words, Bruner finds ethnicity important in the regulation of inter-group behaviour and economic competition. Similarly, he finds ethnic lines clearly defined and boundary maintenance important. This is very different from what we find among the Muslim Tamils. Their ethnicity is not adaptive and has nothing to do with the regulation of inter-group behaviour and economic competition. The process of Islamization that the Muslim Tamils are experiencing is confined to the regulation of inner-relationships among Muslims. It develops as a response to an internal need among Muslims to achieve status where the standards of behaviour are not Tamilian but orthodox. The adaptation and ecology-oriented approach, therefore, fails to provide the perspective necessary to understand Muslim Tamil ethnicity. Shortcomings arise out of the etic nature of the approach. This etic approach carries an analytic bias which, in some cases, leads to insight, while in others, such as the case in point, it obscures the causes of ethnic development. In fact this shortcoming raises the whole question of whether ethnicity can be adequately analyzed without emphasis on the emic view. Without it Muslim Tamil ethnicity is incomprehensible. This is not to deny that political and economic approaches to the study of ethnicity have proved insightful. They have. But an emic approach which views ethnicity as a cultural phenomenon should prove equally fruitful. This is the approach which Deshen (1974:282) calls for and which proves most fruitful in the analysis of the Muslim Tamil's ethnicity.

The main forms of ethnicity that have been recognized by scholars are tribal ethnicity, racial ethnicity and national ethnicity (see Enloe, 1973:23-4). It is clear that the Muslim Tamils do not fit within this tripartite classification. I suggest that a fourth type, 'congeneric ethnicity',[3] which is common to India, be added. Congeneric ethnicity is ethnicity which arises when corporate castes are replaced by non-corporate identities which retain some of the symbolic identity of the original group including, in particular, the general caste name and a sense of separate origin. The Muslim Tamils who moved from their villages have lost their corporate identity but they have retained their sense of a distinct origin as Muslims and, with few exceptions, clearly distinguish themselves biologically in terms of origins from local Hindu castes. They retain instead an identity as Muslims which is much broader than their identity in their native villages. The Islamization process reflects their wider identity base as part of the greater Indian Muslim community. They are seeking identity as Indian Muslims rather than as Tamil Muslims.

Hindus in their turn are undergoing a similar process. Caste fusion has been associated with urbanization in recent years in India. As a result, groups of related castes are joining together on the basis of what they consider common biological origins and forming new caste communities which advocate

[3]My selection of the term congeneric ethnicity is to emphasize the former's similarity to racial and national ethnicity while simultaneously suggesting its differences.

intermarriage within the new group. These new caste identities are also examples of congeneric ethnicity. They retain a common cultural distinctiveness based on caste plus a sense of separate biological origin which to the outside observer appears fabricated. It is nonetheless real to the community members.

In general terms, congeneric ethnicity occurs in India because of the particular nature of its social structure. Caste and religious community form an important aspect of individual identity. A person is always a member of a particular group. In the village this is a corporate *jati* or caste-like group. In the modern Indian city, this corporateness is lost, but the caste appellation or general community identity is retained as in the case of Muslim Tamils. These groups now have a much broader base than the corporate caste groups of the village. Consequently, the boundaries of the new groups are less restrictive in terms of criteria of membership, since the aim is at fusion of groups of people who previously claimed distinctive identities. In addition to the community name of caste appellation, these groups retain a sense of separate biological origin usually expressed in terms of their shared descent from a common ancestor who is viewed as different from the ancestors of any other community. These communities are ethnic groups of the congeneric type, and many modern expressions of caste in urban India are examples of it. Although he does not use the term ethnicity, this is what Hardgrave (1970) describes as the direction of change of the Nadar caste in Tamilnadu. It is also what the Barnetts (1974) describe among the South Indian castes. And it is the pattern which the Muslim Tamils are following. Islamization is an expression of this new identity among the Muslim Tamils. Congeneric ethnicity is its outcome.

Bibliography

Aggarwal, Partap C. (1966), 'A Muslim Sub-Caste of North India: Problems of Cultural Integration', *Economic and Political Weekly*, I, pp 159-67.

Arasaratnam, Sinnappah (1970), *Indians in Malaysia and Singapore*, London, Oxford University Press.

Barnett, Marguerite Ross and Steve Barnett (1974), 'Contemporary

Peasant and Post-Peasant Alternatives in South India: The Ideas of a Militant Untouchable', *Annals of the New York Academy of Sciences*, 220, pp. 385-410.

Barth, Fredrik (1970), 'Introduction', in Fredrik Barth (ed.), *Ethnic Groups and Boundaries: The Social Organization of Cultural Differences*, Boston, Little, Brown and Co.

Bruner, Edward M. (1974), 'The Expression of Ethnicity in Indonesia', in Abner Cohen (ed.), *Urban Ethnicity*, (Assn. Social Anthrop. Monogr. 12), London, Tavistock.

Cohen, Abner (1974), 'Introduction', in Abner Cohen (ed.), *Urban Ethnicity* (Ass. Social Anthrop. Monogr. 12), London, Tavistock.

Deshen, Shlomo (1974), 'Political Ethnicity and Cultural Ethnicity in Israel during the 1960s', in Abner Cohen (ed.), *Urban Ethnicity*, (Ass. Social Anthrop. Monogr. 12), London, Tavistock.

D'souza, Victor (1955), *The Nacayats of Kanara: A Study in Culture Contact* (Kanada Res. Inst. Monogr. 3), Dharwar, Kanada Research Institute.

Enloe, Cynthia H. (1973), *Ethnic Conflict and Political Development*, Boston, Little, Brown and Co.

Hardgrave, Robert L. Jr. (1970), 'Urbanization and the Structure of Caste', in Richard G. Fox (ed.), *Urban India: Society, Space and Image*, (Comp. Stud. Asia, Monogr. *Occ. Pap. Ser.* 10), Durham, Duke University.

Marriott, McKim (1968a), 'Caste Ranking and Food Transactions: A Matrix Analysis', in M. Singer and B.S. Cohn (eds.), *Structure and Change in Indian Society*, Chicago, Aldine.

———(1968b), 'Multiple Reference in Indian Caste Systems', in James Silverberg (ed.), *Social Mobility in the Caste System in India*, Comparative Studies in Society and History, Supplement III, The Hague, Mouton.

Mayer, Peter B. (1970), 'Muslim Political Culture : A Comparison of Attitudes in North and South India', Paper delivered at the 1970 Annual Meeting of the Association for Asian Studies.

Mines, Mattison (1972a), *Muslim Merchants: The Economic Behaviour of an Indian Muslim Community*, New Delhi, Shri Ram Centre for Industrial Relations and Human Resources.

———(1972b), 'Muslim Social Stratification in India : The Basis for Variation', *Southwestren Journal of Anthropology*, 28, pp. 333-49.

———(1973a) : 'Social Stratification Among the Muslim Tamils in Tamilnadu, South India', in Imtiaz Ahmad (ed.), *Caste and Social Stratification Among the Muslims*, Delhi, Manohar Book Service.

———(1973b), 'Tamil Muslim Merchants in India's Industrial Development', in Milton Singer (ed.), *Innovation in Traditional Societies: The Modernization of Occupational Cultures in South Asia*, (Comp. Stud. S. Asia, Monogr. *Occ. Pap. Ser.* 12), Durham, Duke University.

Ryan, N.J. (1967), *The Making of Modern Malaysia: A History From*

Earliest Times to 1966, Kuala Lumpur, Oxford University Press.

Schermerhorn, R.A. (1970), *Comparative Ethnic Relations: A Framework for Theory and Research*, New York, Random House.

Spear, Percival (1967), 'The Position of Muslims Before and After Partition', in Philip Mason (ed.), *India and Ceylon: Unity and Diversity*, New York, Oxford University Press.

Turner, Victor W. (1969), *The Ritual Process: Structure and Anti-Structure*, Chicago, Aldine.

Wright, Theodore P. Jr. (1966), 'The Muslim League in South India since Independence: A Study in Minority Group Political Strategies', *American Political Science Review*, 60, pp. 579-99.

3

Muslim Rituals: Household Rites vs. Public Festivals in Rural India

Lina M. Fruzzetti

For this essay, I have chosen to write about a life cycle rite and the 'festival'[1] of Moharram in an effort to contrast private household rites to public Muslim festivals. The rituals selected for the purpose do not in fact delineate the male/female domains of activities, nor that often loosely defined 'private' *vs.* 'public' division of activities.[2] Life cycle rituals are held in each household whether wealthy, poor, ignorant or educated. The manner of performance can differ, though parts of all life cycle rites are equally prescribed to all Muslim without distinctions of class, occupation, or country of origin. Besides the prescribed Islamic rules concerning life cycle rites, a number of local rules, loosely defined as *desher adat* (customs of the land) accompany the rituals. Both the Islamic and local culture are maintained and followed by the Muslims (local Indian Muslim culture can differ from local Egyptian Muslim culture, within the domain of *adat* activities.)

In this essay, I am not questioning the validity of Islam in

[1] 'Festival' or—to use the Bengali term—*utsob*. Moharram is observed because of the death of Imam Hassan and Hussain, thus the Shiahs observe this occasion in mourning whereas the Sunnis in the rural town of Bishnupur observe Moharram with gaity and mourning.

[2] See Fruzzetti (1976a) and Nelson (1974) for clarification of the concepts and the critique offered.

a secular state nor do I ask what constitutes a Muslim in the classical sense (or in pristine Islamic time). The community in question is an Indian Muslim one which professes to be Muslim and accordingly acts on that belief. Therefore, we will attempt to understand the community within its Indian context.[3]

Muslims in West Bengal have a definite view of their community, their *samaj* (society) or their Muslim *jati* (caste, here taken to mean 'people' or 'group'). Concepts like *samaj, jati*, people, group clearly suggest the idea of a Muslim community in opposition to a non-Muslim one—in this particular case, a 'Bengali' or a 'Hindu' community (in the sense that Muslims do not regard the Hindus as one of them). The idea is consciously held by the Muslims, though it is an abstract notion of an '. . . *umma* Muslima, the Muslim community . . . a society with principles of internal solidarity . . .' and a society which has certain 'conditions for a universal brotherhood on the basis of faith . . .' (Rahman, 1968:19). I argue in this essay that the model of society may not necessarily correspond to the present actual, concrete reality of the Muslim society. Muslims recognize this and they genuinely try to actualize the ideal.

Bengali Muslims adhere simultaneously to the fundamental orthodox principles of Islam and to a Bengali culture. They state that one can be a 'Muslim' and a 'Bengali' without creating any contradiction or conflict between the two spheres, though both the boundaries are sharply defined by their ideology and practice. The social organization of the Muslims in Bishnupur is intricately intertwined with the rest of the Hindu community. Muslims partake in the economic, political and social activities of the town and have a definite role to fulfil. Nonetheless, Muslims will clearly state that they are members of a closed community, the *umma*—an abstract membership of a universal community because of their Islamic faith. But the universalistic aspect of Islam is not the only concern of the Muslims; in everyday practical life, the Muslims share in

[3] Fieldwork was carried out in Bishnupur, West Bengal, India. Generous grants from the Social Science Research Council and the American Institute of Indian Studies made this anthropological research possible.

a 'Bengali culture', which is common to both Hindus and Muslim Bengalis.

We are in fact dealing with a dual system of thought here. First, membership in an all embracing Islamic *umma*, to which all the Muslim faithful belong; and, secondarily, membership in the local culture—Bengali culture. 'The level of ideology (religious ideology) is not separable from that of action. There are certain beliefs and actions which the Muslims regard as *desher niom* (laws or customs of the land, laws in the sense that these are preferred actions relating to religion). Together with the prescribed religious injunctions of Islam, the *desher niom* form a folk religion of Islam unique to Bengal' (Fruzzetti, 1970:81).

Differences from the Hindus are emphasized and at the same time similarities are stressed. A Muslim in Bengal can identify with all Muslims of the world because Islamic law has that 'all embracing character . . . is a system that, more than anything else, made for Islamic solidarity, despite the tremendous differences in the cultures of the lands through which Islam . . . ' spread (Rahman, 1968:xxi). A Muslim's first and primary loyalty is to *dharma* (*din*-Islam) in the ideal model, though that ideology does not preclude action at the local level of activity, since Muslims regard themselves as Bengalis both socially and culturally (through their practice of the *desher niom* or local *adat*). Muslims also emphasize the differences between one group of Muslims and another and not only between Muslims and non-Muslims (Fruzzetti, 1976a).

Through a discussion of the rituals surrounding birth and the festival of Moharram, I will try to elucidate Muslim *values*, and the way these values organize and structure Indian Muslim society.[4] The analysis of the ritual actions and the symbolic interpretation and meaning of the life cycle ritual and the Moharram festival will be considered within the Indian context (see Peters, 1968). Seeking the cultural meaning of specfiic acts, I

[4] See Fruzzetti (1976b). The essay compares two communities in an attempt to understand: (*i*) a Muslim and a Hindu society within the Indian context and the common Indian cultural ground and (*ii*) a Muslim and a Hindu household within ideological difference.

will concentrate on the rituals as performed and will concern myself with the manifest Muslim Bengali interpretation. In the analysis of the Moharram festival, I will show where the local mythology differs from the actual historical fact, though for our purpose I will dwell on the local myths and performance. In a previous essay (Fruzzetti, 1976a), I demonstrated that rituals are the means through which Muslims in this community chose to separate themselves (within the same town) according to specific *paras* and within that locality into clusters of kin-related households or *khandans*. In extreme cases one finds that the *khandan* is further broken up into a yet smaller unit, the nuclear family.

Household rituals are performed privately. Each life cycle rite defines the number of participants, who may or may not participate in them, and who the rituals affect (e.g., in case of pollution). Life cycle rites also define the relationships between one household and another and between the members of the same household to each other and to the ritual. On the other hand, the public festivals are more communal in nature, the central or the main emphasis being on the integration and the solidarity of all Muslims. There are numerous Muslim festivals but for this essay we will concentrate on the Moharram festival. It shall be my contention that the rituals are used to integrate the household, the *khandan* members and sets one household apart from the other; whereas the public festival unites the community. Public rituals are annually celebrated. In this essay, I propose to analyze these two types of rituals within the framework of Islamic precepts and folk Islam (Islam in a non-Muslim country).

Birth Rituals: God's Protection and Rules

Life cycle rituals are divided into two parts. The first part corresponds to the rules laid down by the *din* (religion) of Islam. These rules are followed and an attempt is made to maintain them intact without any possibility of change. The second part of the *rite de passage* falls within the folk element of Islam. Here I am not dealing with written laws but with what is handed down from one generation to the other, within the same line of a number of related households. Furthermore, the birth rituals are divided into two performances—the part that the *moulvi* (equivalent to the priest) performs and that which the women perform on their own without the help of the *moulvi*.

Bengali women state that the aim of marriage is procreation, preferably of a male child, where the birth of the child completes the expectation of women as mothers and wives as well as ensures the continuity of the male line. Bengali women deliver their first born child in their paternal home. Normally, around the fifth month of pregnancy, the *pawati* (mother-to-be) is accompanied by her husband to her father's house and left there until the child is born. The new-born baby will observe its first rice eating ceremony in its father's house in the sixth or seventh month after birth. Thus, the ritual activities discussed in this paper can take place either in one's father's or husband's house.

On the fifth month of pregnancy, the mother is feasted with a lavish meal consisting of five different kinds of cooked curries, sweets, and fruits. The odd numbers 5, 7, and 9 are considered auspicious for women. The local *moulvi* prepares a *maduli* (an amulet). The amulet contains dried flowers from a saint's tomb. Also within the amulet is a piece of paper on which verses from the Koran are written.[3] The amulet is threaded with black thread and is given to the mother to wear around her neck. A second thread of red colour is given to the mother to wear around her waist. Red and black are special colours for both Bengali Hindus and Muslims; both colours appear in other life cycle rituals with similar ethnographic analysis. The first *maduli* must be given by the husband's household to the expectant mother, the purpose of the amulet being to protect mother and child. Pregnancy and birth are considered to be dangerous times for both mother and child, for death lurks around this auspicious life cycle rite. Death is caused by the *pretas* and *bhutas* (spirits) considered to be takers or 'cutters' of life. Just as the red colour is auspicious and represents life and longevity, the black colour acknowledges the fear and the power of death.

The amulet serves to bless the mother (*baraka*, imparted to her from the *pir*). A particularly chosen Muslim saint is selected to protect the expecting mother.

In the ninth month of pregnancy another amulet will be given to the mother. This is the first *maduli* which will be given to the child soon after birth. Also during the ninth month of pregnancy, the mother is given another feast—the ninth month *saade*. Many households do not observe this occasion because of an evil omen, a *badha* (an obstruction), for in the past a mother might have died on that day. The function and aim of this feast is similar to that of the fifth month feast. As the child or the mother could die at childbirth, the mother's desires are sought to be satisfied by the lavish cooking of nine curries, vegetables, sweets and so forth. She is also given gifts of cloth and perhaps jewellery. Another function of this feast is that if a woman were to die during childbirth she might not turn into a vengeful *preta* (spirit). Women try to fulfil and satiate the expecting mother's desires so that (in case of death) she might not retaliate and harm the living. Only in this manner is her soul appeased.

There are no other specific rituals before the actual birth of the child. Following the birth, the important days and the accompanying rituals occur on the first, fourth, fifth, twenty-first and fortieth day. Birth, as a *rite de passage*, is an auspicious occasion although it causes pollution to the members involved. The Muslim mother and the child are polluted for forty days. It is forbidden for the mother to utter the name of Allah or to pray during this period. Thus, Islamic prescriptions and the accompanying code of behaviour for the different life cycle rites differ from the more unrestricted cultural, ritual and social activities of the women within their Bengali centext. Thus, while touching the Koran is forbidden during the forty days of pollution, performing some of the Bengali rituals which centre around the child and mother are part and parcel of a Muslim woman's domain within Bengali culture. Here we refer to *stri-acars*, the married women's rituals that accompany life cycle rites.

The First Day of the Birth

As soon as the mother begins child labour the midwife, who is usually a lower caste Hindu woman, is summoned. She remains within easy reach of the house, and awaits the birth of the child. The mother's stomach is oiled and massaged to lessen the labour pain. When the child is about to be born, a member of the house starts saying *namaz*, so that the first words the child hears are sacred ones. Secondly, noise is created by drums or by another method, introducing the child to noise. After birth, the child remains on the ground, lying on a piece of cloth until the placenta is delivered. Only then is the umbilical cord cut. The *daiima* (midwife) cuts the cord, washes the child, oils him/her and hands the baby to the mother. The placenta is placed in a newly purchased clay pot which is buried within the confines of the house. Five pieces of (whole) turmeric, five cowrie shells and five betel nuts are placed with the placenta and covered before the burial with another new clay pot. Muslim women, like Hindu women, also conceive of the placenta as belonging to the earth. And, therefore, by burying it, it is given back to the earth. The feared spirits and *preta* attack the placenta if it is thrown away and in this manner can harm the mother or the child. The first *maduli* is given to the child for its protection. A red thread is tied around its waist and an iron bangle is put on his/her left arm for additional protection from the spirits. An iron colirium holder is also placed under the child's pillow to protect it from evil forces. A black dot made from a mixture (*nag dana rosa*) of one's own mother's milk, colirium and the leaf of the *naga* tree is placed on children's foreheads and on the soles of their feet. Everyday for six months the mother will apply a dot on the child's forehead and on the soles of his/her feet. This is one of the many ways to ward off evil spirits.

Sometimes a piece of net is tied to the child's left arm. Another piece of net is tied on the window in the room where the child sleeps. The pieces of net must be obtained from the local fishermen's neighbourhood and they must be from the net that the fisherman used for fishing at the time of birth. No effect is produced from a brand new net which has not been used for fishing. As a matter of fact, the net must be stolen, say the women, since *jele* (fishermen) will not volunteer to give it to the women. The nets are used for protection and the *jele* claim that the household's anticipated dangers befall them since it is their nets and their own *mantra* (incantation) that have been taken from them to protect the mother and the child. So, in case people come to ask for pieces of nets needed for ritual purposes, the *jele* have some in store for the occasion. At the end of the nets, one finds small iron-like pellets, also desired objects for protection from spirits. Fishermen's nets and the fishermen's *mantras* are considered to be very powerful. The fishermen work in the middle of the night, a time when the spirits are hovering around looking for mischief. Therefore, anyone who dares the night must do so with the aid of powerful *mantras*. Secondly, the *jele* (fishermen) use the powerful *mantras* to catch fish in their nets. Even though the spirits are very fond of fish, at the same time they are afraid of being caught like the fish in the nets.

The immediate fear of the spirits lasts up to twenty-one days, after which the mother and the child are partially protected by Sasthi, the deity of children. The Hindus say that the child is further under the protection of Sasthi for five years. The spirits and the *preta*, including the destructive *Chutti* (a Hindu godling), inspire the most fear for the newborn babies.

The Period of Pollution

There are two kinds of seclusion due to pollution that the mother and child undergo—*haridia* and *aetur*. *Haridia* means that the mother and the child have gone through an initial period of pollution (though are not completely purified). The second form of seclusion is *chutti*, or keeping *aetur*—the five days period of pollution after which the mother and the child can come outside the room and lie under the sun. The majority of the Muslims observe *chutti*, since *haridia* would mean worshipping Lord Hari in the form of the Tulsi tree (a sacred plant for the Hindus). Ritual activities up to *chutti* day are not elaborate for the Muslims. However, the mother and child cannot leave the room where the baby is born for five days for they are in a state of pollution. In the *aetur ghore* (the room where the birth took place and where they must lie until the end of *chutti*), a fire is lit and kept burning for five days. With the palms of her hands, the midwife applies heat to the mother and the baby (whereas in *haridia* people can lie directly under the sun). After the fifth day, *seke* (heat application) is not applied to the mother. Bengali women claim that the process of childbirth results in the loss of heat for the mother; thus the application of heat through the fire and the consumption of *jhal* (a specially prepared spicy mixture) is one way to compensate for the loss of heat. Since the midwife is the only woman who can touch the mother or the child without being polluted, she is the one who does the massaging. The rest of the household members will not touch the mother or child before the ritual bath on the fifth day, when both will be partially purified. For the Muslims, complete ritual purification occurs on the fortieth day.

While in the *aetur ghore*, the Muslims perform some rituals which parallel those of the Hindus. On the first day of the birth, no rituals are performed. The baby is bathed in turmeric water, oiled and given to its mother. Turmeric is used for many local ritual purposes in different life cycle rites and saint worship. For four days, the mother consumes small quantities of liquid as liquids are believed to further deplete the heat of the mother. A mixture called *jhal* (hot or heat exuding) is made from dried garlic, black pepper and ginger which are then mixed with clarified butter and water, and is consumed by the new mother twice a day. The *jhal* helps dry up the thirty-six *naris* (nerves) which were holding the child. When the child is ready to be born, the nerves release it and the baby is born. As a result, the nerves must be healed and dried by taking *jhal* and very little water or any other liquid. The other source of food for the mother is parched or puffed rice. On the fourth day after the birth, the mother can resume eating cooked rice. The first cooked rice which the mother consumes after birth is given to her by her brother, the child's mother's brother (MB). The meal consists of rice plus fish or meat and a number of other delicious savouries, including sweets. If the child was born in the mother-in-law's house, the money for *jhal bhat* is sent to her by her brother and her in-laws will use it to buy and perpare for the feast. The *jhal bhat* at birth rituals parallels the *mammar bhat* (MB's rice meal) which is the child's first solid meal (for females, celebrated in the seventh month after birth and for males in the sixth month). In both instances, the MB acknowledges his ritual duties and relation to his sister's son or daughter (ZS/D), as he holds a special ritual relation to his ZS/D. For both Hindus and Muslims, the MB's role is important. This importance lies in the continuity of the relationship between the brother and sister (B/Z) or the mother's relationship with her father's side through her brother. Change of residence after the girl's marriage does not entail a change of the maternal or paternal relationships. Ideally, a married Muslim woman never loses her own father's authority over her conduct and behaviour.

The important aspect (and difference from the Hindus) of *jhal bhat* among the Muslims is that a rooster is cooked if it is a male child and a hen if it is a female child. The hen's or the rooster's head is cooked with the rest of the fowl's meat. It is then mixed with cooked rice and offered to the mother. The child is supposed to receive the strength of the rooster or the hen (both of which are admired for their strong and straight heads). This power (*shakti*) is transmitted to the child by the mother through her milk. Breast feeding is thought of as augmenting the child's blood and strengthening the child. Thus, like the Hindus, the Muslim child is created from the male seed as well as from the mother, paralleling the Hindu mother who augments that which is already male. After consuming the meal, the hen's or rooster's head is placed on the roof where it remains to dry in the sun. The length of time that it takes for the head to dry will parallel the time that it will take for the child's neck and body to become strong.

Chutti Din

Muslims in Bengal observe *chutti*, which is more of a celebration. It is the day when the mother will bathe away part of the pollution caused by birth. For the Hindus, *setera* (the sixth) is equivalent to *chutti* (which also means the sixth). Though there is no actual worship of Sasthi on this day, the Muslims say that this is *Sasthir din*—the day of Sasthi. On this day, the mother and child will emerge from the *aetur ghore* to bathe (for the mother this is her first bath since the birth of the child and for the child this is his/her second bath). The dirty clothes which were accumulated in the *aetur ghore* will be washed by the midwife or the *dhoba* (the Hindu washerman caste). Note here that the Muslims use the Hindu midwife and washermen because of their specific caste occupations. Also on *chutti*, the house is cleaned and perhaps whitewashed. The barber woman is called in for *kamano* (pairing of the mother's and child's nails). At this time, the child's head is shaved and the hair is weighed. In the future, an equal amount of the hair's weight in gold or silver will be given to the poor. This will occur on the child's *aqiqa* (naming ceremony). The mother has *alta* (a red dye considered to be auspicious) applied to her feet. *Chutti* occurs on the evening of the fifth day of the birth. Various members of the Muslim household recite a *fatiha* known as *Sasthir fatiha* (a Koranic verse dedicated to Sasthi). Dirty clothes can be washed on this day. Household members are now able to touch the mother and the child without fear of pollution, because of the partial purity which takes place on this day. On the other hand, the midwife will not approach the house nor attend to the *pawati* (the new mother) again. In the evening, a *prodip* (oil lamp) is lit and kept burning for the duration of that night. On this day, the child's future—his/her *karma* will be written. This is the night when Bidata Purush will visit the house where a child is born. How long will the child live? What is his/her fate and chances in the world and so forth? Its entire future will be written down, including whether it will be happy or not, the length of its life, and the day it will die. A *tal pata* (pen made from bamboo), ink and paper or leaf are all placed in a corner of the room next to the lit lamp. The room is cleaned for the occasion and the members of the household are all in a semi-purified state awaiting the arrival of Bidata Purush. He is the giver of life whereas Sasthi (referred to as his consort) is the protectress of children's life. The coming of Bidata and the celebration of *chutti* parallel each other. 'The *Chhatti*, or the celebration of the sixth day after the birth of a child, when the mother takes the bath of purification, actually represents deliverance from the dread of a Hindu godling, *Chhatti*, who personifies the septicaemia which often follows childbirth in unhygienic conditions' (Ahmad, 1969:47). Food offerings are left next to the ink and the *tal pata* for the Bidata. Bidata is an ancestor, a spirit, a higher being with power over people's life. He is the one who ultimately determines the longevity of the newborn child. In the evening, the *moulvi* will recite a *fatiha* before the arrival of Bidata. It is assumed that he arrives on the night of the fifth day (or on the sixth day) after birth.

The next ritual observance does not take place until the twenty-first day after birth. On that day, the mother and child undergo similar ritual purification. Among the Hindus, the twenty-first day bath removes the ritual impurity caused by birth, but this is not the case with the Muslims among whom complete purification is achieved only on the fortieth day. For the duration of forty days, the Muslim mother does not say *namaz* nor touch the Koran because of her impure state. On the fortieth day, she will have to observe some of the Koranic injunctions about her bodily purification, e.g., washing her hair forty times and brushing her teeth with three different sticks forty times. The activities surrounding the bodily purification should be completed before the noon prayers, when the mother will have to say *namaz* again. The purification of the mother and the child is now complete, and the mother can again resume her normal work.

The children remain under the protection of Sasthi and the *feresta* (angels). There is a Muslim saying that conveys the precarious position of the new mother during the forty days of her state of pollution: *Ek pa gore* (mitu=death) *ek pa jamina* (land=life), i.e., the time of birth is like having one foot in the grave and one foot in life. Birth, as a *rite de passage*, incorporates both life and death, especially during the first few days. The possibility of death is very definitely inherent in childbirth. The fear that surrounds the period of birth emanates from the same source both for the Hindus (twenty-one days) and the Muslims (forty days): the dread of the *pret* (the wandering souls) and the *pretas* (the malignant souls). Though the Muslim fundamentalists criticize the general mass of the Muslims for this aspect of local syncretism, the fear of these uncontrollable spirits—the *pretas* and the *bhuttas*—is greater than the fear of criticism, and the rituals surrounding the life cycle rites still persist. The mother (as well as the child), because of their state of impurity, are socially cut off from the rest of society. They remain in seclusion (in a neutral state) where only a low caste woman can touch them without adding or creating problems of pollution because of her specific caste occupation as removers of pollution, or in her role of midwife which neither adds to nor creates pollution during the prescribed period. The *rite de passage* segregates the mother from the rest of the household. This is similar to the three days' segregation when a woman is considered to be in a state of pollution because of her menstrual cycle. When one discards the polluted state one discards with it the items associated with pollution, e.g., the dirty clothes and the jewellery worn at that time (usually cheap glass jewellery is worn when one is in a polluted state). Although birth is a happy occasion and the life cycle rite is an auspicious one, temporary pollution is caused by the presence of and contact with blood. Muslims follow the prescribed Islamic rule for bodily purification as well as the rites for protection in this world.

The Festival of Moharram: Pirs and Martyrs

Through the festival of Moharram, I will attempt to look at the celebrations as one of the ways in which the Muslims in this rural town of West Bengal attempt to unite their community—a community which is divided into thirteen *paras* or neighbourhoods. The role of the martyrs, Hassan and Hussain, who were tragically killed at the battle of Karbala, are used for the purpose of achieving solidarity within the community.

The death of Hassan and Hussain at Karbala marks the split between the Shiahs and the Sunnis in Islam, so that the Shiahs annually observe the death anniversary of the two martyrs. I am suggesting that in this case the Muslims use the tragic death not to remind them of the split in Islam, or the creation of the two sects, but rather to unite all Muslims into one fold and demarcate them from non-Muslims (Thaiss, 1972). Here the abstract concept of the *umma* is actualized for the duration of the Moharram festival. The absence of any Shiah households in the town makes this reversal of the ritual observance of Moharram possible, so that here the Karbala battle symbolically serves to unite Muslims and not to split them into sects (or groups in this particular case).

The pattern of Muslim settlement in the town is relevant to our understanding of the celebration of Moharram. Though the Muslims constitute about 5 to 6 per cent of the total population, the community is split into thirteen *paras* or neighbourhoods. The largest group of Muslims live around the main mosque. This mosque marks the central locality where the celebration will be conducted. According to local history, this was the first settlement of Muslims in this predominantly Hindu area. The Muslims were brought into the town by the then local Rajas. The second concentration of Muslims is found around the area where one of the two major saints of the town is buried. Both localities hold an important place in the celebration of the festival. The Moharram procession always starts from the saint's burial place and proceeds towards the mosque where it stops and where mock fight is staged. When the procession goes out on its way to 'Karbala', (the desert where Imam Hussan died, but in this case the Muslim burial ground in the town) the *tazziya*[5] from the *para* of the mosque will be at the front of the procession and the rest will follow accordingly.

Each of the Muslim *paras* has a sacred structure erected near the centre of its locality. This could be a saint's grave, a mosque, an *idgah*,[6] or perhaps a Koranic school. All the Muslim localities are distinctly marked by these sacred structures. Usually, the houses surround these specific buildings and the *paras* are named after them, e.g., Sheikh *para* where the mosque is situated, Kurbantola where the saint Kurban Shah is buried and so forth.

Moharram is the Muslim month of mourning. It is the first month of the Muslim calendar. Although the Muslims of the town are Sunnis, they celebrate the festival of Moharram with a mixed feeling of gaiety and mourning. Newly bought dresses, a festive atmosphere, men drinking or performing *mataam* (beating one's breast), are all part of the Moharram celebration in this town. Moharram is celebrated publicly by all the Muslims of the town, bringing together the different *paras*, unlike the simaller saint's (*pirs*) feasts or life cycle rituals which are

[5] *Tazziya* is a representation or model of the tomb of the martyrs Hassan & Hussain.

[6] *Idgah* is a place where *Id* prayers can be held.

held privately in the homes. The division of the Muslims into thirteen *paras* or neighbourhoods is clearly evident in this particular festival. Each *para* tries to partake in the festival through diverse means, i.e., by contributing money to the committee of the major mosque in the town, or preparing their own *tazziya* or *duldul*.[7] In many cases two or three *paras* combine their contributions and construct a common *tazziya* to take part in the final procession. Between 1967-69 and 1971-73, only four *paras* had either their own *tazziya* or *duldul* at the Moharram procession. One of the *tazziyas* belonged to a nearby predominantly Muslim village. The *paras* which do not contribute to the procession (in the form of a *tazziya* or *duldul*) would have other obligations to fulfil during the years—e.g., arranging a *pir's urs* from their own *soloanna*[8] contributions—and would therefore be allowed to participate in the procession. Those *paras* who, for economic reasons, would not be able to set up a *tazziya* or to arrange an *urs*, will yet contribute to other *para's tazziyas*. In this sense, no locality (if it does not wish to be excluded) would willingly alienate itself from the rest of the members of the community.

On the first day of Moharram, Muslims cut their nails (a ritual process) and cleanse themselves. On this day, the men start to work on the *tazziya*. In Bishnupur, the tradition of constructing *tazziyas* goes as far back as thirty to forty years, a time when both Hindus and Muslims prepared them jointly. Today, only the Muslims work on the *tazziya*, but the *duldul* is still prepared by the Potidar, who also makes the Hindu clay images of the different Hindu gods and goddesses.

The *tazziya*, supposed to be a replica of Imam Hassan's tomb, has the shape of a mausoleum. Depending on the funds available (which are minimal in most cases), the *tazziya* will be decorated with tinsel and shiny paper. Some of these *tazziya* structures have two or three storeys; others are as many as ten storeys high. The outer frame of the *tazziya* is made from bamboo sticks. Once the frame is completed, the women begin

[7] *Duldul* is a clay horse which commemorates Imam Hussain's horse.

[8] *parasoloana*, a dramatic expression used here, means 'sixteen annas to the rupee', i.e., all neighbourhoods must contribute 100 per cent (16 annas comprised 100 per cent of Re. 1.00).

to decorate it with silver and gold paper. The materials used for decoration are later stored for next year's *tazziya.* A few years back, the whole *tazziya* was buried on the last day at 'Karbala'. The actual decorative materials are of no significance to the Moharram festival. One finds the picture of the Taj Mahal or other Mughal buildings stuck on the *tazziya.* Cut-outs of silver or gold tinsel in the shape of mausoleums are attached to the *tazziya.* A curtain is placed at the entrance of the *tazziya* though the inside is hollow and contains no objects. One of the *paras* prepares a cloth *tazziya.* The frame of this *tazziya* is that of the *bangla* (hut or house, shaped after the local Bengali style houses), and the frame is covered with a red cloth. This type of *tazziya* is a new idea recently introduced to the town.

Moharram and the two other public festivals, *Id* and *Boqrid,* are celebrated collectively unlike the feasts like *Milad* and *Shab-e-brat* which are observed privately. Almost all the Muslims take part in Moharram (with the exception of the women, who stay in the background). In the other two public festivals, men assemble at the main mosque for prayers. One can see that all the three major festivals have a collective quality about them, and the Muslims make an effort to be together for the celebrations.

Every *para* which is going to join in the procession with a *tazziya* or *duldul,* will also have a flag posted near their *asthana* (a holy place which is centrally located in the *para* or Muslim neighbourhood). Every *para* has an *asthana,* even if they have a mosque, a *pir's* grave, or an *idgah* within their locality. An *asthana* is a sacred structure, a shrine or grave of one or more saints but without the bodies of the saints being buried there, e.g., one of the *asthana* contains earth from the graves of five saints, one of which is that of Imam Hassan. The flagpole is made of bamboo sticks, about three feet long. Some are wrapped in red cloth with small pieces of cloth attached to the pole. At the top of the flagpole, a metallic hand (*nisan*) is placed or some feathers are stuck. The hand symbolizes Hassan's child (who died at the battle too) or simply the idea of death. On the first day of Moharram, a small procession goes out from the mosque. The participating parties will hire their own drummers (usually low caste Hindus). The pattern which the procession takes on this day and on the day of Moharram is as follows: the leading party with its *tazziya* or *duldul*, their *para* members and the drummers go first. The next party of men follows the first, keeping a distance of a few feet not for any religious reasons but one which is prescribed by law, to avoid any possible clash. People join the procession as it passes through the town and it finally arrives at the Raja's residence to pay respect (*salaam*) to him. On way to the Raja's house, mock fights are held with red sticks (red is an important colour theme in this festival and denotes death and blood).

The first procession is small and it serves to announce the beginning of the mourning period for the death of Hassan and Hussain and their families. After the procession is over, the parties go back to their *paras* and the flags are posted near the *asthanas* of each locality.

The next day the Muslim do not do any major work in the morning except work on the *tazziyas*. This day is known as *Bisram* (rest). Muslims might tell stories about the troubles that the two Imams and their families went through or they might pray. At night, they celebrate the *urs* of Goriali Shab, the second major *pir* of the town. The death anniversary of this 'hot tempered' (*gorom*) *pir* falls on the second day of the mourning period. The second part of the day is known as *gagron* (to keep vigil all night). The celebration concerning the *pir* lasts until 2 or 3 A.M.[9]

The third day of the celebration is the climax of the Moharram festival and it is on this day that the Muslims go out in procession with the *tazziya*. The Moharram celebration, though it is a period of mourning, is referred to as a *porob* (festival). In the morning, final touches are put to the *tazziyas*. At about 4 P.M., one hears the drums announcing the beginning of the procession. All the Muslims *paras* which are not on the route which the procession takes through the town will meet at the mosque, whereas the others will wait in their *paras* to join in the procession. In the meantime, mock fights are held in front of the mosque with real swords and sticks. Although the fight and the battle is symbolically re-enacted,

[9]See Fruzzetti-Ostar, (1971) for an elaboration of the *pir's* death anniversary.

some of the actors actually get hurt and bleed. Women, who stand and watch from a distance, will acclaim in admiration and the men will clap their hands. The names of the two Imams, Hassan and Hussain, are called out loudly. Before the procession starts, the mosque's *tazziya* is loaned out to Muslim *paras* that don't have one. The *tazziya* is placed next to the specific sacred structure (*asthana*) of the *para* for a short while. In this way, the Muslims of those *paras* can make their food offerings to their *asthanas*. Secondly, due to a partial observance of purdah, the women can also see the *tazziya* and pay their respects to the two saints without having to join the procession. Women of the locality come forward with their covered trays carrying clay horses and elephants, plus some sweets. These trays are placed in front of the *asthana*. Moulvi Saheb puts his cap on and recites a *fatiha* over the offering; the tray is then given back to the donor. In this fashion, the *moulvi* will proceed to each tray of offering before the *tazziya* is taken on to another *para*. On this day, food offerings are made to every *asthana*, and every saint is remembered by his *para* members.

The Moharram Procession

Para A heads the procession. They walk from their *para* to that of *para B* of the big *masjid*. A nearby Muslim village comes to town to celebrate the festival. They meet the two parties at the mosque; they all walk towards 'Karbala'. *Maatam* (beating one's own breast, a sign of mourning and sorrow) begins on this day. As the devotees beat their breasts, they call out the names of Hassan and Hussain. The momentum of *maatam* is slow at first but increases to a climax as it is accompanied by the drums. The procession picks up other parties on its way. It takes them eight hours to reach the Raja's house where they pay respect (*salaam*) to him for the second time. The Raja, who is almost blind, does not come out to meet the procession; he sends his son to represent him. Nowadays, no prize is given to the best decorated *tazziya*, which used to be a tradition associated with Moharram celebrations in this town. The Muslims then proceed to 'Karbala' to bury the flowers which were used to decorate the *tazziyas*, the *tazziyas* themselves being kept for the next year's celebration. Nonetheless, the flowers symbolize the *tazziya* and the two Imams. This is the last act and ends the Moharram celebrations. After the burial of flowers, the *moulvi* will recite a *fatiha* over it, and the people return to their homes.

Moharram is one of the three Muslim festivals (with *Boqrid* and *Id*)[10] in which the Muslims as a whole act as a community. Although many of the middle class Muslims do not actually take part in the procession, they nevertheless cooperate in the festival by keeping their locality illuminated for the Moharram procession which passes through their *paras* or by making monetary contributions to the Moharram committee and so on.

The Moharram festival serves a double purpose: it commemorates the death of the two saints, Hassan and Hussain, and also serves to unite the whole community. The festival becomes a reality and actualizes the *umma* model through the joint efforts of all the Muslims of the town. No locality wants to be left out of the festive activities, especially if it has not got other alternatives, e.g., if a locality has no *pir's urs* to celebrate or does not have a *tazziya* in the procession.

Yet, at the same time, Moharram clearly demarcates the Muslims of the town into *paras* or localities. The different participating parties are in competition to one another. In 1969, a riot broke out on the last day of the Moharram festival between two groups from different *paras*. The police broke up the procession and only three men were allowed to bury the flowers to complete the celebrations. The cause of the fight was small and insignificant but ended in splitting the spatial and social division of the two *paras* even further.

Conclusion

In this essay I have used rituals and festivals to analyze a rural Muslim community. The birth rituals presented us with a private world—the household, its daily concerns, fears of the

[10] See Fruzzetti-Ostar (1970) for an elaboration of the Muslim feasts.

unknown, the beliefs and practices surrounding birth, and ways and methods of approaching the Sacred Being for protection. Rituals surrounding birth contain the Islamic rules regarding bodily purification as well as a number of *desher achar* (local customs) which complement these injunctions.

The Moharram festival celebrated by the Sunnis in the town, though an occasion of mourning which commemorates the death of Hassan and Hussain, was in turn used to create cohesion in the community. The ritual re-enactment of the death scene and the procession to 'Karbala' reflect a disunited Muslims community being brought together (though the reality of such an occasion is temporary). Thaiss' (1972) analysis of the Shiah drama concludes in a similar fashion regarding the annual re-enactment of the drama : 'The persistence of this ritual over time is attributed to the reflective nature of that ritual *vis-ā-vis* the contemporary society—whether it be Umayyad, Abbasid, Safavid, Qajar or Pahlavi' (Thaiss, 1972:364).

Rituals are not performed because of an obsession with tradition. The rituals of Moharram reflect the sentiments of the community. The Muslims are a minority amidst a Hindu majority in this rural Vaisnava town. At the same time, the community is dispersed into many groups who interact with each other on very specific occasions. It is at such times that one can briefly conceive the ideal of the abstract *umma* Muslims. Rituals and myth change over time to suit the specific needs of a community or group. Death of the two saints and their families, which resulted in the emergence of a new Islamic sect, serves to unite the people who are re-enacting the drama. (Again the actual historical mythology changes over time). The saints in turn became *pirs*, i.e., saints who are venerated along with the rest of the town's saints. New meaning and symbols are imparted to the activities of the historical past. All the different Muslim *paras* make an effort to take part in the ritual. All the saints buried in the town are honoured on this day and the sacred structures are cleaned and whitewashed.

The festival of Moharram and the birth rituals incorporate ideas and actions which are part of the local culture. Food offerings to the *tazziya* and the saints are local ways to show honour and respect. The numerous ritual activities during the first seven days of birth, again, can be understood within the framework of Bengali culture.

It is clear that the systems of *desher achar* or *niom* has no clear boundary in that Muslims employ both religious and secular ideas and actions in their daliy life. All practices which are alien to strict Islamic teachings fall under the category of Bengali culture. Here we are not suggesting that the Muslims cannot distinguish between the so-called 'secular' or 'sacred' domains; or, as it is often defined, 'Bengali culture' *vs.* 'Islamic culture'. In this unique manner, they attempt to maintain the purity of Islamic beliefs and practices and prevent it from being infused with ideas that are regarded as being too secular by them.

Muslims do adhere to the fundamental principles of orthodox Islam. They try to keep Islam static, as it has been revealed, and to keep the doctrine unchanged. For the Muslims, Islam need not change since all that is good has already been enunciated by the Koran. Time and time again they recall the Islamic mistrust of change. For these men, Islam is a social code, a '. . . complete way of life rather than being either merely a set of religious rites or pertaining exclusively to the private relationship between the individual and his God' (Rahman, 1968:258).

The Muslims of Bishnupur have forged a unique culture by combining Islamic precepts with the experience of everyday life, its social contexts and the elements that come from a non-Islamic culture. There are points at which these two spheres overlap and, using this as a principle, the Muslims of the town see no contradiction between strictly Islamic and non-Islamic practices. In an abstract sense, they see both as having their concrete parallels in the world of action. We have seen that whatever does not fit into the one fits into the other. Whatever is not in the Koran is *niom* (Bengali), complementing though never contradicting, the spirit of Muslim *dharam*, as the townsmen are aware of Koranic laws regarding the individual's activities in all spheres of life. Local *achars* are also practised though they are understood within the local Bengali culture and not as part of Koranic laws. But this itself is an ideological question, for the boundaries of the two systems are ideally clear. However, on the level of experience, for the purpose of action, there is no need to distinguish them.

We can conclude by stating that the basic source of a Muslim's identity is the observance of Islamic tenets which has the force of defining a concrete community. Doctrine, customs and *desher achar* are all components of these tenets. This also explains the Muslim's negative attitude to social change, change that might directly affect their *dharma*, their religion. Nonetheless, they are aware of the limitations of Islam and its incompatibility with the ideology of a modern state. As regards the experiences of daily living, the Muslims see no conflict in being both Muslims and Bengalis. What is regarded as a universal community, the *umma*, at the level of conceptualization, becomes a series of small groups at the level of concrete action. The universalistic aspect of the *umma* is not the sole concern of Islam; there is another sphere of action on a smaller scale with smaller units involved.

Bibliography

Ahmad, Aziz (1969), *An Intellectual History of Islam in India*, Edinburg, Edinburg University Press.

Fruzzetti-Ostar, Lina (1970), 'The Idea of Community Among West Bengal Muslims' in P. Bertocci (ed.), *Prelude to Crisis: Bengal and Bengal Studies in 1970*, South Asia Series Occasional Paper, No. 18, A Durham, Duke University.

———(1971), *The Social Organization of West Bengal Muslims*, Master's Thesis, University of Chicago.

———(1976a), 'Ritual Status of Muslim women in Rural India', in G. Smith (ed.), *Women in Contemporary Muslims Society*, Bucknell, *Bucknell* University Press.

———(1976b), 'Food and Worship: Analysis of birth rituals'. Submitted for publication in A Ghazi (ed.) Conference Volume, "Hindu and Muslim Interaction", Minneapolis, University of Minnesota Press.

Nelson, C. (1974), 'Public and Private Politics: Women in the Middle Eastern World', *American Ethnologist*, 1, pp.

Peters, E. (1968), 'Sex differentiation in two Arab communities' (Mimeo),

Rahman, Fazlur (1968), *Islam*, New York, Doubleday Anchor and Co.

Thaiss, Gustav (1972), 'Religious Symbolism and Social Change: The Drama of Hussain', in N. Keddie (ed.), *Scholar, Saints and Sufis: Muslim Religious Institutions in the Middle East Since 1500*, Berkeley, University of California Press.

4

Ideal and Reality in the Observance of Moharram: A Behavioural Interpretation

A.R. Saiyid
assisted by
Pathan Mirkhan and Mohammad Talib

The sociological study of syncretic elements present in the religious life of Indian Muslims is a somewhat neglected field.[1] As a result, there has been a lack of proper understanding of the importance and function of this syncretism. In this paper, we have presented empirical data concerning the various 'little' and 'local' traditions that have gathered around the observance of Moharram in certain Sunni Muslim communities, and have made an effort to analyze and interpret the implications of these syncretic elements for the social and social psychological life of these communities and their members. This paper, it may be clarified at the very outset, does not seek to bring under scrutiny the religious aspects or contents of Moharram and/or Islam, nor even of Muslims *per se*. Rather, its concern is with the behavioural aspects of a purely sociological phenomenon. Admittedly, in exercises such as this, the sociological and the purely religious dimensions may intermingle but in

[1] For a classic account of syncretism in the Muslim context, see Clifford Geertz (1960).

terms of focus, approach and analysis there remains a valid and clear distinction between these two dimensions.

Those familiar with the observance of Moharram by Sunni Muslim communities residing in India's rural and semi-rural areas (including small- and medium-sized towns whose ethos is, or has been, essentially rural), are aware of the fact that in many of these communities the first ten days of Moharram are 'celebrated' as if it is some sort of a festival.[2] Several rituals, ceremonies and 'local' traditions are fulfilled which do not have the remotest relationship with Islam. Young and old, men and women, and to an extent even Hindus, are involved in this phenomenon characterized as it is by collective participation and joint 'enjoyment'. Indeed, in many instances rural Sunni Muslim communities, through their enthusiastic observance of Moharram as well as by their sincere fulfilment of its various 'local' traditions, give little inkling to their non-Muslim neighbours that Moharram is not some sort of an Id, but, instead, is a grim reminder of a dastardly tragedy that occurred in the annals of Islam during this month. Ironically enough, in terms of collective participation, it is Moharram that generates public and popular 'celebration' rather than the Id festivals, even though they are more truly a part of Islam's 'great' tradition. All this is not to say that there is unbridled gaiety associated with Moharram or that it is simply an unadulterated festival. Indeed, the observence of Moharram is invariably characterized by certain serious and sombre features also,[3] but many of these

[2] The word 'festival' in this paper has been used in a somewhat special sense. The intended meaning is not simply that of an occasion of joy and gaiety but rather of a season of communal—in the sense of associational—activities and practices, backed by certain beliefs and attitudes. Accordingly, to denote this somewhat different usage, the terms festival, joyous, gaiety, celebration, etc., have been used with quotation marks to emphasize the difference. It is unfortunate that some other suitable terms were not available, or did not occur, to the author.

[3] These generally consist of the recitation of eulogies in praise of Hassan and Hussain. Also, there are various symbolic representations of the Karbala battle. Thus, for example, the *alums* in the Moharram processions represent the flags or standards that had been used. Similarly, the 'Hai Dosh' gyrations (popular in the Marathwada region) are a representation of the protective chains which warriors

largely remain at the level of symbolism and tend to get mixed up with other forms of popular observances. Accordingly, in many communities, Moharram has become a curious amalgam in which the festive and recreational aspects stand out.

Considering, then, that there is an element of sociological oddity and incongruity about Moharram, it is of some interest to the social scientist to explore the factors that may account for this metamorphosis. One explanation which is generally offered to explain away such syncretism is, of course, that of 'Hindu influence'. Admittedly, some of the accretions surrounding the observance of Moharram are Hindu in origin, or at least are influenced by Hindu practices. But it would be too simplistic and palpably inadequate to explain the kind of phenomenon described in this paper (the likes of which are to be found elsewhere in the country too) as a result merely of Hindu influences. In fact, a serious examination of this phenomenon suggests that some deeper dynamics are involved in this unique transformation.

Taking the lead from our empirical data, plus making a reasonable assumption that these data are not entirely unique, an effort has been made to offer an explanation of the Moharram 'festival' within a sociological framework. In this connection, a striking observation—which is at the same time a leading clue to our understanding of Moharram as it is observed today—is the fact that the 'celebration' of Moharram is generally popular (as has already been indicated) in the rural and semi-rural areas. Further, in this environment, it is mostly individuals and groups belonging to the lower socio-economic strata who seem to participate and 'enjoy' the proceedings the most. Another strata of society for whom Moharram appears to be of special interest is women. It thus appears that in order to make a systematic analysis of the underlying dynamics involved in the observance of Moharram as a 'festival', it will be helpful to focus attention upon these sociological categories. Further, it is necessary to consider the existential circumstances impinging upon their lives inasmuch as it is the present author's

of those days used to make in order to save the tents and other material of the army, or the king and his flag. (I am thankful for this clarification to Mr M.K. Shazli, who has been a keen observer of Moharram in Marathwada.)

thesis that the 'festival' of Moharram is a 'need-fulfilment' mechanism for these people.

The harsh, monotonous and insecure living conditions of the rural, and semi-rural, people create a compelling need for occasions like festivals and fairs so that they may find some escape, however temporary, from their drab existence.[4] And, the longer the duration of these diversions the greater is their value. Further, the under-privileged in such communities—be they members of the lower classes or women—desperately need some avenues of recognition and self-expression, or of tension-management. It is the contention of the present author that a number of the 'little' and 'local' traditions concerning Moharram are, in fact, adjustment mechanisms that rural Muslims have created for their psychological stability and security. In addition to this intra-person dimension, such practices are also instrumental for inter-group integration in culturally/religiously pluralistic situations. Hopefully, in the pages that follow, the role of all these existential factors will become evident; and it should also be evident that Moharram has become (or did become) what it is (or was) due to the interplay of these various factors.

One other observation before concluding these introductory remarks. No discussion of the various syncretic elements—like the Moharram 'festival', for example—which have entered into the socio-religious life stream of the Indian Muslims can overlook the important role which these elements have played in the very survival of Islam, especially in the various far-flung

[4] In this connection, it is interesting to note that Dube in his study of Sharmirpet lists no fewer than 13 major Hindu festivals celebrated in the village every year. In addition, there are several other minor festivals that are specific to the various social groups. The Muslims of the same village observe seven festivals. They also join the Hindus in celebrating certain other 'village festivals' which, Dube points out, are not a part of the regular religious calendar of the Hindus or Muslims (1967:111). Another village study, that by Oscar Lewis (1965), lists 19 major and minor Hindu festivals in a north Indian village. It is, incidentally, well known that in contrast to the Hindu calendar, the Muslim calendar is a rather lean affair. According to von Grunebaum (1976:3), the development of festivals in Islam has been limited by the absence of a priestly class. Possibly one other relevant facter is the non-rural and non-peasant base of early Islam.

rural communities of this vast sub-continent. First, syncretism helped the local Muslims to live in an integrated manner with non-Muslim neighbours, even though they had, for some reason or the other, left one religious fold and entered another. Thanks to this syncretism, they did not experience a disruption in their lives or a total break with the past. Second, Islam by being flexible and absorbing, as well as by developing syncretic elements, made itself more attractive to some—and less reprehensible to others. As a result, this syncretism, while 'corrupting' Islam, allowed Muslims to continue existing as a viable group. Moreover, it helped many Muslims—even if they were Muslims in 'name only'—to withstand the overpowering capacity of Hinduism to absorb other individuals and groups. Had the syncretic 'corruption' not facilitated this survival there would, perhaps, today have been considerably fewer Muslims available for Islamization. Hence, in considering the un-Islamic character of the Moharram 'festival' (and other similar aberrations), some unappreciated and unapplauded contributions of syncretism should not be overlooked by those interested in the sociology of Indian Muslims.

Viewed in this light, this paper, while being concerned with a sociological oddity, is, at the same time, also an analysis of a sociological reality; namely, the human proclivity to adapt, survive, and, if possible, to triumph. The 'enjoyment' of Moharram as a festival, is an example *par excellence* of human and social ingenuity in the face of a challenging environment.

Description

Having made these preliminary remarks, it is now proposed to first present two accounts of Moharram 'celebrations' as observed in two different parts of the country,[5] and then to offer

[5] The first description has come from a social survey of the Muslims of Konkan which was directed by the author and in which Mr Pathan Mirkhan had served as the Principal Investigator (1973-74). The data reported here are from Mr Mirkhan's fieldnotes, based on observations made in Fatehpur—a pseudonym. The second description has been provided by Mr Mahammad Talib, a postgraduate student studying at present under the author. Mr Talib's observations

a sociological analysis and interpretation of the empirical data. The focus of attention in the descriptions that follow is more on certain themes and recurrent patterns than upon the 'totality' of ethnographic details. As such, there may appear to be a selectivity in the data. This selectivity is inadvertent; but it is hoped that it will not be misjudged or misunderstood, but, instead, will be considered in the context of the analysis and interpretation that follows.

The first description was a part of a field study carried out in the Konkan region of Maharashtra state. The data presented here are, specifically, from a fishing village, Fatehpur, in Ratnagiri district. The village is predominantly inhabited by Mahigir Muslims. The second description is from Chanorba, a medium-sized Muslim majority town in Moradabad district in Uttar Pradesh. The Muslims of Chanorba are divided into well-defined social layers and Moharram appears to largely involve the various service castes. Fortuitously, just as the first draft of this paper was ready, some additional data from Raichur, a district from Andhra Pradesh, became available.[6] But as it was not quite systematic or comprehensive, it could be more appropriately incorporated in this paper through footnotes.

In Fatehpur, the sighting of the moon which heralds the beginning of the lunar month of Moharram, was a matter of great joy and excitement for the Mahigir Muslims of the village. Young and old were equally eager to see the *Moharram-ka-chand* (the Moharram moon); indeed, their eagerness almost made one feel as if the moon for Ramadan-Id had been sighted![7]

in Chanorba, again a pseudonym, are also firsthand. Certain points, however, were clarified by him, at the author's request, from informants belonging to the town.

[6] Mr S.H. Rizvi, another of the author's postgraduate students, got intersted in the present paper while it was under preparation and provided some observations that he had made in Raichur town in Andhra Pradesh in December 1977. Mr Rizvi's data also fitted in well with the main line of the paper's argument. This additional support has been useful.

[7] In Raichur too, the sighting of the Moharram moon is followed

Soon after the moon had been sighted, the *naqaras* (big drums) that had been stored in rooms adjoining the mosques of each locality were brought out and beaten loudly in front of the various mosques. This was done to inform one and all that Moharram had begun. On subsequent evenings, the *naqaras* were beaten after the *Isha-ki-namaz* (in the night) until the end of the 'celebrations' on the tenth day of the month. The *naqaras*, incidentally, were played somewhat briefly and perfunctorily from the second till the sixth nights, but thereafter it became extremely ethusiastic, frantic and deafening.

On the first evening, apart from the beating of the *naqaras*, some individuals began digging small pits in front of the mosque of each mohalla. In these pits—or *alava*, as they are called—a small *diva* (lamp) was lit every night, and around it the men and children performed a typical dance, which is known as *waye* all over Konkan. The *waye* was performed every night till about midnight to a rhythm set by the *naqaras*. From the seventh night onwards, along with the *naqara* beating, the *waye* too become extremely boisterous. Till the ninth night, the *waye* was danced in front of the mohalla mosque only, but on the ninth night and on the tenth and final day it was performed throughout the mohalla. One norm pertaining to *waye* is that individuals have to perform it only in their own mohalla. If, however, a group is interested in dancing in another mohalla, then they have to give an assurance to the *hodekar* (headman) of that mohalla that they will not misbehave or create any kind of disturbance or foster an intermohalla conflict.

It was observed that in these inter-mohalla visits, the 'visiting' performers did not limit themselves to dancing but

by great excitement. The *ashur-khanas* where the *tazziyas* and *alums* are stored, are cleaned and whitewashed; then, a plaster of red or yellow mud is given on top of which white stripes in the shape of a peacock's tail are drawn for an 'artistic' effect. Lamps and candles are lit and the young and old enthusiastically participate in the digging of the *alava* pits. Certain jewellery items, including the 'jeebes', a crown like silver ornament, are taken out of the storage box (made of iron) and cleaned for use in decorating the *tazziyas*. In the days that follow, there are the usual processions and dances, etc., indulged in with great enthusiasm by members of the lower socio-economic strata.

also indulged in various kinds of comic acts and tomfoolery. Some of them wore wigs and fancy dress and acted out various roles for the entertainment of the sightseers/onlookers.[8] It was not difficult to see that there was a spirit of healthy competition in these performances and also that they were a tremendous source of enjoyment for everyone concerned. When questioned, the villagers appeared to feel that such inter-mohalla competitions enhanced fellow-feeling and intra-village unity.

As if to enhance the gaiety and enjoyment, at least in one mohalla some of the houses were seen to be decorated and Divali-like lights were kept burning near the doors. Some fireworks were also let off. A local *dargah* was also illuminated with electric bulbs during this period.

Women, however, did not participate in dancing the *waye* or in the horseplay. But nor were they indoors. While the menfolk danced and played, most women recited *mercias*, sitting in a circle just a few yards away from where the menfolk were dancing the *waye.* In one mohalla the women sat in a tent on which all kinds of artistic efforts had been lavished. This tent too was erected opposite the mohalla mosque—it was quite spacious and of a squarish shape. There were bulbs of various colours hanging inside. The canvas walls of the tent were painted with colours showing big trees, rivers, grass, etc. Thus, the inside of the tent was made to resemble a garden. In the middle, there was a replica in multi-coloured paper of a monument resembling the Taj Mahal. Beside it there were two other replicas—one of the Kaaba and the other of the tomb of Fatima (the mother of the martyred brothers, Hassan and Hussain). Considerable artistic skills and efforts had gone into making all these things, so that the overall impact was quite impressive and gave evidence of the creative talents of the villagers.[9]

[8] In a number of these acts, fun is often poked at someone's predicament or personal frailty. Thus, Mr Mirkhan has, in a personal communication, mentioned that in some instances in Marathwada, the problems of a hen-pecked husband or of a person with two wives are publicly aired. It would seem, then, that this practice is both an instrument of social control, as well as a source of vicarious pleasures.

[9] It is obvious that there is underlying motif or unity of theme in

While the dancing went on till midnight, the women kept congregating in the tent, locally referred to as *phool-jhaad* (literally, tree of flowers, but perhaps, more correctly 'garden'). A number of women brought sweets of various sorts, as well as sherbet, and deposited them by the side of the replica of Fatima's tomb. When the *waye* finished around midnight, *dua* was recited over the sweets and the sherbet and these were then partaken of by both men and women. In the other mohallas where there were no *phool-jhaad* tents, the women would collect in some spacious house and recite the *mercias*. In all the mohallas, the recitation of the *mercias* continued only up to the eighth night. On the ninth night, when the *waye* was performed not just around the *alava* but throughout the mohalla, the women moved around with the rest of the procession and served as some sort of 'cheer-leaders'. On the tenth and final day too, the women accompanied the *waye* processionists round their respective mohallas. In this way, on the verge of the conclusion of the celebrations, both men and women jointly participated in the 'festivities'.

The next important activity in the community pertained to the *tazziyas*. After the moon had been sighted, meetings were held in each mohalla to discuss the mechanics of constructing the *tazziyas*. Specific responsibilities were allocated and financial arrangements made and agreed upon. However, the actual construction began only on about the sixth day and the various *tazziyas* were completed by the ninth. Interestingly enough, the *tazziyas* were constructed on the premises of the mosques. Accordingly, throughout the ten days the mosques became hubs of endless activity. A striking observation in this connection was that the loudspeakers installed in the mosques were used for a variety of purposes. From time to time, individuals would come to the microphone and recite verses from the Koran; at other times, discs containing similar recitations would be played. Shockingly enough, on other occasions, film music also blared from these loudspeakers.[10]

all these items; they are, to use Sorokin's term, congeries. But they do serve the purpose of creative self-expression and a sense of achievement.

[10] A devout Muslim's sense of horror should be pacified on remembernig that the *actual* religion of the masses reveals some drastic,

Indeed, barring the period of the prayers, these loudspeakers were almost continuously busy.

In Fatehpur, as in other places, the construction of *tazziyas* is facilitated by the fact that the basic wooden structure is never destroyed but is safely preserved in the mosque to be used year after year. Every moharram, this wooden structure is brought out from its storing place, and the bare frame is beautifully and attractively decorated with coloured paper. The final step is to fix a large paper dome on top of the wooden structure, with the result that the *tazziya* begins to resemble a mausoleum. Inside the Fatehpur *tazziyas*, there were replicas of the graves of Hassan and Hussain. Electric illuminations were also provided inside the *tazziyas* so that at night the coloured lights enhanced their attractiveness, and they become a source of wonderment and appreciation for the village childern, women and men. Thus, the *tazziyas* too are products of artistic creativity and skills. And, as may well be imagined, they were a source of mohalla pride and inter-mohalla competitiveness.

An inevitable accompaniment of *tazziyas* is the phenomenon of *mannats*. Men and women, but particularly the latter, visited the *tazziyas* in large numbers and expressed requests for various kinds of favours.[11] Those that come to make these requests appeared to be highly emotionally charged and had a visible air of helplessness. The implorations were made very earnestly, and it was evident that life afforded no other solutions to these simple folks. In return for the grant of favours sought, the favour-seekers promised that they would

and even shocking, departures from the ideal view of religion.

[11]The differing concerns that affect women and men are well reflected here. Women generally seek intervention for, and on behalf of children and ask for marital happiness. For men, employment, success in business and other economic interests are the dominating desires.

In Raichur, it is customary for individuals, both Muslims and Hindus, to ask questions pertaining to their personal problems of the individuals who are holding the *tazziyas* aloft in the procession on the final day. As a fee for this 'consultation', the respondents are paid a *nazrana*. At times, the person at whom the question is directed is unable to provide the answer. In such situations, the *mujawar* (the keeper of the *tazziya*) steps in and answers the question posed.

make cash offerings to the *tazziya* in the subsequent year or years. Obviously, the more acute or intense the emotional state of the favour-seeker, the more lavish he or she is in the promise made. Several informants gave the clear impression that there is a strong feeling that *mannats* made in the presence of *tazziyas* are fulfilled. One interesting observation in this connection was that there were public announcements over the loudspeaker regarding individuals who had donated twenty-five rupees or twenty-five paise in return for the fulfilment of their respective *mannats*.[12] Clearly, such public announcements are supposed to act as encouragement to others. The amount thus collected, it was pointed out, is either spent on the various expenses incurred in connection with the *tazziyas* or split between *tazziya* construction and the maintenance of the mohalla mosque. In addition to such contributions, which are a sort of 'thanksgiving' payment, individuals also made voluntary contributions partly in reponse to the appeal made by those responsible for constructing and maintaining the *tazziya* of the locality, and partly as a matter of respect for, and faith in, the *tazziya*.[13] Overall, there existed a deep religious motivation, and satisfaction, in the support given to the *tazziya*; and, there was a general agreement among those questioned that supporting the *tazziyas* was a religious duty and earned, for the supporters, religious merit.

In Fatehpur, the *tazziyas* were found to be popular among the Hindus also and several of them visited the *tazziyas* for darshan, and made *mannats* and offerings. Thus, insofar as the common problems of life are concerned, Hindus and Muslims were united in seeking solutions through the *tazziyas*. But apart from *tazziyas*, Moharram increased inter-communal

[12] In the Marathwada region, according to Mirkhan, successful *mannats* are repaid in terms of *rotes*, which are hard-baked cakes made from the cream of wheat, and are about the size of an average palm. The *mannats* are made in terms of a specific quantity of *rotes*. Incidentally, according to a popular story in Aurangabad (for which no veracity is claimed), a certain Minister's mother still distributes *rotes* during Moharram for having received a favour from a *tazziya* when her son was young.

[13] In Raichur also, in addition to money, various offerings are made to the *tazziyas* consisting of such items as jewellery and clothes. These offerings are reportedly kept by the *mujawars*.

interaction. During the entire ten days, Hindus, including Brahmans, were found to be visiting Muslim localities and even houses. The Hindu guests were served with various snacks and, in some instances, with alcoholic drinks as well.[14] During the nights, the Hindus were present to witness the *waye*, though they did not appear to participate actively in the dancing. (The *waye*, incidentally, is quite similar to the *govinda* dance of the Maharashtrian Hindus, performed in this region on the occasion of Gokulashtami.)

The Moharram 'celebrations' reached their peak on the ninth day. Till the ninth, the *waye* was performed only opposite the mohalla mosque, but on the ninth night (as has already been mentioned) the entire *mohalla* became the locale of dancing. By now the *tazziyas* were ready and were taken out in a procession throughout the mohalla. These processions went on practically throughout the night and, accordingly, the *waye*, which used to stop around midnight, continued almost non-stop on the ninth night. On this night, many individuals were observed to be wearing new clothes[15] and had also adorned their faces with cosmetics, chief among them being talcum powder! Some males had dressed themselves as females and kept dancing in front of the *tazziyas*. Several women accompanied the procession and appeared to be in high spirits.

On the following day, which was the final day of the Moharram 'celebrations', the unique custom of *posst* was observed. At about 10.30 in the morning, a group of about six persons were seen to be moving about in the mohalla. They had a *naqara* and a *tasha* (a somewhat flat shaped drum with a metallic base) with them with which they were creating a lot of noise. They would stop at every door and collect one rupee and twenty-five paise. This amount was collected from Hindu homes also. The total collections were later spent on

[14] It may, however be added here that inter-communal amity is a special feature of Moharram in Konkan. Traditionally, this region of India has been blessed with exemplary friendliness between the two communities. This friendliness gets further cemented on ocassions like Moharram.

[15] This observation had appeared to be unique to Fatehpur until the Raichur data turned up. There, too, precisely in the processions on the tenth day, people were found to be wearing new clothes.

alcoholic drinks,[16] which were consumed in the process of dancing and merry-making. Incidentally, the drinks were supplied to the dancing men by the womenfolk! This custom of *posst*, it was learnt, is also followed during Dussehra and Diwali, when the Hindus collect the funds and Muslims donate and drink along with the Hindus. These *posst* donations are not compulsory, but traditionally both Hindus and Muslims contribute.

The tenth day, being the day when the *tazziyas* are disposed of, was also a day of processions. Accordingly, after the *posst*, the *tazziyas* in the various localities were taken in processions at about 2.00 P.M. round the respective mohallas. Each procession was characterized by a peak-of-form *waye*. Drinks were freely consumed. In this stage of intoxication and heightened emotional frenzy, the dancers kept shouting various slogans of both a religious and non-religious nature. The music and dancing created a tremendous din throughout the village. However, the noise appeared to be a great source of joy to everyone. All this continued till sunset. At sunset, the processions began to leave their mohallas and head towards a jetty. When all the *tazziyas* reached a point from where they could all be seen simultaneously, the ritual of *salaami* was performed.[17] Therefore,

[16] For most Muslims, this information will indeed be very shocking. To be sure, as individuals many Muslims do drink but public consumption of alcohol is too drastic a violation of one of Islam's best known taboos. It may be clarified, however, that the drinking reported here is not a feature or part of Moharram as such. In fact it is a part of the daily life of most, if not all, Mahigirs. Theirs is a very strenuous occupation which takes them out of their homes in the middle of the night. They are out at sea early in the morning and return to the village, utterly exhausted, only around mid-day. Further, most of them are rather poor and lead a dull and drab existence. Due to the fish lying everywhere, the village is full of a horrible stink. In these conditions, drinking has become a way of life.

Incidentally, according to the Raichur account also, several of those participating in the various processions had drunk freely. Once again, this is a part of lower-class life-style.

[17] The ten days of Moharram being replete with all kinds of rituals and ceremonies, it is to be expected that just prior to the final disposal of the *tazziyas* there should be some sort of valedictory ceremony. Thus, in Raichur the *tazziyas* are initially brought to the disposal

the *tazziya* that was nearest the jetty moved towards it first, followed by the others. At the jetty, water was sprinkled on each *tazziya* to symbolize its 'demise'. The water, incidentally, had been brought from the various mohallas for their respective *tazziyas*. After the water was sprinkled, a *fatihah* was recited. Next, the *dera* (dome) from each *tazziya* was removed and cast into the water. After this coconuts were dashed on the ground and bits of coconut, along with some candy, were distributed among those present. Soon thereafter, the *tazziyas* minus their domes, were brought back to be stored in the *hujras*. The coloured paper used to decorate the *tazziyas* was allowed to remain on the *tazziyas* for another two days.

On the twelfth day of Moharram, a *ziarat* ceremony was observed. This consisted of holding *mauloods* in the evening. After this recitation, the coloured paper was removed from the *tazziyas*. This step signalled the culmination of the Moharram observances. One detail that has not been mentioned concerns the *alavas* in which the *divas* had burnt throughout the first nine nights. These *divas* were extinguished on the evening of the tenth day after the *maghrib ki namaz*. The *alavas* were filled with earth. Later, water was sprinkled on this earth and *agarbattis* were lit and kept burning on the small mounds of earth.

The above description may perhaps have made it evident that the 'celebration' of Moharram is an integral part of the village community's social life, and that it has certain social and psychological meanings for it which are not always evident to the outsider, especially if the outsider is not versed in the task of sociological analysis. In this connection, it is illuminating to know that Moharram continues to attract the

spot in such a formation that they do not face each other, but are lined up with their rears 'facing' each other. Once the *tazziyas* are all lined up, a *milap* ritual is performed. This consists of a movement in which the *tazziyas* are, with a lightening motion, turned around and brought face to face in close proximity. This movement is called *milap*; once it is over, the *tazziyas* resume their original position. But the notable thing about the *milap* is that large numbers of people collect to witness it inasmuch as it is believed that witnessing a *milap* will guarantee a year free from all difficulties and problems. (There perhaps could not have been a more sure mechanism for securing an audience.)

villagers even when they live away from the vIllage. Every effort is made by the inhabitants to return to Fatehpur by the seventh day in order to 'play' *waye* and participate in the other proceedings. In one case, an individual who happened to be only some thirty miles away from Fatehpur and could not get a bus to the village, hired a taxi at a cost of Rs. 80 just to ensure that he would be home on the seventh day. In fact, he boasted that had he been away in Bombay (almost 200 miles away), he would have spent whatever was necessary to return to Fatehpur by the seventh of Moharram. This individual, incidentally, was physically decrepit and was unable to really dance the *waye*. Nevertheless, the spirit was stronger than the flesh, and with the help of intoxicants he tried to enjoy the 'festival' as best as he could. Probably there were some others too who had rushed back from as far away as Bombay. According to informants, individuals who made *mannats* while away from the village and whose *mannats* had been fulfilled, invariably returned to the village during Moharram. As for the vast majority that lived in the village, all fishing activities were suspended from the sixth day onwards; thus for full four days enjoyment and merry-making transcended economic interests.

It was observed that even the village *pesh-imams* (those who customarily lead the prayers in the mosque) were unable to escape participation, excepting that they did not consume alcoholic drinks or perform the *waye*. But they could not avoid being a part of the various processions. Indeed, informants revealed that *pesh-imams* who were opposed to such enjoyment were either not appointed, or, if appointed, were dismissed before Moharram. One significant information in this connection was that a popular Hindu doctor of Fatehpur, who enjoys respect among the Muslims as well, was invited a few years ago to address the Mahigir Muslims on the occasion of Moharram. In his address, he criticized the consumption of liquor, the blaring of loudspeakers in the mosques, and the generally boisterous enjoyment of Moharram. He pointed out that such an observance of Moharram was un-Islamic. But he only succeeded in evoking a negative reaction and since then he has not been invited to participate in the Moharram 'festivities'. Indeed, the very practice of inviting guest speakers on this occasion has been abandoned to avoid such unsavoury and conscience pricking homilies.

We shall now describe Moharram as it is observed in Chanorba. In Chanorba, agriculture is the dominant occupation. The Muslim population is divided into various status groups, including such service castes as the Julahas (weavers), Qasais (butchers), Saqqas (water-carriers) and Faqirs (traditionally beggars, but who now also work as casual labourers and domestic servants). In the upper echelons are the traditional elite, the moulvis (literally scholars, but here landlords), and an intermediary group of peasant farmers, the Chaudharies. Moharram in Chanorba primarily preoccupies the lower status groups, but the elite is not entirely divorced from the various ramifications of the Moharram 'celebrations'.

From the day the month of Moharram begins, the Muslims belonging to the various service castes don green *kurtas* (longish shirts) and green caps. This green attire is held to symbolize the fact that with the advent of Moharram all status differences in the community have been obliterated and that all Muslims can participate in the festival without any distinctions. (Of course, this is only a pious hope inasmuch as the elite reveals no such desire and does not participate in the planning and execution of the various Moharram activities.)

From the very first night of Moharram, the residents of the various mohallas gather together in their respective localities (after the *Isha-ki-namaz*) to participate in what is known as *maatam*. While *maatam* generally involves the beating of breasts, in Chanorba there is only a slow rhythmic beating of drums. Those present merely sway to the rhythm. The *maatam* gatherings occur every night for the first five nights, and are more in the nature of social get-togethers. From the sixth to the ninth of Moharram, the community witnesses various kinds of processions. First, in the evenings there are the *alum* processions followed in the night by *mehdi* processions. And finally, there are also the *tazziya* processions. The construction of the *mehdis* and *tazziyas* is an elaborate affair in Chanorba and those involved in these tasks work at them almost throughout the year. The *mehdi* is a local creation. It is in the shape of a big *doli*, or palanquin, and is spectacularly decorated with multicoloured and shiny papers which are artistically pieced together in numerous designs and patterns. It rests on two long bamboo shafts and is carried by four persons. In a sense, the *mehdi* is another form of *tazziya* but is all the same a distinct entity with its own norms. Thus, in Chanorba the *tazziyas* are only ready on the tenth day and are taken out in procession later that evening. But the *mehdis* are prepared earlier and they can, therefore, be taken out in processions right from the initial days. They seem to serve the function of building up a tempo from the very beginning. The various *mehdis* are linked with the different occupational groups and in this way they provide an accepted machanism of inter-group rivalry in terms of creative self-expression. The *mehdis* are taken out in nocturnal processions according to an agreed schedule and each night is designated by the name of the occupational group whose *mehdi* is going to make the rounds that night. As with *tazziyas* so also with *mehdis*, it is considered to be an act of religious merit to give 'one's shoulder' to the *mehdi* during the procession.

Unlike Fatehpur where the various activities pertaining to Moharram had their locus in the locality or mohalla, in Chanorba the *alums, mehdis* and *tazziyas* are caste-centred. As such, they are linked with specific occupational groups like water-carriers and so on. Accordingly, the competitive spirit underlying the *tazziyas* and *mehdis* is also caste oriented. This inter-group competitiveness, incidentally, is not limited to the *mehdis* and *tazziyas* only; there are two other institutionalized competitions that are a vital part of the Moharram 'celebrations' in this town. First, there is *mercia-goi* and then there is *patey-baazi*. The former refers to a display of competence in the recitation of eulogies in the memory and honour of Hassan and Hussain, while the latter is a pseudo sword fencing competition which is held with sticks that are carved out as swords. The fencers initiate a small battle scene symbolizing Imam Hussain's battle with his enemies.[18] Both *mercia-goi* and *patey-baazi* have, over the years, been raised to the status of fine arts

[18] Something similar takes place in Raichur also. But here, unlike in Chanorba, open knives, swords and other weapons are used in the various processions. The participants also include body builders and other physical culturists of the various localities. The *tazziya*

which are learnt, practised and displayed with exemplary zeal and dedication. In fact, the potential competitors keep practising one or the other of these throughout the year so as to be in a fit condition when Moharram comes round. While the learning of *mercia-goi* is largely an individual effort, skill and perfection in *patey-baazi* are a matter of training under a skilful *ustad* (teacher). (There are usually three or four such *ustads* in Chanorba, and they command the respect and admiration of the entire community.)

The opportunity for the public display of talent and skills in these two enterprises comes when the *mehdi* or *tazziya* processions are going round the various localities. It is customary for these processions to halt in front of the homes of the rich and prominent members of the community, who generally limit their participation to the grant of cash assistance for the construction of *tazziyas* or *mehdis*. In token of appreciation, therefore, the processions halt before the homes of such individuals and performances of *mercia-goi* and *patey-baazi* are given. The intensity of interest and seriousness of these performances is heightened by the fact that the members of the elite group witness and patronize the 'show'. While *patey-baazi* is in progress, there is a continuous and loud beating of drums and blowing of trumpets to a certain rhythm; this accompaniment is infectious inasmuch as the spectators too begin to gyrate their bodies in a slow rhythmic manner. When the *mercia-goi* and *patey-baazi* are over, the participants are given an appreciative pat and are also served with some snacks and refreshments, provided by the individuals who are honoured by the halts and performances in front of their *havelis* (mansions). Thereafter, the procession moves on to its next halt.

From the above, it will be evident that even though the elite members of the Muslim community in Chanorba do not participate in the Moharram 'festivities', nevertheless, in a covert manner, their interest and support are extended; and, it is a matter of personal gratification for them that they are personally recognized and honoured through the performances of

processions are opportunities for these people to exhibit their strength and gain admiration and acclamation.

mercia-goi and *patey-baazi*. In a feudalistic set-up, such recognition and honour are of ineffable value for the self-esteem of the elite. Consequently, the elite too encourages all the traditions of Chanorba's Moharram and this support, obviously, is a source of encouragement and legitimation for lower castes to 'celebrate' Moharram with pomp and pageantry. One interesting point that needs to be mentioned here is that young children of the elite families are especially woken up even at very late hours of the night to witness the various processions. Indeed, this is a part of child's socialization in these families. In this way, conscious efforts are made to inculcate an interest in, and enthusiasm for, the local Moharram. This practice amply supports the observations concerning the elite.

In the preceding description of Fatehpur's Moharram, it was mentioned that *tazziyas* were instruments of blind faith when it came to illness and other personal crises. In Chanorba too the people have a strong belief that *tazziyas* and *mehdis* can, and do, help overcome illnesses, especially the incurable ones. However, instead of making *mannats*, there is a local tradition whereby children are made to pass from under the *tazziya* or the *mehdi*. This passing through the empty space (under the *tazziya*) is believed to be beneficial for effective cure. In fact, the popular belief is that the more often one goes under the *tazziya* stroke the greater the benefit that one will derive. Accordingly, it is seen that the moment the procession stops somewhere, there is a stampede in which individuals, particularly children, try to get below the *tazziya* or the *mehdi*. Mothers of ailing children especially congregate so as to encourage and push their children in the space below. This belief is shared by the Hindus also, and they pass from under the *tazziyas* and *mehdis*.

As in Fatehpur so in Chanorba, the excitement begins to mount after the first six days. On the seventh day, the processions have an added feature in the form of a giant black figure (which may well be confused for Ravana by an undiscerning eye) which is supposed to represent Jaffar, the mythical king of the Jinnas. He is believed to have come to the rescue of Hussain in the blood-bath of Karbala, but Hussian refused to be helped. On the eighth day, the duration of the procession is prolonged inordinately because two, rather than one, *mehdis* are on show, and hence, there are two processions which take up the entire night. A competition—involving the usual *mercia-goi* and *patey-baazi*—is arranged between the two processions, and the winners have the satisfaction of becoming the toast of the community. For several days after the actual performance, people keep discussing the merits and demerits of the respective performers, and the decision of the panel of judges, which is constituted for this purpose, is supported and criticized in various quarters. On the following day, that is, the ninth, there used to be an interesting source of amusement (which has now been given up). An individual of a moronic disposition was selected and dressed up to resemble a *langoor* (lemur).[19] This *langoor* was expected to entertain the spectators while the procession was in progress. Towards this end, the disguised individual had a great deal of freedom to resort to any 'monkey tricks'; he even enjoyed the freedom to violate some of the accepted norms of behaviour, including sex-segregation norms. Thus, he could chase girls and try to embrace them. In the ensuing confusion, others too would seize the opportunity to violate some of the sex-taboos, though, of course, they had to be unobtrusive about it. The general rush and pandemonium, however, provide an opportunity whereby such deviant behaviour could pass by unnoticed or unprotested.

The tenth and final day, as everywhere, is the day of bringing the Moharram 'festival' to an end. As part of the last round of enjoyment and merriment, a small fair is organized and children especially are given money to spend in this fair. The shops and stalls that are set up in this fair belong to the Hindus. In this way, the Hindus benefit economically from this particular feature of Chanorba's Moharram. It may also

[19] Animal impersonation is found in other regions as well. In the mid and late thirties, while I was growing up in Poona (now Pune), I remember seeing men dressed up as tigers and lemurs roaming round the streets. There would be a drummer with them, and the routine was to stop opposite both Muslim and Hindu shops and perform a typical dance after which they would collect money from those witnessing the performance and then move to another shop. The reason behind the assumption of the animal form is not clear except that it gives certain anonymity to those who wish to earn an extra buck on the side.

be mentioned here that since the surrounding villages have a sparse Muslim population, they cannot afford to organize their own Moharram festivities. Consequently, the Muslims from these villages come to Chanorba to participate in its Moharram and thereby increase the scale of Chanorba's 'festivities'. In addition, as in the case of Fatehpur, the residents of Chanorba who have taken up jobs in places as far away as Calcutta try to return home during Moharram and they are often in the mood to spend lavishly. This general influx of individuals during the final days of Moharram serves as a windfall for the Hindu shopkeepers. Not surprisingly, these Hindus help the 'festival' by donating money for the *tazziyas* and by providing illuminations on the procession routes.

The culminating procession on the tenth day provides an interesting commentary on the reality of the social differentiation among the Chanorba Muslims. It has already been mentioned that in Chanorba the *tazziyas* are not constructed by each mohalla or residential locality but by occupational groups which, it need hardly be mentioned, are hierarchically organized. Significantly enough, the order in which the *tazziyas* are lined up in the final procession reflects the social hierarchy. Since there is no river or stream near Chanorba the *tazziyas* are not immersed in water but are buried on the premises of the *Imambada*.

The two descriptions given above, along with the supporting evidence provided from the Andhra Pradesh town in the footnotes, reveal certain striking similarities. To be sure, details do vary from region to region but the above account appears to indicate that these variations are of lesser consequence than the parallels in the generalities, and it is the latter that deserves attention for herein lies the meat of the sociological enterprise. Of course, the limited data presented here do not warrant any universal generalizations; nonetheless, they do provide some meaningful insights on the basis of which certain significant conclusions may be drawn. Accordingly what follows is an attempt to offer a theoretically relevant explanation in the hope that other scholars will unearth more data and thereby help in the task of validating or negating the present tentative explanation.

Discussion

It is now proposed to go beyond mere description and to analyze and interpret the data in order to realize the more abstract sociological and social psychological implications of the Moharram 'festival'.

The two descriptions have indicated that Moharram affords an excellent opportunity for mass participation and collective celebration on a joint basis. Such an opportunity is not afforded by the two leading Muslim festivals namely, the two Ids. This is an important point because a major reason for the peculiar metamorphosis of the 'great' tradition of Moharram, it may be suggested, was its potential for a prolonged and joint observance. Mass religious observances, collective celebration of festivals and their corollary, village fairs, have played a special role and enjoy a special significance in the lives of rural and other simple communities. In these communities, not only are there several such occasions, but efforts are made to prolong the duration of these occasions. (Note here the fact that marriages too are long-drawn affairs, and, at the same time, occasions of much enjoyment and entertainment.) To be sure, one reason for this phenomenon is that in all such communities and societies there has been no premium on time, a season and not hours, or even days, has been the relevant unit of time. But this is hardly the 'cause' of lengthy mass enjoyment of festivals. The real reason, it may be asserted, has been the quality of life (in such human groupings) characterized as they have been by great scarcity, harshness, monotony and insecurity. Given this situation, Yang has pointed out, 'The universal observance of festivals led to the renewing of energy and spirit of the hard working masses, presenting a sense of relative abundance and reward' (1967:94).

But physical harshness, monotony, and the various frustrations are not the only deprivations to be borne and suffered—there is a resultant strain on social relationships as well. Thus, Kluckhohn has observed: 'Where people live under constant threat from the physical environment, where small groups are geographically isolated and "emotional inbreeding" with the extended family group is at a maximum, interpersonal tensions and hostilities are inevitably intense' (1965:156). Obviously, such situations require mechanisms that will allow for the release and resolution of social and psychological tensions in addition, of course, to providing diversions that will distract from the grim reality of sheer physical survival. Festivals—religious and secular—have been the physical, social and psychological 'comfort cushions' of the non-urbanized and non-modernized societies and communities, where life has few other attractions and escapes. And, given the quality of 'mechanical solidarity' that characterizes such groupings, the collective celebration of festivals is an inevitable phenomenon. Thus, if Moharram with its ten-day period was not available, possibly something else would have been invented in its place!

The fact that Moharram has become mixed up with numerous and unrelated pseudo-religious and non-religious incongruities is not difficult to understand in the light of what is known about the relationship between 'great' and 'little' traditions. In this connection, McKim Marriott's experience is instructive. His observations in Kishan Garhi led Marriott to conclude:

> Behind their Sanskritik names and multiple great-traditional rationales, the festivals of Kishan Garhi contain much ritual, which has no evident connection with the great tradition. The festival of Lights, for example, as it is celebrated in Kishan Garhi, contains many elements which are not connected either with a celebration of Ram's triumphal return from Lanka or with a celebration of Lakshmi's wedding. (1966:194)

Once the basic need to celebrate festivals with a mass base is appreciated, it is not difficult to perceive its extension into the other spheres of institutional life. Thus, commenting on the village fairs of traditional China, Yang has pointed out, '. . . religious worship, economic transactions and recreational activities intertwined to provide an occasion to bring the individuals out of their family-centred routine activities, to enable relatives and friends to meet and renew their social ties . . .'

(1967:85). In the case of Moharram 'festivities' in both Fatehpur and Chanorba, it has been seen that those who were away from their homes tried to return to their native places to participate in Moharram. But this is only the manifest reason; the latent reason obviously is to be back among family and friends.

Turning now to the integrative aspects of the Moharram 'festival'. It should, perhaps, have been clear by now that the various activities connected with the observance of Moharram are ideally suited to promote intra-group and inter-group cohesion. The various stages and phases through which the *tazziyas* and *mehdis* pass, right from the time of the preliminary discussions concerning their construction to final disposal, are all opportunities for joint decision-making, mutual cooperation, and the promotion of group pride.[20] The desire to put up one's best becomes a matter of honour for each group that is involved, be it on the basis of locality or occupation. Simultaneously, with the promotion of this intra-group fraternal feeling, community solidarity is forged and a 'Muslim identity' comes to the fore. After all, in the minds of the participants, everything that is being done at Moharram is the 'right' and 'correct' religion; and, through these activities, the participants have the satisfaction that they have contributed to the greater glory of their religion.

The various activities surrounding Moharram observances have an intra-personal dimension as well. Given its puritanical ethos, Islam has provided a somewhat limited scope for an individual's creative self-expression through the channels of 'artistic' accomplishments. Architecture, caligraphy, etc., have been the few avenues open to Muslims and these have generally found expression in the urban environment. But the human urge for creativity is no less compelling in the rural environment. Fortunately, the intricate construction and decoration of the *tazziyas* and *mehdis* affords an opportunity to the artistically inclined and the skilful, to reveal their gifts and attain a sense of achievement. In addition, the various performances and competitions that have become a part of the Moharram celebrations are also a channel of self-realization.

[20] For an insightful analysis concerning this point (in the context of the Memorial Day observed in America), see Lloyd Warner (1953:).

The institutionalization of these various forms of self-expression has also made it possible to earn public approbation and acclamation, and thus reinforce the natural need for creativity and recognition. Such intra-personal satisfaction further enhances a sense of loyalty and commitment to the entire phenomenon of Moharram as a festival. In this connection, it is important to recall that in Chanorba people practice and train for *patey-baazi* throughout the year.

Incidentally, it is not only those gifted with artistic talents that find opportunities for self-expression and to attain local fame; the village bumpkin and the moron also acquire roles that draw attention. The lemur of Chanorba, for example, was invariably the local idiot who did precious little for the rest of the year. Similarly, those who dance and prance and indulge in horseplay and tomfoolery in Fatehpur are obviously individuals of no great consequence; often, some of them are also the socially undesirable. But on this occasion they are, even though for a few fleeting moments, the cynosure of all eyes. It is difficult to adequately express the satisfying and reassuring impact of this recognition on the egos of such individuals.[21] Without Moharram, many of these people would have remained psychologically deprived.

There is yet another dimension at the intra-personal level that spills over into the inter-group level of interaction. As a collective 'festival', Moharram cuts across the barriers of the social structure. Its various processions, competitions and *melas*, etc., bring together persons of all categories. In this joining together, even though temporarily, differences of rank and status recede into the background and for a change everyone comes together as a 'Muslim'. Indeed, it is worth noting here that not only caste and class distinctions get blurred but even the usually rigid norms of sex-segregation get relaxed. Women watch their men with spontaneous amusement as they dance and perform. In an otherwise rigidly structured situation, this occasional relaxation serves as a safety-valve and provides some much needed psychological relief.

Thanks to the phenomenon of *mannats*, the value of

[21] I am indebted to Lloyd Warner's analysis (1953) for this line of thought.

Moharram, particularly for women, cannot be gainsaid. In the kind of socio-cultural set-up with which we are here concerned, women are the victims of several well-known social and psychological tensions, frustrations and insecurities, and the social structure and culture afford little scope for the control and solution of them. In addition to women, there are several men too who suffer from some misfortune or helplessness, and for whom there is no succour in view. For such individuals, tension-management in their predicaments is more easily affor-ded by intermediaries, whether they be saintly persons or reli-giously imbued 'sacred' objects or symbols. These are proxi-mate and visible and as such more measuring than a remote and abstract deity. Accordingly, the faith in *tazziyas* and *mehdis* (along with *dargahs*) as agencies of tension-management, cures, and other solutions, was only a natural development. Indeed, given the relative lack of intellectual sophistication, scientific knowledge and facilities, the uncertainties and calamities of life could be faced without a total abandonment of hope and courage only through reliance on the afore-mentioned agencies.

Concerning the generally close relationship between women and *mannats*, a point of sociological interest is that wherever the social structure is characterized by a relatively rigid sex-segregation, women have tended to develop their own rituals and myths, and the freedom to tackle, within the socio-religi-ous framework, the problems that affect them.[22] And, concern-ing the question as to why men should also resort to *mannats* Fernea and Fernea (1972:401) have provided a clue by pointing out that all men pass through the world of women and inevitably come under the influence of their mothers, sisters and grandmothers.

Reverting to the role of *tazziyas* and *mehdis*, it had earlier been pointed out that they serve a functional purpose for the

[22] Note in this connection the following commentary of Fernea and Fernea : 'However sexually segregated the Middle-East communities have been, religion has normally provided women with a legitimate area of activity outside the home; in many instances, women have utilized this freedom to develop meaningful rituals that reflect their own needs and concerns. Their freedom to do this has per-haps been enhanced by a greater distance from the ulema ...' (Keddie, 1972:401).

secular needs of groups as well as individuals. But this is not their only dimension. As has just been discussed, they are the focal points for *mannats* as well. As such, they also have a religio-magical aspect and satisfy the need for miracles and magic. Now, it is well-known that faith in miracles and magic is an important constituent of the general ethos of the non-industrial way of life but what is less will-known or appreciated is that 'high' Islam is not quite compatible with this sort of ethos.[23] In this situation, *tazziyas* and *mehdis* (along, of course, with *dargahs*) have amply filled up the vacuum. The experience of those individuals whose *mannats* have (accidently) been fulfilled, or have experienced similar coincidences, have further served to strengthen faith in these objects and symbols. Pertinent here is Malinowski's observation that wherever there is a connection between some extraordinary good and magic, there 'an ever nascent tradition is found to surround famous magicians or famous systems of magic with a halo of supernatural reputation' (1965:110).

Incidentally, in this very context, Malinowski has pointed out yet another phenomenon, namely, the 'competitive boasting of one community against another' (1965:110). The significance of this observation may be seen in another context, namely, that of the religious pluralism that exists in our country. No great persuasion would be needed to agree that in such a context an established system of magic and miracles is extremely functional for maintaining the morale of each community *vis-ā-vis* other communities; but the precise mechanism through which this morale is perpetuated and maintained is 'competitive boasting'. The success stories of the various *mannats* are an essential ingredient of this aspect and each miracle performed by the *tazziya* provides fuel to competitive boasting.[24] More, the *tazziyas* are also able to attract the attention and devotion of the Hindus, with obvious consequences for Muslim morale.

[23] In this connection, see Mujeeb's comment as quoted by Gustav Mensching (1964:269-73).

[24] It may be suggested that the element of 'competitive boasting' is present in the various displays of fencing and strength, etc. In a latent way, this is an effort to let the 'other' community know that 'we' have strength and saviours. I understand that some Hindu processions are also marked by such displays.

However, competitiveness is not the only relevant dimension here, because religious pluralism cannot for long be contained on the basis of competitiveness alone. Indeed, like all pluralism, religious multiplicity in any societal situation is laden with hostility, both manifest and latent. Hence, integrative mechanisms like festivals that will permit joint celebrations are highly essential.[25] Insofar as the Muslim festivals are concerned, the two Ids are characterized by too strong a religious content to easily permit an integrative function. Indeed, Bakrid with its emphasis on animal sacrifice even goes against the Hindu grain. Moreover, the Ids are too short and not exactly suited to collective or joint celebrations. Moharram, on the other hand, not being a rigorously defined religious event, could be more easily torn out of its real—an essentially political/historical—context and transformed into a mass festival. Its ten-day duration was another facilitating factor; the 'little' and 'local' traditions could seep in easily thanks to its extended duration, and make possible the collective participation of the masses. It is not surprising, therefore, that in the context of Indian rural life, Moharram eventually came to be what it is (or until recently was). Apart from fulfilling the various existential needs of the Muslim social system, Moharram also succeeded, to an extent, in binding Hindus and Muslims together. At the same time, it has also given the latter community the satisfaction that in competition with collective celebrations like Dassehra and Ganesh-puja, it too has a similar festival in its fold.

In the light of the analysis offered here, it will not be difficult to perceive that as the conditions of life change, and as modernization[26] and Islamization gather momentum, the entire

[25] The relevance of this observation can be more clearly appreciated when it is remembered that in India festivals occasionally tend to erupt in strife and violence. Interestingly, even in a highly secularized society like the American society, festivals are apt to create psychological tensions.

[26] I include urbanization and education in the modernization process. Modernization is gradually bringing about fundamental changes in the quality of life of the communities with which we have here been concerned. As a result of this primarily, I think, changes in the observation of Moharram will occur and are occurring. It is widely believed

character of Moharram as it is celebrated today will undergo drastic changes. In fact, this has already begun to occur. For the sociologist, these changes and their social implications should be a matter of interest.

One final comment: The sociologists' reliance on empirical data plus the kind of analysis and interpretation that has been presented here points towards the need for the sociologist and the Islamicist to work in greater cooperation than they have hitherto done. Sociologists, in response to the need and nature of their discipline, are more concerned with 'popular' religion than with formal or textual religion, and it is essential to remember that in the cosmological outlook of the Muslim masses, the former plays as important a part as the latter. To neglect this reality is to thwart a proper and more complete understanding of Islam or any other religion.

that the process of Islamization has been responsible for several changes in the 'celebration' of Moharram as well as in the discarding of many Hindu practices and beliefs. This, however, is a point that needs further study. Some very limited data at my disposal (from the Konkan study) leads me to hypothesize that Islamization *per se* appears to work where the forces of modernization have already first made their impact. In other words, for Islamization to work there must first be the readiness for change. In the Konkan study, it was somewhat striking to observe that as we moved from the remote villages to places closer to Bombay, the syncretic elements were less in evidence. In any event, we urgently need to study Islamization in the context of modernization to empirically clarify many of these issues.

Bibliography

Dube, S.C. (1967), *Indian Village*, New York, Harper and Row.

Fernea, Robert A., and Elizabeth W. Fernea (1972), 'Variations in Religious Observance among Islamic Women', in Nikkie R. Keddie (ed.), *Saints, Scholars and Sufis: Muslim Religious Institutions in the Middle East Since 1500*, Berkeley, University of California Press.

Geertz, Clifford (1960), *The Religion of Java*, New York, Free Press.

Gerson, Walter M. (1969), 'Jews at Christmas Time: Role Strain and Strain Reducing Mechanisms', in Walter M. Gerson (ed.), *Social Problems in a Changing World: A Comparative Reader*, New York, Thomas Y. Crowell Co.

Grunebaum, G.E. von (1976), *Muhammadan Festivals*, London, Curzon Press.

Kluckhohn, Clyde (1965), 'Myths and Rituals', in William A. Lessa and Evon Z. Vogt (eds.), *Reader in Comparative Religion*, New York, Harper and Row.

Lewis, Oscar (1965), *Village Life in Northern India*, New York, Random House.

Malinowsky, Bronislaw (1965), 'The Role of Magic and Religion', in William A. Lessa and Evon Z. Vogt (eds.), *Reader in Comparative Religion*, New York, Harper and Row.

Marriott, McKim (1966), 'Little Communities in an Indigenous Civilization', in McKim Marriott (ed.), *Village India: Studies in the Little Community*, Chicago, University of Chicago Press.

Mensching, Gustav (1964), 'The Masses, Folk Belief and Universal Religion', in Louis Schneider (ed.), *Religion, Culture and Society*, New York, John Wiley and Sons.

Warner, W. Lloyd (1953), *American Life*, Chicago, University of Chicago Press.

Yang, C.K. (1967), *Religion in Chinese Society*, Berkeley, University of California Press.

5

Saint Worship in Indian Islam: The Legend of the Martyr Salar Masud Ghazi

Kerrin Graefin V. Schwerin

Islamic folk religion in India appears to have been under the influence of pre-Islamic[1] and Hindu traditions. This influence manifests itself mainly in saint worship which is also widespread in the regions of the origin of Islam and in Persia, Turkey, etc. The Arabic tribes practised ancestor and hero worship[2] which after Islamization was transformed into the saint worship of learned and exemplary Derwesh or Sufi teachers. Those who fought to spread the creed, the so-called *shahids* or martyrs, are also found among the saints. These men had often travelled abroad and died far away from their homes. They were worshipped not only at the place of their death, but also where they had lived, teaching and fighting. Thousands of pilgrims visited their graves expecting to be freed from illness and suffering or hoping

[1] By the term 'pre-Islamic', we understand the following traditions: the tribal religions of the Arabic regions; and tribal and Hindu traditions which were practised by tribes and castes before their conversion to Islam.

[2] Cf. Goldziher: 'The deceased tribal hero was credited with the same attributes and virtues after death as distinguished him while alive, and his grave was believed to benefit people seeking protection and help in the same way as did the tent of the living man' (1967:213).

to have a much wanted child. Each saint was known for special healing powers such as the healing of leprosy, snake bite or sterility.

The most important festival—*Urs*—was celebrated on the occasion of the date of the saint's death. In pre-Islamic times, the *dargah* or place of burial occasionally possessed sacral importance. *Dargahs* are often located under ancient and particularly holy trees, on the bank of rivers, etc. (Hartmann, 1944: 128-33). It is also significant that in India the date of the *urs* festival is often not determined by the Islamic lunar calendar, but by the solar calendar.

Saint worship is generally performed by all social classes of Indian Muslims. In practices we find, however, characteristic differences according to their social background and membership of religious sects. The Sufi tradition in India has brought forth a voluminous theological literature which represents the mysticism of an intellectually and spiritually pretentious social group. Popular saint worship appeals more to the lower Muslim castes, also called Ajlaf or common folk. At the *urs* festival and also on each *jummah-rat* (Thursday night) after sunset, *qawwali* singers with their hymns addressed to the specific saint transfer their devotees into a state approaching trance; at times one of them, particularly in the Chishti order, actually falls into a genuine trance and begins to dance (*sama*).

A high percentage of north Indian Muslims lives in cities and are, due to their close contact with Muslim institutions, such as the mosque and *dargah*, quite familar with the ritual practice of Islam. Muslims living in the villages, however, often lack basic knowledge of the contents and practice of their religion because they have never been completely alienated from their Hindu or tribal traditions and because they have no standards on which to orientate their beliefs and conduct. Therefore, the folk religion of this social group of Indian Muslims exhibits strong degree traces of pre-Islamic influences. The Meos who live south of Delhi are a good example of a rural Muslim community with a low degree of Islamization. It was only during the course of the twentieth century that Mohammad Iliyas, the organizer of the Faith Movement, tried to complete the process (Haq, 1972: 115). The Meos also belong to that group of Muslims who worship Salar Masud Ghazi, the object of this study.

The cult which has grown up around Salar Masud or Ghazi Miyan gives evidence not only of a process of Islamization having taken place among the North Indian lower castes and of the existence of an Islamic folk religion, but also of the continuity of pre-Islamic and Hindu influences. It is certain that in the course of the Muslim conquest of Indian regions, forced conversions occurred on a large scale. But the majority of indigenous Indian Muslims was probably converted peacefully by wandering faqirs and Sufis. Indian temples and sacred places were taken over by Muslims who sometimes converted them into Islamic pilgrim centres. The local, not yet converted, inhabitants continued to visit these places or began to try their luck with newly founded *dargahs*, were consequently converted, or incorporated the Islamic cult into their system of beliefs by identifying the Muslim saint with one of the gods already familiar to them.

British ethnographers and census officials found it difficult to make a clear distinction between Hindus and Muslims of the lower castes that had gained access to Islam via these *dargahs*. Briggs shows how fluid the transition of identification was. In Hing Laj (Muslim sanctuary in the West of India), he observes, 'a Musalmani (woman) used to mark their foreheads with a tika thus making them Musalmans. Consequently, on their way back from the shrine, they stopped at Koteshwar (Shiva temple) and received their brandmark of Mahadeva as proof that he had remade them Hindus' (Briggs, 1938: 109).

While the majority of the *dargahs* in India are hardly documented in ethnographic literature, the cult of Syed[3] Salar Masud or Ghazi Miyan in Bahraich, a northeastern district in the Indian state of Uttar Pradesh, has been described in various sources. It can be assumed that some of the authors based their accounts on previous descriptions. But we also find among them the reports of eye-witnesses of the nineteenth and twentieth century (see, for example, Sleeman, 1858, vols. 1 & 2 and Rockey, 1913:250-56).

[3] Ibbetson (1919: 1:13-14) states that *shahid* (martyr) was often mixed up with Syed (Sayyid). Therefore, we cannot be sure that Salar Masud was a Syed.

The Legend of the Life and Death of Salar Masud

The life history of Salar Masud is legendary in character. At least, there are no contemporary sources which would allow the conclusion that he did actually exist. He is first mentioned 200 years after his death.[4] Several sources more or less agree in their narrative:

Salar Masud was the son of Salar Salm (Salu) and the nephew of the military leader Mahmud of Ghazna (see Nasim, 1931; Habib, 1927) who many times swooped down into North India, plundering, destroying and killing. Salar Masud was only 16 years old when he joined one of these expeditions in 1030 and came as far as eastern U.P. where he collided with the local population, the Bhars.[5] He passed through Lahore, Delhi, Meerut, and Kanauj up to Satrikh near Bara Banki in Oudh where he set up his headquarters. From there he and his officers raided the surrounding villages up to Bahraich in the north. In 1033, two of his officers, Syed Saif-ud-Din and Miyan Rajab, received an order to conquer and plunder Bahraich. Meanwhile, the king of the Bhars, Sohel Dev, had succeeded in collecting a large number of his subjects and in carrying the war into the enemy's camp. The two officers, therefore, asked for reinforcements from Satrikh. Salar Masud himself took command of his army and marched off to Bahraich. There he set up his camp underneath a Mahua tree[6] near a sun or Mahadev temple and is said to have remarked that he liked the place and desired to settle there after having removed the idol.

The battle between the Bhars under the leadership of Sohel Dev and the Muslims was fought on the bank of the Kosala

[4] The legends of Salar Masud were collected by Abdul Rahman Chishti in the *Mirat-i-Masudi* (see Nizami, 1961:306).

[5] The Bhars are an ancient tribe of India. 'Legends', writes Oppert, 'associate their name with the earliest Aryan heroes, e.g., with Rama and his sons, but the Bhars suddenly disappear from the scene and, so far as history is concerned, reappear just previously to the Mohammedan invasions of India, at which period they certainly possessed a vast territory, and were indeed the real owners of the soil' (1972:37ff). Further, '. . . their name still survives in Bahar, Bahraich, Bara, etc.' (1893:39).

[6] The Mahua tree is sacred. It is inhabited by spirits. Alcohol is made out of its fruits (see Briggs, 1920).

river. Salar Masud and a great number of his soldiers were killed. The young general who had just turned 19 and was still unmarried was buried under the Mahua tree near the sun temple.[7]

The repeated attacks of the Muslims had thoroughly shaken the framework of political authority in this region so that it had not recovered even by the time of the next assault from the northwest led by the Ghoris. Remnants of Salar Masud's Muslim army supposedly remained in the area around Satrikh. The graves found in surrounding villages indicate that Salar Masud's soldiers and officers were buried there after the battle. A number of Muslims who survived the battle may have settled down, built the graves and preserved the story of Salar Masud. A few place names also speak in favour of this assumption (Siddiqui, 1950:73). Some of the soldiers killed in battle were worshipped as saints, but they never attained the popularity of their general, Salar Masud. His younger brother, Amir Nasirulla, is said to have been buried in Dekauli. Also, his father was supposedly killed in one of his campaigns (*Encylopaedia of Islam*, 1960:2:1047). There is a story about the officer Malik Amber that he rode back without his head from the battlefield near Bahraich to Bijnor where he was buried together with his horse.[8] The fact that a number of landowning families in Oudh trace their origin to this very time also could support the assumption that remnants of the army and hangers-on remained in the region (Siddiqui, 1950:110, Nevill, 1904a:153).

The exact date of the construction of Salar Masud's first grave cannot be asserted.[9] It is also not known when it first began to be visited by pilgrims. The poet Amir Khusrau, who

[7] See Siddiqui (1950:71) and Crooke (1968:1:207). Crooke writes, 'He was, it was said, buried by some of his followers in the place which he had chosen for his resting place, and tradition avers that his head rests on the image of the sun, the worship of which he had given his life to destroy.'

[8] This story is regarded as unhistoric since Bijnor was supposedly conquered only in the twelfth century by Qazi Adam, the ancestor of the Pirzadas of Bijnor (see Nevill, 1904b).

[9] Siddiqui (1950:73) maintains that Nasir-ud-Din Mahmud had the first *dargah* constructed. Nizami (1961:77), on the other hand, states that Nasir-ud-Din resided in Bahraich, but that the *dargah* was not mentioned in his history, *Tabaqat-i-Nasiri*.

lived in the second part of the thirteenth century, was the first to comment on the popularity of Salar Masud (Nizami, 1961: 306). Since the spot where he was buried had been sacred before his appearance, it seems probable that the local population continued to visit it and that Salar Masud, whom they had learnt to fear and respect, had become the object of their devotion.

Zohra Bibi and the Wedding of Salar Masud

It is also quite impossible to date the second part of the legend concerning Salar Masud. The healing powers of his grave must have been known among the Muslims of the region whether they were immigrants or local converts when Zohra Bibi, the unmarried and blind daughter of the merchant Syed Jamal-ud-Din of Rudauli near Lucknow, went on a pilgrimage to his grave hoping to regain her eyesight (Nevill, 1903:149). She was cured and out of gratitude decided to construct a *dargah* on the former site of the sun temple in the village Parasi, some one-and-a-half miles outside Bahraich. Besides it, she had another grave constructed for herself. Shortly afterwards, she died, and her parents and relatives established the custom of making a pilgrimage to Bahraich in the month of *jeth* (Hindu month May/June) in order to celebrate a post-mortem wedding of the two unmarried deceased. Zohra Bibi was thus betrothed to the hero Salar Masud and the number of pilgrims began to grow. Another shrine in memory of Zohra Bibi was established in Rudauli and an *urs* festival is celebrated there at the same time as in Bahraich.

It is possible that the first solid *dargah* was constructed by Nasir-ud-Din Mahmud, the son of Sultan Iletmish and governor of the region (*Encyclopaedia of Islam*, 1960:1047). It is obviously he who also colonized the town of Bahraich and led it to prosperity. Mohammad bin Tughlaq was probably the first Muslim ruler of Delhi who visited the shrine (1340) (Nizami, 1961:77). In 1378, Feroz Shah Tughlaq made a pilgrimage to Bahraich and was deeply touched by the spiritual atmosphere of the place. He is said to have had his hair cut and to have turned towards mysticism (*Encyclopaedia of Islam*, 1960:1047).

He granted buildings and a *jagir* for the maintenance of the shrine. Copperplates on the *dargah* provide evidence that in the eighteenth century Akbar II also contributed money to the annual *mela* (Siddiqui, 1950:73). Another ruler of Delhi, Sikander Lodi, known for his puratanism, prohibited the procession to the grave of Salar Masud and the custom among women to make offerings at Muslim shrines (Briggs, 1908:1:587). The *dargah* of Salar Masud was rather small at that time; it was built of brick and surrounded by trees. It was obviously rebuilt at a later date.[10]

The Festival

Salar Masud is worshipped by Hindus and Muslims in North India, Rajasthan, Punjab, Bihar and Bengal. However, the local ceremonies vary considerably. The central festival which draws between 50,000 and 100,000 devotees from all parts of North India takes place on the first Sunday in the month of *Jeth* (May/June). The festivities and the *bazaar* continue over a period of several days. The most important ceremony, the wedding, is performed on Sunday night.

One of the more important processions originates in Rudauli, the birthplace of Zohra Bibi, the bride. The local leader of the untouchable sweeper caste has the privilege of carrying the bridal bed (*palang perhi*) to Bahraich.[11] *Hijras* or eunuchs play the part of the parents at the wedding (Mujeeb, 1966:13). Other processions bring further presents from Banaras, Jaunpur and Mirzapur. The generally chosen form is cash for the dowry of the bride. *Charhana Mazar Sharif* is a religious offering or present from the groom to his bride and consists of cash or merchandise. A particularly popular gift seems to be a chicken. In May/June the price for chicken rises considerably in the eastern part of the province due to increased demand (Rockey, 1913: 253). *Qalandari*, on the other hand, are copper coins which the

[10] See Garcon de Tassey (1869:73) and Herklots (1972:67). The picture of the *dargah* shows a dome and arches in the style of a later period.

[11] See Nevill, (1903:53) and Garcon de Tassey (1869:74). Garcon de Tassey maintains that this was the privilege of a tradesman.

pilgrims throw at the dome of the *dargah*. To hit the golden pinnacle of the dome is considered a special blessing (Nevill, 1903:149).

Rockey estimated the amount of money thus collected by the *dargah* at one hundred English Pounds per day (Rockey, 1913:253). These donations consist of copper cons, and silver, and sometimes gold and jewellery. The *khaḍim* of the *dargah* used to administer this income and look after the buildings. In 1876, a committee under the chairmanship of the British deputy commissioner of the district replaced him. A school and a dispensary were then founded and maintained from the income of the *dargah* (Nevill, 1903:149).

The many groups approaching the *dargah* carry banners and are accompanied by drummers. Some of these banners are green (the colour of the Shiahs) and others red (the colour of the martyr). These banners are fastened on to a lance or bamboo pole and carried upright. On top of the pole are copper coins wrapped in cloth, with which the pilgrims touch the dome of the shrine after having arrived at Bahraich. Briggs, however, states that the poles were decorated with locks of hair symbolizing the head of the martyr (Briggs, 1953:481). In any case, the banner stands for Salar Masud who led his soldiers into battle. Rockey describes such a banner, forty feet long and fifteen feet in width which was carried from Gonda. 'It was', he writes, 'a wonder of small figures of ridiculous conception, and was carried on a bamboo, erect, the whole 38 miles and back again, by admiring devotees' (Rockey, 1913:253). The banner remained at the *dargah* if the wish of the bearer was fulfilled. Otherwise, it was carried back to its place of origin where it became an object of devotion after a few years. The banners and poles that remained at the shrine were sold; they possessed sacral value. The takings from them are considerable.

The wedding takes place on Sunday night and the place is profusely illuminated. The pilgrims push forward to enter the *dargah*; others hangs suspended from nearby trees, having tied ropes around their hands, feet and necks. For this self-torment they hope to receive special blessings from Salar Masud (Garcon de Tassey, 1869:74). Unfortunately, there is no account of the actual wedding ceremony.

On the occasion of the *urs* festival a *mela* or *bazaar* takes place in the locality where traders from neighbouring villages offer merchandize for sale. It seems that indulgence in liquor was common and quite excessive (Garcon de Tassey, 1869:30). The motive for a pilgrimage to Bahraich therefore varies. Some groups are there to play their traditional role in the wedding ceremony; others are traders. The majority of pilgrims is, however, made up of those who are looking for help of some kind or the other, and who often offer all their belongings to the *dargah* hoping for relief or cure of illness. These are blind, crippled, lame or leprose, since Salar Masud is particularly known for his power of healing these very infirmities.

There is an imitation of the *dargah* of Bahraich in Banaras which is frequented by the Doms. Two other shrines exist in Amroha (Moradabad district in U.P.) and Jaleshwar (Etawa district); the former being called 'Bara Miyan', the latter 'Chota Miyan'. Here the pilgrims, particularly Dhanuks, a sub-caste of the Doms, hope to be cured of sterility. The Sansiyas on the other hand believe Ghazi Miyan to be the king of snakes (Briggs, 1953:481).

The Panch Pirs

Another form of devotion of Salar Masud is that of the *Panch Pirs*. The classical *Panch Pirs* are Shiite, and consist of Muhammad, the Prophet, and his family members—Fatima, Ali, Hasan and Husain. These five names are depicted in Ali's hand on the Muharram standards and in Shiite shrines, like on the boulders that line the ascent to the shrine of Maula Ali near Hyderabad. The hand recurs in the local cult of *Panch Pirs*. Among the Hindus, the cult of the Five appears under the name of *Panch Devata*. In Indian popular usage, a variety of combinations of Muslim *Pirs* and Hindu gods is found, each put together by local and individual preferences.[12] In the Punjab, the following *Pirs* belong to the Five: Khwaja Qutb-ud-Din, Khwaja Moin-ud-Din Chisthi, Nizam-ud-Din

[12] Among others, Bhairava and Kalika belonged to those frequently mentioned Hindu gods of the Panch Pirs (Ibbetson, 1919:1:572).

Auliya, Sultan Nasir-ud-Din Mahmud and Nasir-ud-Din Abu Khair. At other places two of them are replaced by Kwaja Khizr and Farid Shakarganj. The Bhatti caste prefers its own patrons. The dyers worship Pir Ali Rangrez, the Lohars Hazrat Daud, the Mehtars Lal Pir, etc. (Crooke, 1968:1:203). 'The same list will contain Sultan, Devi, the Guru, Khwaja and Guga Pir., . . . The five saints are in fact any five personages the worshipper likes to mention; and the fact that a man describes himself as a Panch Piria implies generally that he is indifferent as to the saints whom he worships and is probably a man of the lower orders (Ibbetson, 1919:1:572).

Salar Masud or Ghazi Miyan is very frequently found among the *Panch Pirs*. In Rohtak district near Delhi he is worshipped in the form of a mound crowned by a banner. The mound is usually located near a pond or a Jal tree outside the village. The cult resembles that of the Guga Pir.[13] The first inhabitants of a new settlement who dies becomes a *Panch Pir*. Briggs comments: 'In the Punjab the "Five" often is a single personality' (1953:489). In Hindu cults also one comes across a unification of several gods in a single god. In the case of Rohtak there is no specific reference to the martyr Ghazi Miyan, but it is possible that the pole or flag on top of the mound represents him as it does elsewhere.

The Meos around Delhi, who maintain that they were converted to Islam by Salar Masud, erect such a standard (*nishan*) once a year and celebrate a festival. The standard is carried from village to village by people singing and collecting grain from the peasants. There is, however, no grave or fixed location to serve as the point of worship of Salar Masud (Ibbetson, 1919:1:624; Mujeeb, 1966:10-11).

In eastern UP the worship of the *Panch Pirs* is also quite widespread, particularly among the lowest Hindu castes. Crooke complained that it was impossible to find a common explanation for this cult: '. . . the whole cult has become imbedded in a mass of the wildest legends and mythology' (Crooke, 1968:

[13] See Briggs (1938:235) and Crooke (1968:1:211). Crooke writes, 'Guga was killed in a battle with Firoz Shah (1351-88) of Delhi . . . Guga who became a saint is now considered a snake godling and is well known and popular in the Punjab, in fact in all North India. He is worshipped especially by the lower castes.'

1: 205). In Banaras there are five different versions of the *Panch Pirs*, but in each case Ghazi Miyan tops the list, a proof of the popularity of the Bahraich legend in the area.

The priests of the cult belong to the drummer caste of Dafali who wander around singing, beating the drum and narrating the story of Ghazi Miyan. These drummers also lead the wedding procession at Bharaich. An iron wire, an abstract form of the standard or hand, wrapped in red cloth and decorated with flowers, represents Ghazi Miyan and is carried by the drummers from house to house.

The lowest castes—the Pasis and Chamars (Crooke, 1968: 1:206)—worship Ghazi Miyan and the other four *Pirs* in the form of five wooden piles set up in the yard of the house. The Bharwars erect an altar in the shape of a grave inside their houses in front of which they offer a chicken in the month of August while Muslim drummers proceed from house to house collecting a kind of cake.

In other regions also local festivities take place in which the banner of Salar Masud reoccurs. Earthen mounds and the standard/pole appear again and again in the worship of the *Panch Pirs* and Ghazi Miyan. Briggs describes the place of worship as an earthen platform, set up in the northwest corner of the room. A piece of metal is stuck on top of the mound representing a hand; each finger symbolizes one of the saints. A yellow cloth is wrapped around the 'wrist'. Every Wednesday the mound is washed and decorated with flowers; incense is burnt or a *huqqa* lit. On special occasions a goat or rooster is offered. The Dafali caste carries out this ceremony (Briggs, 1953:489; Herklots, 1972:67).

Speculations on the Continuity of Hindu and Tribal Cults

The cult surrounding Salar Masud and the *Panch Pirs* in North India clearly bears influences of Hindu and tribal traditions. It was not only practised by Muslims, but also by a large number of Hindus. Rockey believed that on one occasion which he witnessed half the pilgrims coming to Bahraich had been Hindus (Rockey, 1913:254). Also, Sleeman was surprised to find that of all the saints a Muslim warrior of the quality of Salar

Musud was worshipped by Hindus, whose ancestors had suffered heavily at his hands. He explained this attraction of the Hindus of the lower castes with that ever-present fear of everything powerful and their endeavour to pacify this evil by making offerings (Sleeman, 1858:1:48). Conscientious and educated Hindus, however, declared: 'These invaders, however merciless and destructive to the Hindu race, say they must have been sent on their mission by God for some great and useful purpose, or could not have succeeded as they did; had their proceedings not been sanctioned by Him, he could have at any moment destroyed them all, or have interposed to arrest their progress' (Sleeman, 1858:2:324). Crooke, on the other hand, suggests that the cult in question was a non-Aryan fertility cult (Crooke, 1968:2:324).

Balmik and Lal Beg

The majority of Ghazi Miyan's and the *Panch Pirs*' devotees are the lower caste Hindus (Doms, Nats, Mirasis) and those converted from the lower castes to Islam (Lal Begis, Julahas, etc.). These groups were essentially tribals who had only just settled down and begun to take up professions such as musician (Dafali),[14] sweeper (Doms), beggar, artist, prostitute, etc.

A legend among the Doms which concerns their ancestor, Valmiki, shows that one can establish a continuity between pre-Islamic traditions and later developments. According to the legend, Balmik, or Valmiki, the hunter and robber, one day raised his weapon against Brahma who consequently condemned him to incessantly utter the name of Rama. During this long exercise, Balmik was completely eaten up by termites. When Brahma returned after 60,000 years, he heard the voice of Valmiki emanating from underneath an anthill. He called Indra and asked the god to rain upon the mound and thereby to free Balmik, i.e., to awaken him to new life. Brahma then asked Balmik to compose the Ramayana (Briggs, 1953:55). Balmik

[14] The Dafali are a sub-caste of the Mirasi (musicians) (see Briggs, 1953:2; Crooke, 1968:1:206).

also means anthill. The anthill is of great significance in Indian folk and tribal religion.[15]

Balmik was also the procreator of Lal Beg. 'Balmik is a saint who gave to a worshipper a son whom she called Lal Beg' (Briggs, 1953:461). Lal Beg was a warrior. Some sub-castes of the Doms identify Lal Beg with Ghazi Miyan. It could further be concluded that Ghazi Miyan (Lal Beg) was regarded by those castes that worship him as their ancestor; other caste ancestors such as Dhanuk and Sansiya, sons of Balmik, gave their names to the castes of Dhanuks and Sansiyas which are partly Muslim.

It is also possible to prove a relation between Balmik and Ghazi Miyan in the case of the mound or anthill. The mound or anthill stands out prominently in the worship of Ghazi Miyan in all the regions (Bengal, Chota Nagpur, Madhya Pradesh, UP, Punjab). The rain-shower sent by Indra to bring Balmik back to life is symbolized by the washing of the mound or anthill. The mound can be understood as the feminine child bearing element.

The lance on top of the mound is also a common object of devotion among the lower castes. The Doms, but particularly the Sansiyas, are partly basket weavers. They worship the bamboo which provides their livelihood (Briggs, 1953:85). Bamboo is also a symbol of fertility at wedding ceremonies. The belief that Shiva turned his snake into a bamboo suggests that the lance in question is a male fertility symbol (Briggs, 1953:68). As already mentioned, Ghazi Miyan is worshipped as a saint who cures sterility. Furthermore, Valmiki and Ghazi Miyan are both identified with the snake of Shiva.

Worship of the Sun

The participation of Hindus in the festivities at Bahraich can be explained by another factor. The sources frequently mention that Salar Masud was buried at the original site of a sun or Mahadev temple.

[15] Crooke notes; 'The anthill is . . . used as an altar by some of the Dravidian tribes . . . . Ants . . . .are regarded as in some way connected with the souls of the sainted dead' (Crooke, 1968:2:2:256).

The worship of the sun goes back to Vedic times (Bhandarkar, 1913:151). It seems to have reached the peak of its influence in North India in the centuries after Christ's birth. This form of the sun cult was brought to India from Iran where its priests, the Nagas, also originated. It existed up to the seventeenth century when it was destroyed by the Mughal emperor Aurangzeb.[16] The history of the origin of the sun cult tells of Samba, the son of Krishna, whose father condemned him to be a leper in punishment for a sin. 'Since those women who saw your handsome figure became all excited, therefore you shall be punished with leprosy' (Stietencron, 1966:130). At another place the curing powers of the sun are mentioned: 'The deaf, the blind, and those suffering from leprosy, the lame, stiff and immobile, you cure them all, O God, who is a friend of your devotees' (Stietencron, 1966:135).

Unlike other Muslim martyrs who are known as malevolent (Ibbetson, 1919:1:123), Salar Masud is benevolent. He possesses the same healing powers as the sun god. Thus, the cult of the sun god was transferred upon him. While the special day of Muslim martyrs is usually Thursday or Monday, in the case of Salar Masud at Bahraich Sunday (Ibbetson, 1919:1:14), the day of the sun god, was maintained.

The fact that the temple at Bahraich was also identified with Mahadev (Shiva) is explained by the absorption of the sun cult by Shaivism. In Jejuri near Poona, Martand (the sun god) is identified with the Shaivite Khandoba (Gupta, 1919:18-21). As Stietencron says: 'The sun God, however, moves into the background to make room for Shiva who is now worshipped as the highest god' (1966:17, 252).

During the phase of its decline, the sun cult was merely performed by the lower castes who are also devotees of Ghazi Miyan. Furthermore, Shiva, in the shape of Mahadev, shares many attributes with Ghazi Miyan: 'He was a powerful, wrathful and impetuous god, but generous and bountiful and spared nothing when he was propitiated. Whenever a man conceived

[16] The sun cult is, however, still alive among the female population in eastern India. The younger women worship the sun only once a week, on Sundays, while the older women worship it everyday because of their age, as the sun protects and cures illness (Information received from Dr. Erika Moser).

a desire for anything, he was the god to be appealed to for its fulfilment' (Bhandarkar, 1913:114).

DULHA DEV

The annual wedding of Salar Masud with Zohra Bibi appears to be un-Islamic. Crooke tries to draw a parallel between Salar Masud and Krishna or Dulha Dev 'snatched away by an untimely and tragical fate in the prime of boyish beauty' (Crooke, 1897:95). Dulha Dev is the spirit of the bridegroom who is tragically killed by lightning or a tiger on the eve of his wedding. 'In the Central Provinces he has his place in the house, represented by a bit of stone or iron kept in an earthen pot' (Briggs, 1953:476). There is also a tale of Ghazi Miyan being killed by fire on the eve of his wedding (Briggs, 1953:481). The wedding festival reminds us of ceremonies common in Hinduism when the god and his consort/wife are brought together in an annually repeated festival. The wife in question is very often a *bhakta* or female devotee such as Zohra Bibi herself was.

Islamization and Political Solidarity

The cult around Salar Masud represents a complex of various traditions of the lower Muslim and Hindu caste in North India which allows us to observe the sequence of its historial development. It is well-known that in the process of 'Aryanization' the influence of Brahmans on tribal populations and lower castes led to an identification of tribal godlings and totems with Brahmanic gods (e.g., the marriage of a Brahmanic god with a tribal goddess). Social mobility inside the social system corresponds to this process of identification. 'This conglomeration goes on forever', Kosambi remarks, 'while all the tales put together form a senseless, chaotic mass. The importance of the process, however should not be underestimated.... The marriage of the gods imply human marriage as a recognized institution, and would be impossible without social fusion of their formerly separate and even inimical devotees, (Kosambi, 1965:170). The integration of foreign and often socially antagonistic elements led to a neutralization of social conflicts.

Islam, the religion of Salar Masud, as represented by the upper class Indian Muslims, exhibited and still exhibits a considerable factor of conflict in India, because it has to safeguard itself against such an integration. Muslim society inside Hindu society remained in the diaspora and had to resist such a fusion in order to maintain its identity. From the foregoing discussion it is, however, clear that the folk religion of Islam as represented by saint worship had been integrated into an already existing religious framework by the lower castes so that the latent conflict created by the conversion of members of these castes to Islam was neutralized. This integration prevented social groups from breaking away from the existing order.

This process of integration of various Indian religious traditions came to an end during the last two centuries due to political developments. It is often said that the lower castes hoped for social liberation when converting to Islam. Mobility in Indian Muslim society is admittedly easier than in the Hindu caste system. The economic success of converted Muslims is often accompanied by their becoming members of the Ashraf or upper class and by a process of Islamization.[17] But it seems equally certain that the conversion of untouchables and other low castes to Islam hardly changes their social and economic situation. While Islam theoretically propagates the destruction of social barriers, in actual practice it has not succeeded in making the lower castes equal partners of the upper class. The low degree of Islamization among these castes was a consequence of social and economic deprivation and aggravated the social gulf between Ashraf and Ajlaf.

The Census Report of 1931 (India, 1931:515) registered the decreasing popularity of the cult of Ghazi Miyan and put the blame for it on the attempts of Muslim preachers to cleanse the folk religion of all Hindu influences. Since the Indian Muslims lost political power in the eighteenth and nineteenth centuries, a process of religious and political solidarization set in. The

[17] See Vreede de Stuers (1968). She distinguishes between 'Ashrafization, a process of social mobility, and 'Islamization', a process of purification from non-Islamic usages.

Tabligh movement, elections, the growth of political parties, etc., led to a solidarity of the lower class Muslims with their religious community which found its theological guides among the fundamentalists and its political leadership among lawyers and landlords. This religious minority feared that in consequence of the introduction of democratic principles the Hindus, being in the majority, would monopolize all positions of influence, and tried to gain political allies among the lower caste Muslims.

Studies of social change among the urban Muslim middle class show that, by adopting neo-traditionalism, by purifying their beliefs and customs, i.e., by intensifying Islamization, it tries to strengthen its identity *vis-ā-vis* Hindu society and to screen off all corrupting influences from outside, either of Western or Hindu origin. Thus, purdah has become the symbol of correct Islamic conduct (Vreede de Steurs, 1968:99). A study of Islamic missionary efforts among lower Muslim castes points in the same direction.[18] As is well known, converts usually insist more fanatically and inflexibly on the observation of rules of conduct. The Meos serve as a good example of this generalization. This type of Islamization, however, is not the consequence of economic or social mobility, but of a political process. The identification of the propagated ideals of Islam during the course of the freedom movement in India resulted in the religious and political solidarity of these lower social classes with the Muslim upper class in the Pakistan movement and was directed against the Hindu dominated Congress Party, and therefore it intensified religious and political conflicts. This ideological solidarity of socially and economically conflagrating Muslim classes is essentially conservative, since it was used by the upper class for the realization of its own class interests, i.e., the foundation of a Muslim state.[19] It still prevents the social and economic

[18] The missionary work of Muslim organizations was accompanied by communal riots, the cause of which usually was the playing of music before mosques and cow slaughter; the Hindu equivalent was the *Suddhi* and *Sangathan* movements of the Arya Samaj and the Hindu Mahasabha.

[19] Mujeeb states: 'This is, I beileve, sufficient indication that the needs which found political expression were not the needs of the community as a whole but those of a class, which consisted of the big and small landlords, and the lawyers, doctors, government servants who belonged to the families of these landlords' (Philips and Wainwright, 1970:410).

cooperation of lower Muslim castes with Hindus of identical economic status.

Bibliography

Bhandarkar, R.G. (1913), *Vaisnavism, Saivism and Minor Religious Systems*, Strassburg, Trubner.

Briggs, J. (1908), *History of the Rise of the Muhammedan Power in India till the Year 1612*, 2 Vols., Calcutta, R. Cambray & Co.

———(1920), *The Chamars*, London, Oxford University Press.

———(1938), *Gorakhnath and the Kanphata Yogis*, Culcutta, YMCA Publishing House.

———(1953), *The Doms and their Near Relations*, Mysore, Wesley Press.

Crooke, W. (1897), *The North-Western Provinces of India*, London, Methuen.

———(1968), *The Popular Religion and Folklore of Northern India*, 2 Vols., (Reprint), Delhi, Munshiram Manoharlal.

Encyclopaedia of Islam, (1960), London, E. J. Bill.

Garcon de Tassey, M. (1869), *Memoir sur les Particularites de la Religion Musalmane dans l'Inde d'apres les ouverage Hindustanis*, Paris, Labitte.

Goldziher, Iqnaz (1967), *Muslim Studies*, S.M. Stelin (ed.), London.

Gupta, B.A. (1919), *Hindu Holidays and Ceremonials*, Calcutta, Thacker Spink.

Habib, Muhammad (1951), *Mahmud of Ghazna*, 2nd ed., Delhi, S. Chand & Co.

Haq, M. Anwarul (1972), *The Faith Movement of Mawlana Muhammad Iliyas*, London, University of Chicago Press.

Hartmann, R. (1944), *Die Religion des Islam*, Berlin, E.S. Mittler & Sohn.

Herklots, G.A. (1972), *Islam in India: The Customs of the Musalmans of India*, (reprint), New Delhi, Oriental Book Reprint Co.

Ibbetson, D. (1919), *A Glossary of the Tribes and Castes of the Punjab and the North-West Frontier Provinces*, 2 vols., Lahore, Superintendent Government Printing.

India, Government of (1931), *Census of India*, 1931, vol. xviii, *United Provisions*, Pt. 1, Report, Delhi, Superintendent Government Printing.

Kosambi, D.D. (1965), *The Culture and Civilization of Ancient India in Historical Outline*, London, Routledge and Kegan Paul.

Mujeeb, M. (1966), *The Indian Muslims*, London, George Allen and Unwin.

Nasim, M. (1971), *The Life and Times of Sultan Mahmud of Ghazna*, (reprint), Delhi, Munshiram Manoharlal

Nevill, H.R. (ed.) (1903), *Bahraich: A Gazetteer, District Gazetteer of U.P.*, Vol. XLV, Allahabad, Superintendent Government Printing.

———(1904a), *Barabanki: A Gazetteer, District Gazetteer of U.P.*, vol. XXXVIII, Lucknow, Superintendent Government Printing.

———(1940b), *Lucknow: A Gazetteer, District Gazetteer of U.P.*, Vol. XXXVI, Lucknow, Superintendent Government Printing.

Nizami, K.A. (1961), *Some Aspects of Religion and Politics in India during the Thirteenth Century*, Aligarh, Department of History, Aligarh Muslim University.

Oppert, G. (1972), *On the Original Inhabitants of Bharatvarsa or India*, (Reprint), Delhi, Oriental.

Philips, C.H. and M.D. Wainwright, (eds.) (1970), *The Partition of India: Policies and Perspectives*, London, George Allen and Unwin.

Rockey, N.L. (1913), 'Progress of Islam in Oudh', *Muslim World*, 3, pp. 250-56.

Siddiqui, N.H. (1950), *Landlords of Agra and Oudh*, Lucknow, Anwarul Hasan Siddiqi.

Sleeman, W.H. (1958), *A Journey through the Kingdom of Oudh*, 2 vols, London, R. Bentley.

Stietencorn, Hencry V. (1966), *Indische Sonnenpriester: Samba and the Sakadvipiya Brahmana*, Wiesbaden, O. Harrassowitz.

Vreede de Steurs, Cora (1968), *Parda—A study of Muslim Women's Life in Northern India*, Assen, Von Gorkum.

6

Creating a Scene: The Disruption of Ceremonial in a Sufi Shrine

Patricia Jeffery

Analyses of ritual practices abound in anthropological and sociological literature, but few of them can be related to my concerns here. For one thing, there is little material about large-scale public ceremonials (in this case, those which took place at a Sufi shrine in India) which draw huge crowds of devotees and in which there is a sharp distinction between 'actors' and 'audience'. Secondly, here I am more concerned with the disruptions rather than the ceremonies, and so I shall not be exploring the symbolic content of the ceremonials which I discuss. Rather, I want to focus on the clues which the disruptions can give about other aspects of the organization of the shrine.[1]

The arena where these public ceremonials take place is the shrine (*Dargah Sharif* or *Astana Sharif*) of Hazrat Nizamuddin Auliya which is some five miles south of Old Delhi.[2] Hazrat

1 The research on which this paper is based was funded by the Social Science Research Council of the U.K. I am grateful to colleagues who made useful comments on earlier versions of this paper. In referring to *Pirzade* in the course of the paper, I have used pseudonyms.

2 The words *dargah* and *astana* both mean threshold or doorway, and they have been similarly extended to mean the abode of a holy man or the tomb of a saint.

Nizamuddin was one of the most famous Sufi saints of India. He was one of the saints in the Chishti *silsilah* (chain, connection) and was the Khalifa (successor) of Baba Farid (Shaikh Fariduddin Ganj-i-Shakar) who is buried at Pak Pattan (now in Pakistan). Also in this *silsilah* was Moinuddin Chishti who established it in India, and who is buried at Ajmer. The Khalifa of Hazrat Nizamuddin included Nasiruddin Chiragh Delhi (see Begg, 1972; India, 1961; Mujeeb, 1967; Nizami, 1973 and 1974). The poet Amir Khusro was also a disciple of Hazrat Nizamuddin and is buried a few yards away from him in the *Dargah Sharif.* Hazrat Nizamuddin died in 1325 AD (725 AH) and Amir Khusro died within six months.[3] Since their deaths, many prominent Muslims have made architectural contributions to the memory of these two men, and many powerful people, including members of the Mughal royal family, have chosen to be buried in the precincts of the *Dargah Sharif* (see Fanshawe, 1902; India 1922; and S.S., 1976). Faithful pilgrims, by no means exclusively Muslims, come to the *Dargah Sharif,* believing in the efficacy of approaching God through some saintly intermediary. Some Muslims consider that the devotion of such pilgrims verges on idolatry and gross heterodoxy, since it strikes at the orthodox belief in God's immediacy. However, throughout the Islamic world, many Muslims continue to take their troubles to revered saints.

The custodians of the *Dargah Sharif* are the *pirzade*, who see to the upkeep of the buildings, guide and help pilgrims and organise the public ceremonials. The term *pirzada* (pl. *pirzade*) means literally the son or the disciple (spiritual son) of a pir, or person who acts as a spiritual guide and may be the founder of a religious order. In general parlance, though, a *pirzada* is a person attached to a shrine or mosque who does not necessarily claim descent from the saint.

At the *Dargah Sharif,* the *pirzade* recount how Hazrat Nizamuddin's disciples wanted to know what would become of them after he died: he replied that he would put none of them under any compulsion to remain by his side after his death, but he undertook to entreat God not to let any who chose to stay to go *nanga ya bhuka* (naked or hungry). According to

[3] India (1975) contains accounts of his life and writings.

the *pirzade*, this prayer has continued to be answered right down to today, for they claim to be the descendants of several men who remained at the tomb after Hazrat Nizamuddin died.

Originally, there were four *khandans* (patrilineage, dynasty) all of which claim to be Syed, that is, descended from the prophet Muhammad through his daughter Fatima, which is undoubtedly a good way of asserting the propriety of an occupation which is not universally accorded legitimacy by Islamic scholars. The *pirzade* claim that their lines have been living in India for about 700 years, for their ancestors fled Iran and Turkestan during the time of Genghiz Khan. All four *khandans* are said to be connected to Hazrat Nizamuddin through descent from his sister, or descent from one of his special disciples, or both. They are called *Haroonian*, *Hindustanian*, *Nabera-gan* and *Qazi-zad-gan*. The *Haroonian* died out sometime in the last hundred years for want of male heirs. In 1947 about half of the then *pirzade* moved to Pakistan, and it is possible that the *Dargah Sharif* also lost part of its population after the Mutiny in 1857. Currently, there are about 250 *pirzade* (men, women and children) attached to the *Dargah Sharif*.

Defaced Scripts

During the Islamic calendar, the *Dargah Sharif* is the site of several major events which draw large crowds of pilgrims who watch and participate in the proceedings. In this context, we can regard the *pirzade* as the promoters of theatrical spectaculars. Throughout the year, however, small numbers of pilgrims visit the *Dargah Sharif* to consult their pir about some spiritual, medical or marital problem, or simply to do *ziyarat* (pilgrimage), or to fulfil a *mannat* (vow) in gratitude for a wish which has been granted. The large-scale public ceremonials with which I am concerned here are the highlights of the year: some of them stretch over several days and pilgrims are numbered in their thousands rather than scores.

In looking at the ceremonials, I intend to take my cue from the dramaturgical analogy employed by Goffman (1969). For one thing, his analogy seems particularly apt when dealing with people who are presenting a performance to an audience in the way the *pirzade* do during the festivals at the *Dargah Sharif*. Moreover, certain passages of his exposition are more suggestive for my purposes than any I have found in the more traditional anthropological literature dealing with 'ritual'. This is because I am interested in ceremonials which 'go wrong'. My informants could provide descriptions of what ought to happen, and produce a script for the ceremonials; but on several occasions the reality departed from the ideal, and the informants themselves were explicit about disruptions and interruptions which 'should not' have happened, in which they felt that their scripts had been defaced.

I shall leave the commentary to the final part of the paper and here simply describe what happened to disrupt the ceremonials. These interrupted ceremonials occurred during the year while I was doing fieldwork, though the *pirzade* admitted that disruptions had occurred in previous years, sometimes during the very ceremonials which were disrupted while I was present, sometimes during others. The disruptions are not only seen as such by the *pirzade*, but are also apparently rather unpredictable. In this paper, I want to explore how to make sense of this sort of event. Clearly, if the disruptions can be dismissed as the result of bad rehearsal, there would be little point in this exercise, but I want to argue that the disruptions are important clues to questions beyond the context of the immediate ceremonial.

Disrupted Ceremonials

The ceremonials I shall describe are *Bara Wafat*, which is commonly celebrated by Muslims in the Indian subcontinent and is made somewhat special at the *Dargah Sharif* by the annual showing of holy relics; the *urs* for Amir Khusro and Hazrat Nizamuddin Auliya, which draw the largest crowds of the year to commemorate the two saints; and the festival of Basant which is usually particularly associated with Hindus but has a special place in the Nizamuddin repertoire. I shall present these accounts in the order in which they occurred.

The Urs for Amir Khusro

There are two main *urs* at the *Dargah Sharif*, one for Hazrat Nizamuddin and one for Amir Khusro. The latter takes place according to the lunar calendar betwean 16 and 20 Shawwal, with the major events scheduled for the 18th, which is the supposed day of the saint's death.[4] The word *urs* originally meant nuptials, particularly the taking of the bride to the groom; but in this context it means the death anniversary, in the sense of the saint being united through death with the supreme spirit.[5] There is an annual commemoration of each *urs* and these two affairs draw by far the largest crowds to the *Dargah Sharif*. Pilgrims eat and sleep in the courtyards of the *dargah*, which is ornately decorated and lit for the occasion. Outside, there is a temporary bazaar and a fun fair, and in the evenings there are *mushaira* programmes under the patronage of three *pirzade*, with the programmes predominanty taken up with *qawwali* (devotional singing) rather than poetry.

The two *urs* follow the same pattern.[6] After *maghrib-ki-namaz* (prayers said after sunset) on the 16th, there is *fatiha* prayer in the name of the saint.[7] After *isha-ki-namaz* (evening prayer) on the 17th there is *fatiha* and programme of *qawwali*. Early in the morning of the 18th, the *chaddar* (mantle) covering the tombs of the two saints and the other drapes and curtains are replaced with new ones, and at 11 A.M. there is *bara qul* (conclusion)[8] followed by a *qawwali* programme. This is replicated

[4] India (1961:29) is incorrect in saying that the *urs* of Amir Khusro is timed according to the Gregorian calendar. Both *urs* are held according to the lunar calendar. Further, both men are said to have died on the 18th of the month and not the 17th as reported there.

[5] For the meaning of *urs* see Platts (1911:760) where he gives both meanings, and also India (1961); *Encyclopaedia of Islam* (IV:1038) only gives details of wedding ceremonies.

[6] The ensuing account differs somewhat from that given in India (1961:29-30).

[7] The *fatiha* is the opening *surah* of the *Qu'ran Sharif* and is believed to be worthy of frequent repetition. The word is also used to refer to prayers made for the dead or in the name of a saint.

[8] *Qul* (say) is the first word of several *surah* of the *Qu'ran Sharif*, and any or all of these may be read, such as at *fatiha* and the conclusion of commemorative festivals.

on the 19th; and finally on the 20th when the *khatam* (termination)[9] takes place on the third day after death.

During the *urs* of Amir Khusro, two disruptions occurred within about five minutes on the 18th Shawwal. Before the *fatiha* was said by the Imam a large crowd of pilgrims settled themselves around the older *pirzada* men in the main court of the *Dargah Sharif*, to participate in *Qu'ran Khwani* (recitation of *Qu'ran Sharif*).[10] One of the men from the 'party' on duty that day (the *Nabera-gan*), Hidayat Ali, took charge of the proceeding so that each reciter would keep his turn and only one person would be speaking at one time. For several minutes, things went as directed, but then one man stood up and began to recite out of turn. He was interrupted, and drowned out, so he sat down. When his interrupter had finished, he stood up again and began to recite, only to be interrupted again. Again he sat down and waited, again he stood up to recite and was interrupted. Hidayat Ali was clearly not going to permit him to recite, and, humiliated, he sat down and made no further attempt to recite. This man was not a *pirzada* himself, but is regarded as the *chamcha* (follower, sponger) of Hazoor Baksh (from the *Qazi-zad-gan*) who was absent on this occasion. This incident is a good example of the way in which a *pirzada's* followers may be resented by the other *pirzade*, and may be a source of weakness rather than strength.

After *fatiha* and the distribution of sweets to the pilgrims, several men recited extempore prayers, and then the scene was shifted for the *qawwali* programme. The *qawwals* arranged themselves in a group facing the entrance to Hazrat Nizamuddin's tomb and the *pirzade* began to sit in two rows between the *qawwals* and the tomb. Hardly had the *qawwals* begun to sing and play when shouting arose among the *pirzade*. The *qawwals* had appealed to the men on duty that Burhanuddin (of the *Hindustanian*) had seated himself slightly ahead of the others

[9] *Khatam* means the complete recitation of the *Qu'ran Sharif*, but in this context there only the *fatiha* and some other verses are recited.

[10] *Qu'ran Khwani* means recitation of the *Qu'ran Sharif*, though here all that is entailed is the recitation from memory of several important *surah* by individuals. *Qu'ran Khwani* are also held in homes, often in fulfilment of a vow, when several women simultaneously read different *surah* until the *Qu'ran Sharif* has been read in its entirety.

and refused to move back to make the lines straight. Most of the men on duty agreed and wanted Burhanuddin to move back. However, Burhanuddin's *chamcha*, Rustam Ali, happened to be one of those on duty and by dint of taking his turban off and gesticulating wildly, he managed to thwart the efforts of the others on duty to restrain him and he persuaded the *qawwals* to continue their singing. All the other men on duty stormed out of the *Dargah Sharif*, piqued that Burhanuddin had been able to retain his conspicous position while they were supposed to be in charge. Here we can see how a follower may indeed be a source of strength to a *pirzada*, for the centrepiece of the dispute sat silently through all the turmoil. Further, we get a glimpse of the position of the *qawwals* at the *Dargah Sharif*: many public functions require their services, while conversely they depend on being permitted to perform and collect *nazrana* (offerings). Thus, they must keep in the good books of the *pirzade* : in this case and another, which will be considered below (the Basant festival), their performances were interrupted and they rapidly had to assess which party they should obey. In each case, they followed Burhanuddin.[11]

The Basant Festival

This is the only festival at the shrine which is timed according to the solar calendar. It is generally considered to be a Hindu spring festival, though Mrs. Meer Hassan Ali does refer to the celebration of the 'bussund' festival in Lucknow in the early nineteenth century (1973, 1:287-88). The *pirzade* agree that Basant is mainly a Hindu festival and say that *basanti* (bright yellow) is particularly associated with the yellow blossoms of spring. Traditionally, they used to wear *basanti* coloured clothes on this day (as also described by Mrs. Meer Hassan Ali, 1973:1:287-88 and Platts, 1911:156), though hardly anyone now wears more than a single *basanti* coloured item, such as glass bangles for the women, or kerchiefs, hats or turbans for the men. *Nizami Bansri* contains the tradition

[11] Burhanuddin is a patron of *mushairas* which are broadcast on All India Radio, and the *qawwals* undoubtedly value any opportunity to obtain a wider audience.

about the celebration of Basant in Nizamuddin.[12] Hazrat Nizamuddin was greatly grieved by the early death of his relative and disciple, Taqiuddin Nooh. On the day of Basant, while he was mourning near the grave, Amir Khusro came along with some friends, clutching some mustard flowers. Amir Khusro tilted his hat and began to dance, and Hazrat Nizamuddin smiled for the first time since Taqiuddin Nooh's death. Amir Khusro explained that he had come to offer flowers to his idol (in the way the Hindus were also doing) and he began to sing in Persian:

Ashk-rez amed ast abre bahar,
Saqia gul barez-o-bade beyar.

(While shedding tears, the spring cloud has come, 'O, Giver of Wine, scatter the flowers and bring the wine!)[13]

Hazrat Nizamuddin began to cry and went into ecstasy and later the party took the flowers to the grave of Taqiuddin Nooh and repeated the verse which had so affected Hazrat Nizamuddin. It is this event which is re-enacted each year, though now the *qawwals* who sing the couplet stop to sing at several tombs around the village and in the *Dargah Sharif*, including those of Hazrat Nizamuddin and Amir Khusro, whose tombs are covered with *basanti* coloured mantles for the day.

On the day in question, some twenty men and boys gathered by the *Koshak Lal* after *asr-ki-namaz*. The Imam did *niyaz*, flowers were placed on the stone where Hazrat Nizamuddin is believed to have sat, and the *qawwals* began to sing. The procession then moved on to the tomb of Taqiuddin Nooh, where more *qawwali* was performed and flowers were placed on the grave. Then, in the *Dargah Sharif*, the party stopped outside

[12] See *Nizami Bansri* (1960:209-16). I am grateful to Mohammad Nasimuddin, who helped translate this and other material for me.

[13] See gist of *Tarikh-e-Nizami* (1388 AH). I am grateful to Hooshang Philsooph for elucidating this couplet for me. *Saqi* (bringer of wine) usually connotes a young and inferior person, but it is possible that this is a reference to Hazrat Nizamuddin himself; the reference to tears may be a more direct reference to his grief than the translation suggests.

the tomb of Hazrat Nizamuddin and several men went inside to throw blossoms into the *basanti* coloured *chaddar* covering the grave, while the *qawwals* performed outside. Flowers were also placed on the graves of Amir Khusro and his sister's son who is buried in the same enclosure. As the party moved towards the corner of the court to visit another tomb, it was suddenly halted. The *qawwals* stopped performing and an affray broke out between Burhanuddin and Hazoor Baksh and their sons. Punches were aimed, insults hurled, and Burhanuddin even had his turban knocked off. Burhanuddin had wanted the *qawwals* to go first to his *hujra* (cell), but Hazoor Baksh tried to intervene to persuade them to go to his cell first. Burhanuddin retorted that this would entail a pointless retracing of steps, and ordered the *qawwals* to continue. When they did so, Hazoor Baksh and his sons stalked out shouting abusive ripostes over their shoulders at Burhanuddin and one of his followers who had been impertinent to contribute his own comments. The proceedings ended at this point in disarray, though informants said that several other tombs should have been visited by the *qawwals*.

One *pirzada* who had tried to stop the fighting, and others who were not involved, talked of a long-term *izzat-ki-dushmani* (enmity of honour) or *daulat-ki-bat* (question of domination) between Burhanuddin and Hazoor Baksh, and they considered it wrong to fight in front of strangers like that, for the reputation of the shrine would be tarnished.

BARA WAFAT

This festival takes place on the 11th and 12th of *Rabi-al-awwal*. The term means 'twelve demise' and is taken to signify the death of the Prophet Muhammad after twelve days of sickness. However, several *pirzade* insisted that the festival commemorates the anniversary of his birth and not his death. Indeed, the day is also called *Eid-al-Meelad-al-Nabi*, or the festival of the birth of the Prophet.[14] Either way, the day is an

[14] For *Bara Wafat* as the death anniversary, see Crooke (ed.) (1972: 188-90) and Platts (1911:1197); for *Bara Wafat* as both death and birth anniversary, see *Encyclopaedia of Islam* (I:651 and III:419).

important one to all Muslims, and particularly so to the *pirzade*.

The programme at the *Dargah Sharif* is held during the afternoon of 11th *Rabi-al-awwal* and continues through the *shab* (night) of the 12th. It consists of *meelad Sharif* until *asr-ki-namaz* (afternoon prayer) which is followed briefly by *Qu'ran Khwani* (recitation of the *Qu'ran Sharif*), and the showing of the various relics to the pilgrims until the *azan* (call to prayer) for *maghrib-ki-namaz* (prayers just after sunset). The relics are said to have been given into the safe-keeping of the *Dargah Sharif* by Bahadur Shah Zafar shortly before he was arrested near Humanyun's tomb in 1857. Mehdi Husain (1958:*xix-xx, xxviii-xxix* and 280-81) repeats this tradition, but I have found no further reference to this yet, and Bahadur Shah Zafar made no reference during his trial to going to the *Dargah Sharif* shortly before his arrest (see Parliamentary Papers, 1858-59). Whatever their source, the relics consist of several hair from the beard of the Prophet (set in wax on silver bases), a small brick of baked Karbala mud (the scene of the massacre of Hussain and his party), a small piece of leather (said to be the final remnant of a book written by Hazrat Ali), and a *qadam-e sharif* (footprint of the Prophet). They are only brought out of the store-room once a year, and each relic is shown in turn to different segments of the gathered pilgrims who sit in the court around the tomb of Hazrat Nizamuddin.

Although the *Nabera-gan* were on duty, a loud argument arose among the *pirzade* before the relics could be brought out of the *toshey-khana* (store-room). The problem was who should be the first among them to have the chance to hold up each relic in turn to show the gathered devotees, and where each *pirzada* should stand on the raised platform so that the pilgrims would be able to get the best view of the relics. After five minutes of wrangling in full view of the pilgrims, the *pirzade* sorted out the order in which the older men among them would show the relics. From that point, the performance continued smoothly: the Imam did *niyaz* over some huge *thalis* (metal trays) covered with satin or velvet cloths and containing sweets which the *pirzade* later distributed as *tabarruk* (blessed food) to the pilgrims. The *Qu'ran Khwani* followed, and for about ten minutes men stood up in turn to recite passages of the *Qu'ran Sharif* from memory.

Then a *pirzada* emerged from the main doorway to the *masjid*, supporting a silver casket on his head and guided through the throng of seated pilgrims by another *pirzada*. He put down the casket between several *pirzade* on the western side of the platform around the tomb of Hazarat Nizamuddin. Two of them reverently opened it, took out and gently unwrapped the relics one by one and washed each of them in *kewra* (rose water) before handing them separately to Burhanuddin who was to be first to show each relic to the pilgrims. He first explained in some detail the relic he would be showing, and then, holding the relic in his out-stretched hand, slowly described a wide arc right over the pilgrims seated beneath him. The relic was then passed to four other *pirzade*, one of whom was Hazoor Baksh. In this fashion, each relic was shown to pilgrims sitting around the tomb of Hazrat Nizamuddin and the last *pirzada* to show each relic returned them to the *pirzada* seated by the casket whose job was to wash them again and replace them in the casket. Once all the relics had been shown, Barhanuddin and Hazoor Baksh were mobbed by pilgrims eager to touch the hands which had held the relics, and may be even to receive a small pieces of cotton wool soaked in the *kewra* in which the relics were washed before and after being soaked. Other *pirzade* distributed portions of *tabarruk*, and many pilgrims meanwhile crowded round the *qadam-e-sharif*, which had been filled with *kewra*. One *pirzada* dipped a piece of cotton wool into the *kewra* and squeezed some into the right hand of each pilgrim, who would drink a little and wipe his face, head and body with the remainder. The programme was brought to a close with the *azan* for *maghrib-ki-namaz* and pilgrims and *pirzade* alike prepared to pray. Later that evening, another *meelad shariff* was held in the same part of the *Dargah Shariff* until after midnight.

The Urs of Hazrat Nizamuddin

This *urs* takes place between 16 and 20 *Rabi-us-sani*, and the incident which concerns me took place on the final day, when Burhanuddin and his follower, Rustam Ali, were on duty together. After the *Qu'ran khwani* and *fatiha*, several men made extempore prayers, the last of these being one of Burhanuddin's guests. He prayed first in Arabic, and then (with each phrase being endorsed by *amin* from the pilgrims) he prayed in Urdu, asking that all children who were not yet married would be well-married in due course, that couples with no children should be granted children by Allah, and that Hazrat Nizamuddin would grant the wishes of those who petition him. Finally, he wanted to make a prayer for the well-being of the *sajjada-nashin*[15] of the *Dargah Sharif*, Pir Bur.... But before he could finish, Hidayat Ali had leapt to his feet, pointed his right hand accusingly and shouted, 'And who gave you permission to mention any name in our *Dargah Sharif*?' The proceedings came to an abrupt halt, the price which Hidayat Ali was prepared to pay for preventing Burhanuddin's name from being singled out before the pilgrims by an outsider. *Pirzade* and pilgrims shuffled around for a few minutes until preparations for the *qawwali* session were complete.

Commentary

I have so far described some disrupted ceremonials, and now the task is to make sense of these interruptions. In some respects, doing so will echo the natural history of my fieldwork. From the first days I had some hint of trouble: Hazoor Baksh refused to introduce me to his wife as she only speaks Persian. When I mentioned this, other *pirzade* told me that his wife is a *pirzada* herself, and Hazoor Baksh was just annoyed that I had already visited Burhanuddin's home. These two men have figured in all the scenes described above, though not always in direct confrontation with one another. The first incident occurred only a few weeks after I began my fieldwork: suddenly, the atmosphere of reverence and decorum was shattered. Clearly, all was not well and even the *pirzade* would admit that. This put me on a trail which lasted throughout my fieldwork, with subsequent scenes acting as talking-points which enabled me to pursue the clues further.

In themselves, the scenes may appear rather trivial, and

[15] A *sajjada-nashin* is a spiritual superior at a mosque or religious endowment such as a shrine. I discuss this in more detail below.

certainly the drama was generally over in a few minutes if not seconds. There was a very brief, but significant, slipping of the mask. After the event, many of the *pirzade* were prepared to make mountains out of these apparent molehills. As my work evolved, it became clearer that these tiny incidents are actually vital pieces of information which provide glimpses behind the veneer and help to unfold the sources of the disruptions.

Clearly, we are not going to advance at all if we take as our starting-point an assumption that rituals draw people together and renew solidarity among them. May be that *ought* to have been happening, but it was not. My informants were emphatic that things had gone wrong in the ceremonials in question and that conflict had been expressed which should not have come to the surface in this sort of context.

So, what of conflict in ritual? Could it be that the approaches of Gluckman (1963:110-36; 1965a:109-36; 1965b:250-59) and Turner (1974:155-98) are helpful here, particularly in their consideration of rituals of rebellion or rituals of status reversal or elevation ? Gluckman argues that protest may be instituted in openly expressed ritual and social tensions. He suggests that such rituals are ways of handling social conflicts within an unquestioned social order: rituals of rebellion in fact strengthen the social order. In similar vein, Turner talks about rituals of status reversal which contain 'robust verbal and non-verbal behaviour, in which inferiors revile and even physically maltreat superiors' (1974:156). Often these are calendrical rituals in which inferiors are permitted for a short period to act in ways which would normally be unacceptable. He also talks of rituals of status elevation, in which future incumbents of high position must behave humbly and are often subjected to devastating degradation at the hands of their future inferiors.

While conflicts are being brought to the fore in these scenes, there are several reasons why Gluckman and Turner cannot help out here. They are both dealing with contexts in which there is regular and scripted abusive behaviour which is considered integral to the ritual by the actors. On the other hand, I am dealing with cases in which the incidents are not regular and actors consider that something has gone sadly wrong with their presentation. We are not dealing here with situations in which normally unacceptable behaviour becomes briefly permissible. There are also grounds for suggesting that the conflicts enacted during the ceremonials are anything but abnormal, for it is by no means self-evident that the social order is unquestioned by all the actors. Nor are we dealing with rituals of status reversal or status elevation, for the crucial reason that no *pirzada* considers himself inferior to any other, though there are several who try to make out that they are superior to the rest. This assertiveness does not go unchallenged. Here is the meat of the matter: sense can be made of these rather bizarre intrruptions only if our perspective goes beyond the immediate ceremonial context.

For this purpose, I have found Goffman (1969) more useful than the traditional anthropological literature on ritual. Goffman presents an analogy between social life and the acting out of a drama. This is directly pertinent to the *pirzade* acting in front of an audience during the public ceremonials. But in Goffman's sense, the analogy has much more extensive relevance to the *Dargah Sharif*, for the *pirzade* are always orienting to an audience. Their day-to-day work entails making impressions and maintaining a convincing presentation to an audience, whether of one or of many. The *pirzade* are a team presenting a routine to an audience. Since the audience will always tend to judge by appearances, the team has to be circumspect in its presentation, and the team may have to suppress backstage behaviour while on stage, so that their image is not tarnished and the audience does not obtain information which might contradict and devalue the image which the actors are trying to convey. There are many ways (which Goffman talks about at length) in which precautions may be taken, but performances are very fragile, and 'wrong impressions' are sometimes conveyed.

When disruptive events occur, the usual result is embarrassment, and even loss of reputation. Teams are especially vulnerable to renegade colleagues who let the side down, particularly if the team's party-line is unequally congenial to all the members of the team. There are, writes Goffman, 'situations, often called "scenes", in which an individual acts in such a way as to destroy or seriously threaten the polite appearance of consensus, and while he may not act simply in order to create such dissonance, he acts with the knowledge that this sort of dissonance is likely to result' (1969:185). While many disruptions may be accidental, or the result of incompetence, others 'create a scene'; for, sometimes individuals 'will feel obliged to destroy an interaction in order to save their honour and their face' (Goffman, 1969:216).

If we move in this direction, we then have to ask why the party-line is uncongenial to some *pirzade*, why there is disagreement over stage-directions and casting, why some *pirzade* are prepared to 'create a scene', and why there might be some chinks in their armour which they may want to conceal from their audience?

The Origins of the Pirzada Khandans

As far as the *pirzade* are concerned, the disruptions are to be explained in terms of the origins of the *pirzade khandans*, which they explicitly link up with issues of relative holiness and legitimacy and the question of the *sajjada-nashin* of the *Dargah Sharif*.

While parties not directly involved in the scenes were generally more forthcoming about them, all the *pirzade* are passionately interested in the question of the *khandan* origins. One man inisited that I must begin my research with this question and then everything else would fall into place neatly. Figures 1 and 2a, b, c, d and e show some of the genealogical connections involved and can indicate some of the issues which the *pirzade* raise. All this material comes from printed sources; the *pirzade* are enthusiastic producers of political tracts about the *Dargah Sharif* and their own position in it.[16]

QAZI-ZAD-GAN (ALSO KNOWN AS KASHANI)

Most of the printed material which refers to the *Qazi-zad-gan* simply suggests that this *khandan* was founded by a Qazi

[16] The genealogical material presented here is all obtained from books published in Urdu. In order to conceal the identity of the authors, I have omitted their true names and have simply appended their *khandan* membership.

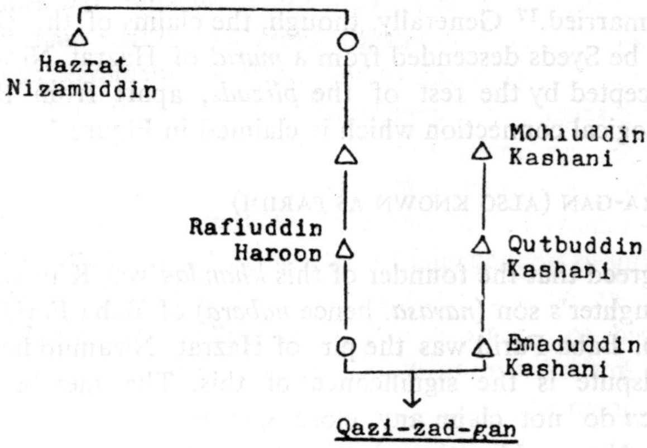

Fig. 1: Qazi-zad-gan (also known as Kashani)
(*from* Sirat-e-Nizami, *n.d.*, *circa 1900*, *by member of* Qazi-zad-gan)

(lawyer) called Mohiuddin Kashani because he came from Khorassan (in Iran). Generally, he is described as a *murid* (aspirant, disciple) of Hazrat Nizamuddin. Only the version shown in Figure 1 (which was written by a member of the *khandan*) suggests that there was quite such a close connection between this *khandan* and that of Rafiuddin Haroon. Present members of the *khandan* describe themselves as the *awlad* or descendants of Hazrat Nizamuddin's sister.

The version presented in Figure 1 is not accepted by Burhanuddin (a member of the *Hindustanian*), but it must be recollected that his rival, Hazoor Baksh, is a *Qazi-zad-gan*. Burhanuddin argues that Mohiuddin Kashani died before Haz rat Nizamuddin and so could in no sense be called his successor. Further, descent from Rafiuddin's daughter's son gives no right to the inheritance of position at the *Dargah Sharif*. Moreover, he argues, the *khandan* is probably not even Syed: a book written by one of their members about two hundred years ago (*Matlub-al-talibin*) prefaces the names with 'Shaikh' rather than 'Syed', and the *shijra* (family tree) contains too few generations. Another of Hazoor Baksh's rivals, Nadir Ali (a member of the *Nabera-gan*, who has not figured in the scenes described above), asserts that the *Qazi-zad-gan* are frauds, for the *shijra* contains the name of a man who, according to the *Tarikh-e-Burhanpur*, never married.[17] Generally, though, the claims of the *Qazi-zadgan* to be Syeds descended from a *murid* of Hazrat Nizamuddin are accepted by the rest of the *pirzade*, apart from the close genealogical connection which is claimed in Figure 1.

Nabera-gan (also known as Faridi)

It is agreed that the founder of this *khandan* was Khwaja Imam, the daughter's son (*navasa*, hence *nabera*) of Baba Farid (hence *Faridi*). Baba Farid was the pir of Hazrat Nizamuddin,. What is at dispute is the significance of this. The members of the *khandan* do not claim any close genealogical connection with Hazrat Nizamuddin, though they do lay claims to 'blood' connection to two men spiritually connected to the saint. On the one hand, some of them assert that their descent from a saint greater than Hazart Nizamuddin himself gives them a special position at the *Dargah Sharif*, and further that Khwaja Imam was in fact Hazrat Nizamuddin's closest and most spiritually endowed *murid* who became his special servant and, ultimately, successor. Nadir Ali goes further than this: he claims that the *khandan* is superior to the others since it is the only really Indian one. He believes that one of the wives of Baba Farid was a daughter of the king Ghyasuddin Balban.[18] Within the *khandan*, Nadir Ali asserts his own superiority on the grounds that men in another line are descended from an adopted son, while those in a different line are the descendants of a man who died before his father (which would disqualify them from claims to property or succession rights within the *khandan*).

Rustam Ali (the follower of Burhanuddin) is generally considered to be of this *khandan*, and is said to have presented papers at court claiming that he is the only *Nabera-gan* still living in the village. In conversation, though, he denied his membership of this *khandan*, preferring to stress his links to Burhanuddin, who is his mother's father's step-brother's son's son. Meanwhile,

[17] Nadir Ali takes very little active part in the activities at the *Dargah Sharif*: other *pirzade* joke that he will die in the law courts, for he spends his days in litigation against other *pirzade*, many of the cases revolving around the genealogical material presented here.

[18] This is a tradition which is often repeated, but Begg (1972:89) question its validity.

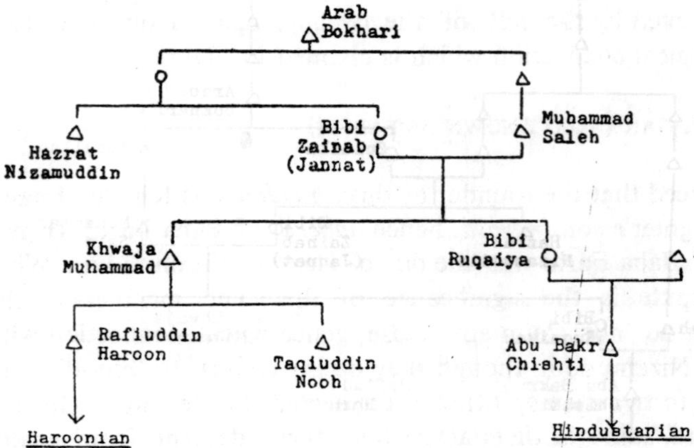

Fig. 2a: Haroonian and Hindustanian
(*from* Sirat-e-Nizami, *n.d., circa 1900, yy member of* Qazi-zad-gan)

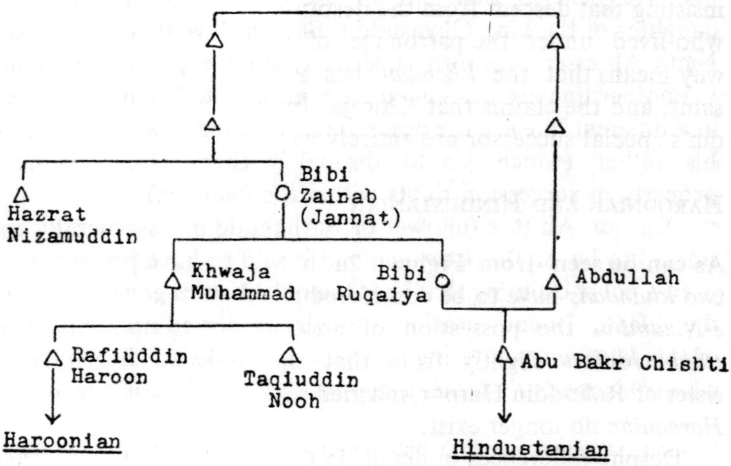

Fig. 2b: Haroonian and Hindustanian
(*from* Nizami Bansri, *n.d., circa 1942, by member of* Nabera-gan)

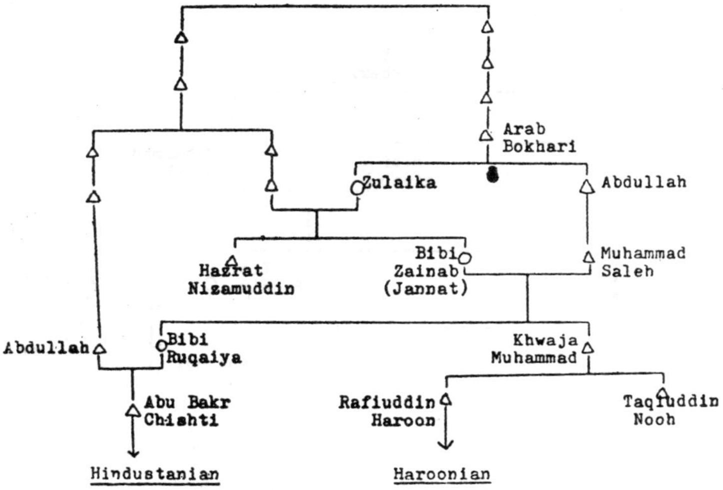

Fig. 2c: Haroonian and Hindustanian
(from Tabqat-e-Nizami, *a manuscript originally written in the 18th century, updated during the 19th and now in the possession of the Imam of the* Dargah Sharif)

Burhanuddin himself belittles the claims of the *Nabera-gan* by insisting that descent from the destitute grandson of Baba Farid who lived under the patronage of Hazrat Nizamuddin in no way means that the *khandan* has inherited anything from the saint, and the claims that Khwaja Imam was Hazrat Nizamuddin's special successor are entirely without foundation.

HAROONIAN AND HINDUSTANIAN

As can be seen from Figures 2a, b and c, the origins of these two *khandans* have to be considered together. A copy of *Tabqat-e-Nizami* in the possession of another member of the *Hindustanian* differs slightly from that shown here, for it shows a sister of Rafiuddin Haroon married to Abu Bakr Chishti. The *Haroonian* no longer exist.

Despite differences in detail in the versions reported in the *Sirat-e-Nizami*, the *Nizami Bansri* and the *Tabqat-e-Nizami*, the essential message is the same: the *Haroonian* were descended from the saint's sister's son, while the *Hindustanian* are descendants of the sister's daughter's son. The issue has been greatly

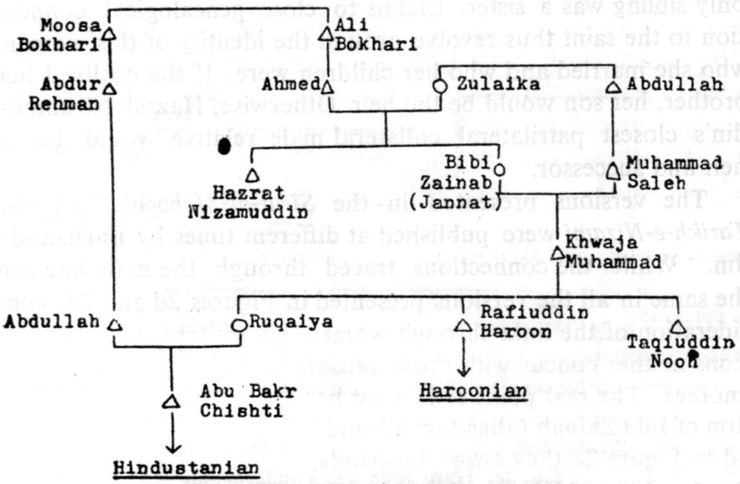

Fig. 2d: Haroonian and Hindustanian
(from Sirat-ul-Mehboob, *n.d., circa 1942, by member of* Hindustanian)

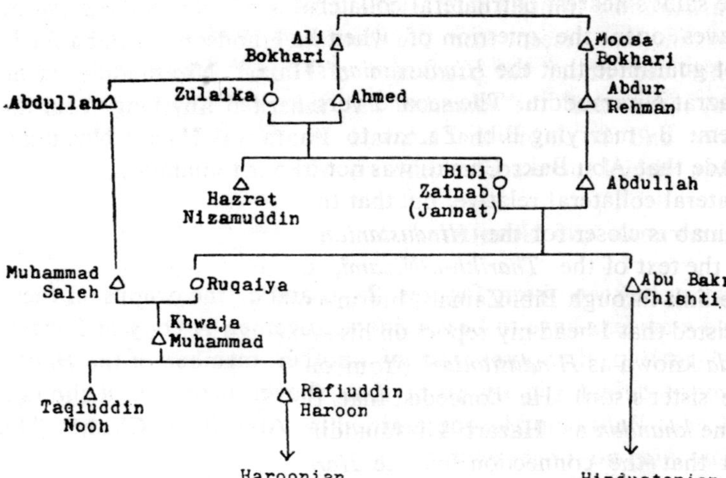

Fig. 2e: Haroonian and Hindustanian
(from Tarikh-e-Niazmi, *n.d., circa 1960, by member of* Hindustanian)

confused because Hazrat Nizamuddin never married and his only sibling was a sister. Claims to close genealogical connection to the saint thus revolve around the identity of this woman, who she married and who her children were. If she outlived her brother, her son would be the heir. Otherwise, Hazrat Nizamuddin's closest patrilateral collateral male relative would be his heir and successor.

The versions presented in the *Sirat-al-Mehboob* and the *Tarikh-e-Nizami* were published at different times by Burhanuddin. While the connections traced through the male line are the same in all the versions presented in Figures 2d and 2e, consideration of the links through women shows that the two versions neither concur with those presented earlier, nor with one another. The real point of interest here lies in the shifts in position of Bibi Zainab (alias Jannat) and Bibi Ruqaiya. From Figure 2d to Figure 2e they swop husbands, and Ruqaiya ceases to be the daughter of Khwaja Muhammad and becomes his mother instead. The implications of this shift are clear. In the first version, the *Haroonian* are closer to the saint than the *Hindustanian* (though the link is through a woman), and Abu Bakr Chishti is the saint's nearest patrilateral collateral relative. This, however, leaves open the question of when Bibi Zainab died, and does not guarantee that the *Hindustanian* should be the successors to Hazrat Nizamuddin. The second version neatly solves this problem. By marrying Bibi Zainab to Abdullah, the claim can be made that Abu Bakr Chishti was not only the saint's closests patrilateral collateral relative, but that the connection through Bibi Zainab is closer for the *Hindustanian* than for the *Haroonian*. In the text of the *Tharikh-e-Nizami*, greatest stress is put on the link through Bibi Zainab, but in conversation Burhanuddin insisted that I head my report on his *khandan* '*yak-jaddi khwahar-zada* known as *Hindustanian*' (from one grandfather and from the sister's son). He conceded that the *Haroonian* are of the same *khandan* as Hazart Nizamuddin and Abu Bakr Chishti, but that the connection of the *Haroonian* with the saint is distant.

Burhanuddin is quite alone in making these claims for the *Hindustanian*. Even members of his own *knandan*, who are closely related to him, say that his purpose in re-writing history is merely to advertise himself to the public, and those of other *khandans* agree. One member of the *Qazi-zad-gan* considers that there were many Abu Bakrs around at the time of Hazrat Nizamuddin and that Burhanuddin's ancestor was certainly not the son of the saint's real sister. Hazoor Baksh, not surprisingly, gives as good as he gets, for, according to him, Burhanuddin's father's father was merely a servant in the village in 1857. He sided with the British and later received substantial rewards which enabled him to make his utterly false claims about his ancestry seem plausible to outsiders.

There are, then, substantial disagreements about the origins of the *pirzada khandans* and how they are connected to Hazrat Nizamuddin. These differences matter intensely to the *pirzade*, so much so that several of them are involved in court cases with one another over these very issues. The background to this sort of disputation is that the question of *khandan* origin is often entwined with that of the *sajjada-nashin* of the *Dargah Sharif*. This word literally means 'a person sitting on a prayer mat in adoration', and is applied to the spiritual heir or successor of a saint, who tends the grave and cares for the devotees' needs. The central question is whether there can be several, or only one, *sajjada-nashin* at one *Dargah Sharif*.

Most of the *pirzade* deny that there is any one among them who can justify a claim to precedence as the only *sajjada-nashin*. Their position rests on the belief that Hazrat Nizamuddin himself created no leaders and that the present *pirzade* are not entitled to make differentiations which were considered unnecessary by the saint. Further, they argue, Hazart Nizamuddin left no property which could have been inherited and passed down through any one of the *pirzade khandans*. Moreover, all the *khandans* can claim close connection to Hazart Nizamuddin, and any slight inequalities which might have existed long ago have been erased, because the *khandan* have greatly intermarried over the past 700 years. While the *Haroonian* (the *khandan* which died out) might have been able to claim closest connection to the saint, there is no cause to differentiate on that score among the three *khandans* which remain. Consequently, they say, every *pirzada* is entitled to append *sajjada-nashin* (head priest) to his name. According to this view, *pirzada*, *sajjada-nashin* and *Khadim* (servant) are virtually synonymous and applicable to all the *pirzade* equally.

On the other hand, some *pirzade* have severally argued that there can only be one *sajjada-nashin* at the *Dargah Sharif*. These include Nadir Ali, Hazoor Baksh, and Burhanuddin. As we have seen, the latter has produced an elaborate argument to assert that he of all the *pirzade* has the closest links to Hazrat Nizamuddin, and thus has special rights at the *Dargah Sharif* through inheritance. The details of his case have varied, but the essence remains the same: he is the sole *sajjada-nashin*, and the other soi-disant *pirzade* are mere *khadim*, who are not entitled to call themselves *pirzada* let alone *sajjada-nashin*. Interestingly, these claims appear to be accepted outside the *Dargah Sharif* to an extent which they are not inside.[19]

The whole issue is shrouded in confusion and dispute, none of which can be cleared up after this distance in time. Moreover, while the *pirzade* tend to present the matter as an academic exercise in mediaeval history, it is vital not to be taken in by this mystification. They pitch the debate around the relative holiness of the different *pirzade*, but it is also about something else. It would be simple to conclude that the mass of *pirzade* cannot be wrong in their denials of the claims of others to preeminence, but we should not do so. We have to explore how the egalitarians and elitists alike might be influenced in taking up the positions they hold.

Behind the Veneer

If we examine the sources of income at the *Dargah Sharif*, we can begin to see why there should be such strong opposition to any suggestions that one person alone is supreme there. Equally, we can begin to understand why individual *pirzade* might like to press such a case, for if they succeed in convincing the public of their special claims to holiness, they can hope to draw a large following. As some of the less successful *pirzade* point out, money follows money. The *pirzada* with a dominant spiritual position can buttress it with a commanding economic one,

[19] It is clear, for instance, that India (1961) has accepted his account further, of the *mushairas* presented during the major *urs* at the *Dargah Sharif*, only those held under his patronage are broadcast over the radio.

which feeds back onto his spiritual claims, and make them all the more probable in the eyes of the pilgrims.

There are good reasons why the *pirzade* want to keep their cards close to their chests on this sort of question. During the whole fieldwork period, I drew a virtual blank when it came to money matters, for the *pirzade* would side-step the topic by asserting that they are mere *faqirs* who neither have money nor any interest in it. This *faqir* ideology lies behind a great deal of the image-maintenance in which the *pirzade* spent their days. One aspect of this is ensuring that those who watch the *pirzade* should go away assured that they are simple *faqirs* with no care for the morrow since they have faith in the bounty of Allah and their saint. No doubt all informants everywhere put up fronts against intruding social scientists, but in a sense the *pirzade* are experts in the craft of image-creating. Their livelihood depends on successfully persuading their audience to believe in them. Indeed, it might well have taken much longer to disentangle their disputes had it not been for the scenes described above and the talking points which they created.

The point here is that the *pirzade* do not depend on some centralized salary-paying body at the *Dargah Sharif*. Unlike many Sufi shrines in India, there are no *jagirs* (grants of land or villages), the rents from which could be used for the upkeep of the *Dargah Sharif* and the support of the *pirzade*. Hazrat Nizamuddin rejected contacts with statesmen and refused any *jagirs* and gifts which were offered to him. Consequently, all expenses have ultimately to be met from the donations of pilgrims, though some *pirzade* own land and houses in their own right. As Syeds closely connected to Hazrat Nizamuddin, and as Sufis who have chosen to cherish his memory, the *pirzade* consider themselves entitled to rewards in the form of *nazrana* (offerings) for the services which they perform for pilgrims. In their work, the *pirzade* are generally individual entrepreneurs in competition with one another. In fact, few are explicit about the competition for income until there was some disturbance, so what follows represents my own piecing together.

There are four main sources of income at the *Dargah Sharif*: the *bari-dari Nizam*, the flower and book shops, the system of *wakil* and their *mehman*, and *piri-muridi*.

BARI-DARI NIZAM[20]

Of the income which comes to the *Dargah Sharif*, only that which comes through the *bari-dari Nizam* virtually excludes competition. Outside each of the two main tombs, pilgrims may place donations in a trunk kept for the purpose. The takings are shared out among the *pirzade* according to a rota. The original four-week rota (relating to the four *khandans*) has become fragmented, and now there 96 turns which run from Wednesday to the following Tuesday, for each of which there are specified *bari-dar* and *hysse-dar* (co-parceners) who organize the shrine's activities and share out the cash donated during the week, provided that they 'sit' on duty in the *Dargah Sharif*. There are still some disputes surrounding the ownership of shares which changed hands in 1947 when some *pirzade* went to Pakistan; there are sometimes disputes about the sighting of the moon, for this may have a bearing on which set of *bari-dar* will be on duty during a major festival; and there are even accusations by those on duty during a festival that other *pirzade* used the cover of crowds to pilfer donations from the trunks. Generally, however, the system allows rather little room for manoeuvre. Further, with a 96 week rota superimposed on a cycle of festivals based on the lunar year, the chances of being on duty while many pilgrims are visiting the *Dargah Sharif* relate closely to the number and distribution of shares owned. Some *pirzade* control few shares, and the *bari-dari Nizam* can be no more than a minor part of their income. Burhanuddin is one of those who own many shares, and one of his sons is permanently deputed to 'sit' when their turns come round.

Within each of the three other sources of income, we can consider the *pirzade* in competition with one another, though members of one household may be involved in enterprises in each of these spheres.

[20] According to Platts (1911:120-21 and 500-1), *bari* means a turn of duty and *dari* means having or possessing: thus a *bari-dar* means a person who is entitled to wait in turn. It is in this sense that the *pirzade* talk about the *bari-dari Nizam*, though Platts also indicates that the compound *bari:dari* means fruitfulness.

Flower Shops

Most of the flower shops are located near the two main entrances to the *Dargah Sharif* (one is inside the main precincts), and each stocks a virtually identical range of items for the pilgrims to buy: there are petals to throw on the graves, joss sticks to place beside them, sweets for *niyaz* and bottles of *itr*. Two other shops, run by the same man, sell books, plaques with quotations from the *Qu'ran Sharif*, *tasbih* (rosaries), *ta'wiz* (amulets) and prayer caps. Competition among these shops normally only consists of shouting and beckoning the arriving pilgrims. When one man took advantage of his already superior site by moving his stall forward and out of line with the others, this was considered unfair competition and ultimately he was forced to move back into line.

Vakil and Mehman

A *vakil* (agent, pleader) gives advice on spiritual and everyday matters to his *mehman* (guest), and he expects financial contributions (*nazrana*) in return. Permissible competition in this sphere is over new pilgrims to the *Dargah Sharif*. Some new pilgrims arrive with directions from *pirzade* at other shrines referring them to a particular *pirzada* in Hazrat Nizamuddin. However, many pilgrims arrive unprepared, and the *pirzade* are very alive to the possibilities: the pilgrim will be swarmed by eager *pirzade*, trying to monopolize his attention, guiding him around the *Dargah Sharif*, helping him with his devotions, and finally trying to persuade him to sign their register of *mehman* and present *nazrana*. Once a person has become a guest in this fashion, he should only go to that *pirzada* thereafter. It is even common for a *mehman* to be 'inherited' by his *vakil's* son, and, equally, a pilgrim may go to his father's *vakil*, though there is no necessity for this.

However, if a pilgrim is unaware of the etiquette of commitment to a particular *pirzada*, and especially if he returns after several years and goes unrecognized by his *vakil*, there is plenty of room for poaching. There are many accusations of stealing guests, even of copying their names out of their true *vakil's* register, or simply of forgetting to inform the *vakil* that his *mehman* had presented *nazrana* to be handed over to him. One such accusation was made by a member of the *Qazi-zad-gan* who claimed that the late Mujib-ur-Rahman had become his guest while a young man of no political importance. After he had become Prime Minister of Bangladesh, this *pirzada* claims that Burhanuddin and Hazoor Baksh both managed to extract *nazrana* from him during one of his visits, which by rights they should have handed over to him. While some *pirzade* are on sufficiently good terms with one another so that they can collect the *nazrana* presented by their *mehmans* when they are absent, there are plenty of opportunities for those who want to exploit the system.

This system of *vakil* and *mehman* is the lynchpin of the incomes of the *pirzade.* The monthly net income from the flower shops probably exceeds Rs. 200 only when there are major festivals at the *Dargah Sharif.* The *pirzade* often say that having a shop brings very little income, for there are too many of them selling identical products, and most families who run a shop also rely heavily on the *nazrana* from their *mehman.* A pilgrim buying some flower petals and joss sticks may do so for under Rs. 5, while *vakils* who are lucky enough to have cultivated wealthy *mehman* may receive hundreds (or even thousands) of rupees. Even very ordinary people may regularly send money-orders to their *vakil* if they cannot make a pilgrimage often, and during slack times at the *Dargah Sharif*, *vakils* may go 'on tour', in order to keep in touch with their *mehman.*

PIRI-MURIDI

This entails the attachment of a *murid* (aspirant) to a pir to learn the path of spiritual advancement. In Hazrat Nizamuddin, those *pirzade* who practise *piri-muridi* in fact mostly give advice on social, marital, and medical matters and prescribe remedies. The success of a pir rests firmly on personal qualities and skill, particularly on his ability to inspire confidence in his advice and convince his *murid* of the efficacy of his diagnosis and counsel. It is an activity in which there may be spectacular pay-offs, but there are also risks. The pir must make detailed study of manuals which deal with diagnosis and the administration of *ta'wiz* (amulets) and other remedies. If he makes mistakes in his prescriptions, his errors will rebound on him: the wife of one *pirzada* was said to have died because he had written out a *ta'wiz* wrongly. Moreover, the *murid* becomes an innocent before his pir, and lays on his pir's shoulders all his cares and sins. On the other hand, the able pir can hope to make a lot of money, and have his *hujra* (cell) constantly packed with people bringing their troubles to him. Among these, some will no doubt be especially impressed by his insight and gradually over the years a pir may build up a reputation and a following of faithful *murids.* This is precisely what Burhanuddin and Hazoor Baksh have been doing for the last thirty years.

The Cleft Stick

This all highlights a crucial dilemma for the *pirzade.* On the one hand, they depend largely on their own individual and competitive efforts to entice pilgrims to buy *their* flowers, to become *their* guests, or to place faith in *their* diagnostic skills. For the ambitious, there is the dream of attaining supremacy by capturing a larger market; for the less successful, there is the fear of being left with a reduced slice of the cake. Since the major ceremonials at the *Dargah Sharif* draw such crowds, they are important to all the *pirzade* on economic grounds alone. The throngs from India and beyond are attracted partly by the reverence in which Hazrat Nizamuddin and Amir Khusro are so widely held, and partly by the knowledge that wealthy Muslims give large sums of money at such times for the preparation of *langar* (free food) for the poor.

According to the rhetorics of some *pirzade* (generally those not directly involved in the scenes described above) there is another factor: the pulling power of the *pirzade* themselves. This line of argument goes as follows: to be convincing, the *pirzade* have to create an impression of holiness, an image of other-worldly, saintly *faqirs*, who possess spiritual qualities by virtue of their connection to Hazrat Nizamuddin and are consequently entitled to be supported by the faithful. *Pirzade* who adopt this line said they were greatly shamed and worried by the behaviour of those who caused public disturbance during the ceremonials. Of course, it could be that their response was more that of men deprived of the limelight than of men who had genuine evidence that the *pirzade* might be vulnerable to consumer resistance. However, they claimed to be convinced that the numbers of pilgrims visiting the *Dargah Sharif* could easily fall off if such disturbances became well-known.

On the other hand, while a single-team presentation might give a good impression to the pilgrims, and provide them with no grounds for slacking in their attendance, it would also leave them with an impression which several *pirzade* feel unable to endorse, for most of them would suffer if the pilgrims came to accept any one of them as supreme. They are caught in the cross-pressures of feeling that they have to give the impression of being cooperative while in reality being in competition. While a united front might give a false impression, disputation in public gives a bad one.

In view of the pervasive disagreements among the *pirzade* about genealogical matters and questions of precedence, as well as the reality of competition among them, it is perhaps surprising that the *Dargah Sharif* continues to function at all. There are, however some reasons why the disruptions can not be permitted to be more destructive than they already are. Firstly, there has been a considerable amount of intermarriage among the *pirzade*, and the cross-cutting ties may help to defuse the divisions which exist. While this may have some effect, there are no sanctions against marriages with outsiders, provided there is prior consent from the other *pirzade*. This is said to be a guarantee of the 'good' status of in-marrying women, and is normally freely given. Somewhere between a quarter and a half of the marriages of the *pirzade* take place outside. It is pertinent to note here that of Burhanuddin's seven married children, five of them have been married to outsiders (*pirzade* at other shrines), and of the two sons who have married 'inside' (one to his FSD and one to his MBD) one of them lives in Pakistan. Burhanuddin's wife laments sending her daughters away, but he is awake to the leverage which could be pulled by affines inside, as well the benefits of having important affines outside. By contrast, only two of Hazoor Baksh's married children have been married outside the village. It would be wrong to lay too much stress on the cooling effects of cross-cutting ties which result from marriage within the village, for they are evidently not able to prevent expensive and acrimonious legal wrangles over *khandan* origins and other questions. Perhaps the most that can be said is that Burhanuddin's tactics in arranging the marriages of his children detach him from local affinal obligations and enable him to manoeuvre more freely in *Dargah Sharif* politics.

A more important reason behind the continuation of the *Dargah Sharif* is the indivisibility of Hazrat Nizamuddin Auliya himself. Without him, the *pirzade* are nothing. Apart from some young men who have received lengthy schooling, there are few among the *pirzade* who could easily earn a livelihood except at the *Dargah Sharif*. Indeed, during my fieldwork, the village was under threat of demolition, and there were even fears that the *Dargah Sharif* might be taken over by the Waqf Board (though this is unlikely, since there are no *jagirs* attached to the *Dargah Sharif* or any other sources of regular income other than the pilgrims).[21] Few of the *pirzade* are in a position to offer an alternative 'product' to pilgrims. Three brothers, lucky enough to have had a scholarly and popular father, are doing just that, and are clearly making something of a success of their catering 'up-market': there may be fewer devotees attending their father's *urs*, but they are all conspicuously well-heeled, unlike the more varied pilgrims who attend the *urs* of Hazrat Nizamuddin and Amir Khusro. Another man has special charge over the western Sufis who visit the tomb of Inayat Khan, which lies on the outskirts of the village. And, meanwhile, Burhanuddin and Hazoor Baksh are contesting the ownership of the tomb of a man to whom both of them are distantly related. For the rest though, all their livelihood comes to them because of Hazrat Nizamuddin's entreaty to Allah—and without their saint, they would have nothing. Awareness of this sets limits on the type and extent of disputation which is conducted among the *pirzade* during their competition with one another.

Conclusion

To a causal visitor at the *Dargah Sharif*, the scenes which I

[21] The Waqf Board administers Muslim trusts and charities in India.

have documented might appear rather trivial in themselves, but I have suggested that they cannot be understood within the ceremonial context alone. These fleeting signs of discord were vital elements in the 'natural history' of my fieldwork, for the momentary slipping of the mask revealed crucial insights behind the scenes at the *Dargah Sharif*, and forced me to pursue their ramifications into the realms of genealogical disputation and the economic organization of the *Dargah Sharif*. For the *pirzade*, the scenes outlined above are tied up with questions of precedence, relative holiness and closeness to Hazrat Nizamud-din, but I have argued that this conceals an underlying and important dilemma for the *pirzade*, since they compete with one another for income, while, at the same time, as *faqirs* they ought not to appear concerned with everyday matters such as seeking a livelihood.

Bibliography

Begg, W.D. (1972), *The Big Five of India in Sufism*, Topdara (Ajmer, India), W.D. Begg, W.D. Begg's Office.

Crooke, W. (ed.) (1972), *Islam in India or Qanun-i-Islam*, by Ja'far Sharif and G.S. Herklots (reprint of 1921 ed.), London and Dublin, Curzon Press.

Encyclopaedia of Islam (1913, 1927, 1936 and 1934), 4 vols., Leiden and London, Luzac and Co.

Fanshawe, H.C. (1902), *Delhi Past and Present*, London, John Murray.

Gluckman, M. (1963), *Order and Rebellion in Tribal Africa*, London, Cohen and West.

———(1965a), *Custom and Conflict in Africa*, Oxford, Basil Blackwell.

———(1965b), *Politics, Law and Ritual in Tribal Society*, Oxford, Basil Blackwell.

Goffman, E. (1969), *The Presentation of Self in Everyday Life*, London Allen Lane.

Hassan Ali, Mrs. M. (1973), *Observations on the Mussulmauns of India: descriptive of their manners, customs, habits and religious opinions* (reprint of 1832 ed.). Delhi, Idarah-i-adabiyat-i-Delli.

Husain, Mehdi (1959), *Bahadur Shah II and the War of 1857 in Delhi and its Unforgettable Scenes*, Delhi, Atma Ram and Sons.

India, Archaeological Survey of (1922), *A Guide to Nizam-ud-din*, by Maulavi Zafar Hasan, Memoir No. 10, Calcutta.

India, Registrar General of (1961), *Beliefs and Practices associated with Muslim Pirs in Two Cities of India (Delhi and Lucknow)*, Monograph Series Part VII-B, Monograph No. 1, Delhi, Registrar

General of India, Ministry of Home Affairs, Government of India.

India, Government of (1975), *Amir Khusrau Memorial Volume*, New Delhi, Director, Publications Division, Ministry of Information and Broadcasting, Government of India.

Mujeeb, M. (1967), *The Indian Muslims*, London, George Allen and Unwin.

Nizami, K.A. (1973), *The Life and Times of Shaikh Farid-ud-din Ganj-i-Shakar*, Delhi, Idarah-i-adabiyat-i-Delli.

———(1974), *Some Aspects of Religion and Politics in India during the Thirteenth Century*, Delhi, Idarah-i-adabiyat-i-Delli.

Parliamentary Papers (1858-59), *East India Affairs: Mutiny. East India* (*King of Delhi*), Return to an order of the Honourable The House of Commons dated 24 March 1858: A copy of the evidence taken before the Court appointed for the trial of the King of Delhi.

Platts, J. (1911), *A Dictionary of Urdu, Classical Hindi and English*, London, Crosby and Lockwood and Sons.

S.S. (1976), 'A Neglected Treasure', *Sunday Standard*, January 11, 1976.

Turner, V. (1974), *The Ritual Process: Structure and Anti-Structure*, Harmondsworth (England), Penguin Books.

7

Mira Datar Dargah: The Psychiatry of a Muslim Shrine

Beatrix Pfleiderer

Muslim shrines in northern India are an aspect of Sufism. Sufism was brought to India from the north in the eleventh century. Shaikh Moinuddin Chishti established himself around 1219 AD at Ajmer (Shah, 1977:106), probably a little after the decisive battle between Shihabuddin Ghori and Prithvi Raj (Mujeeb, 1967:116). He was one of the important spiritual leaders in the twelfth century (Mujeeb, 1967:116). His tomb at Ajmer, which became famous under the rule of Akbar (1556-1605) (Rashid, 1978:112), is still one of the major attractions for pilgrims in northern India.

By the thirteenth century, Sufism had become a movement which consisted of the following basic elements:

1. The routine of prayers;
2. the institution of Shaikh or Pir (master, saintly person);
3. and his disciple (*murid*); and
4. the community life of the *khanqah* (monastery) (Mujeeb, 1967:117).

A Shaikh (or Sufi) was expected to exhibit the following characteristics:

1. He must be of spiritual eminence;

2. he must have high ethical standards;
3. he must be able to resist his desires;
4. he must be able to instruct the *murids*;
5. he is supposed to be a *wali* (protector, benefactor, companion, friend); and
6. he should have *karamah* (supernatural power, which gives him knowledge without study, which enables him to see waking what people see in dreams, and the power of prediction).

Karamah enables a saint to perform miracles and to generally exhibit the same powers as supernaturals. We have to keep this in mind since this power is not lost at the saint's death, but is retained and later attributed to his tomb in the *dargah*. *Karamah* is also used to legitimize the saint's authority. But legitimation of saintliness is also achieved by tracing one's descent to Ali, the son-in-law of the prophet.

The typical tasks of the saints were to oversee their *murids*' spiritual education. In addition, they had to receive a large number of people who came to have, say, an ailment cured or a wish fulfilled. It was at this time that saints started to write *ta'widhs* for this purpose (Mujeeb, 1967:126).[1]

In the beginning the Sufi-saints did not feel that they needed to settle down at a particular place in order to perform their functions, nor did they agree about the form they should give to their public life if they did settle down. But the advantages of working over a long period in a particular community were obvious. The *khanqah* or *dargah* thus became an institution among those Sufis who belonged to an order. As an institution it lasted longer than the lives of its founders and individual inmates, and was liable to develop characteristics that did not harmonize with the principles and ideals for the service of which it was founded. It must therefore be judged by itself (Mujeeb, 1967:147).

As the *khanqahs* developed they experienced certain experimental forms of community living. When they eventually

[1] Writing *ta'widhs* is a very common practice among traditional healers (*faqir*) of the non-academic variety of Unan imedicine.

received more permanent forms, they started expanding as well. Mujeeb writes :

> It could be said generally of every *khanqah* that even in the bad days a person who waited long enough was sure to get some sort of meal and, with luck, a share of money or goods distributed as charity that would take him over the next crisis. It was the shaikh and those dedicated to the spiritual who starved; inmates of the *khanqah* got what they wanted, sometimes less than was sufficient, sometimes in abundance. The small group that collected round Shaikh Nizamuddin at Delhi began with courses in starvation, but gradually the physical conditions improved. The shaikh continued his practice of 'concealed' starvation to the end of his days; his chief *murids* did the same. But food and charitable gifts became an attraction of his *khanqah* as of every other. In every *khanqah* ideals of austerity fought against satisfaction of physical needs. . . . A feature of *khanqah* life which is by no means admirable is the opportunity it provided to large numbers of people to live on generosity of well-to-do admirers of the shaikh, and thus introduce into the *khanqah* the odour of parasitism (Mujeeb, 1967:147ff).

So the *khanqahs* might be said to have served as a mediating institution between the Shaikh and his saintly qualities on the one hand and the masses on the other. Via a *khanqah*, a saint could definitely reach many more persons than he could have reached otherwise. Other functions of the *khanqah* included the distribution of money, food and goods. The goods might have been donations made by a near-by worldly ruler and were distributed among needy pilgrims and the poor people of the neighbourhood.

Apart from spiritual guidance and distribution of food to the destitutes, a *khanqah* or *dargah* had several other functions to fulfil. Being handed over to a Khalifah after the Pir's death, the main task of the successors is to cherish the memory of the dead saint, to observe the proper rites at his tomb and to guide pilgrims and visitors to the tomb in order to receive the saintly blessings of the dead Pir via mediation by his successors. It was important for the successors of a Pir to legitimate their alleged (or constructed) closeness to the saint as soon as possible after his death. This was done by stressing blood ties either with the saint himself or with his nominated successors (Khalifahs). In most shrines there was constant quarreling on this matter (see also Jeffery's paper in this volume).

The attraction of a Muslim shrine is defined by the supernatural power of the saint's (Pir) spirit, who is buried in the tomb inside the *dargah*. This power is recognized by both Hindus and Muslims as well as other communities like Christians and Parsis. The holiness inside the *dargah* increases as one comes closer to the tomb. This question will be relevant in the discussion of our own shrine. In most shrines women are not admitted into the interior of the tomb. They have to perform prayers, burn incense and make offerings outside the walls of the inner sanctum. The tomb, which is in most cases built of white marble and situated in a domed marble hall, is surrounded by a large courtyard covered with marble stones. This is the place where public rituals are performed. Most shrines consist of several tombs, where those who were related to the saint by blood ties or by marriage are buried. The courtyard is surrounded by the pilgrims' quarters and those of the permanent inmates. The mosque is situated on one side. In most shrines a Unani dispensary is located close to the main entrance. The main functions of the *dargahs* can be subsumed under the following headings:

1. Social Functions

Depending on the popularity and power of the venerated Pir, the number of daily visitors may vary from 50 to 100 per day and up to many thousands during Moharram and the annual *urs* when fairs are held (*Times of India*, January 11, 1979). This is especially true for famous shrines like Ajmer, where thousands of Muslims from all over India come to attend the fairs. Lesser known shrines may have only some twenty visitors on a routine day and several thousands during the fair. The fairs held at the *dargahs* serve as social events for the surrounding rural and urban population. The annual *urs* celebration is an occasion for amusement of all sorts for devotees and vistiors. Thousands of '. . . pilgrims are entertained by games, merry-go-rounds, music and plenty of food. In Sakhi Sarwar the Baluchis used to meet, to sing and dance and enjoy horse races' (Schwerin, 1978:2). Furthermore, when the social well-being of a family is endangered or disturbed, they might decide to go to a *dargah* in order to re-establish equanimity under the guidance of one of the *mujawars* (assistants), who mediates the blessings of the Pir. The poor, the destitute, and the socially isolated people of the community might find the *dargah* a proper place to stay in, in order to adjust to their social handicap. Also, couples who are afflicted with the problem of childlessness may bring a red thread, have it blessed by the *mujawar* who is looking after them, and have it tied to the secluding wall of the tomb. Also, people in debt might seek the blessings of the Pir.

2. Entertainment

Some *dargahs* maintain public kitchens which distribute free food (*langar*) to the poor and to travellers. The *langar* is also an essential feature of the annual *urs* celebration. The duration of the service and the amount of food cooked depends upon the amount of money donated by individuals for this particular purpose (Schwerin, 1978:2). For example, in the Dargah Khawaja Saheb at Ajmer there are two big *deghs* (cauldrons) in which food is cooked whenever some visitor to the *dargah* volunteers to pay the cost (Rashid, 1978:122). Although this kind of mass cooking is mainly an affair of the pilgrims, it has yet some side benefits for the local community: 'All the men who take part in the "looting the deg" are swathed up to the eyes in clothes to avoid the effect of the scalding mess. When the cauldron is nearly empty, the Inderkotis (a local sect) tumble in together and scratch it clean . . .' (Rashid, 1978:122).

Most of the *dargahs* provide their visitors with *qawwali* singing every Thursday night. A group of musicians sings of the life and death of the Pir as also more popular songs of the Sufi-tradition. The *qawwali* singers are either rewarded with food or by contributions from the audience, usually one rupee notes placed upon the steps of the *dargah* or presented through an intermediary to the leader of the group (Schwerin, 1978:2).

3. *Education*

Education is another function of most of the *dargahs*. Koranic schools are attached to *dargahs* where Koran reciting and reading and the writing of Urdu texts is taught, especially to children of the neighbourhood (Schwerin, 1978:2).

4. *Redistribution of goods*

We have already mentioned in this context the public cooking which may be financed by a single visitor and distributed to all the visitors for free. Further redistribution takes place during market days: 'During the annual *urs* celebration administrators of the *dargahs* rent out land around the *dargah* to tradesmen for fixed rates per square meter' (Schwerin, 1978:2). It is during this occasion that the administrators (or *mujawars*) also collect those contributions that guarantee the regular functioning of the *dargah* as well as the income of its servants. While the smaller sums (*nazar*) are deposited in front of an attending *mujawar*, the bigger donations in notes are placed directly on the tomb of the Pir. Some *dargahs* stick to the old custom and distribute these presents immediately to the needy who are always present. Other *dargahs* that need to plan a budget keep it (Schwerin, 1978:2).

In most shrines, long feuds have been going on over the distribution of wealth among the *mujawars*. In some cases, considerable misuse has developed (see Jeffery's paper in this volume). By misuse we mean that *mujawars* pocket the devotees' contributions instead of giving them away for charitable purposes which is what they are meant for. A series of waqf laws were framed during British rule to prevent extensive misuse of donations.[2] A further redistributive mechanism is the renting

[2] The problems and the ritual consequences of the economic position of the 'full-time' *mujawars* is discussed in P. Jeffery's paper in this volume. For further information on the administration and economy of *dargahs*, see Rashid (1978: 111-26).

of lands belonging to the waqf[3] to local peasants or shopowners. Another redistributive aspect of *dargahs* is begging on *dargah* premises. Since the accumulation of beggars suffering from infectious diseases was prohibited in the *dargah* of Ajmer in 1958[4] because of the danger of infection, a Committee of Enquiry[5] suggested: 'Begging within the dargah premises shall be strictly prohibited. Beggars suffering from any infectious disease shall be ejected from the dargah premises . . . (others) shall be kept and maintained in a home specially provided for them' (Rashid, 1978:124). A last redistributive aspect to be mentioned here is the providing of accommodation to large numbers of pilgrims. This task is partially met on the *dargah* premises itself.

5. *Religious guidance and healing*

Dargahs are centres of pilgrimage whose reputation spreads far beyond their local community. Though they serve as nighbourhood and regional centres in the four functions mentioned above, their main function and attraction is, however, to meet the religious and psychic needs of pilgrims. This function of the *dargah* not only attracts simple people, but people of all social classes of both the Hindu and Muslim communities.

Pilgrims are normally looking for one or other of the following:

1. Social well-being;
2. psychic well-being;
3. physical well-being;
4. guidance and counsel for social problems;
5. appeasement in cases of psychic problems; and
6. healing of psychiatrically recognized illnesses.

Pirs are known for their special powers and abilities. In accordance with their special reputation, they attract 'cases' from all over the country. Information concerning the special

[3] Taxfree donation for charitable or communal use.

[4] Vide By-law of the Dargah Khwaja Sahib By-laws, 1978. For details, see Rashid, 1978:124.

[5] In 1949, the Central Government constituted a Committee of Enquiry to examine the affairs of the Ajmer Dargah (see Rashid, 1978:129)

'skills' of a particular saint seems to spread among pilgrims by word of mouth. As mentioned earlier, during a saint's lifetime the special power of *karamah* was attributed to him (in the case of martyrs, their special power is derived from the circumstances of their death). During the saint's lifetime people would come for blessings *and* for the cure of their ailments, which was done by issuing *ta'widhs*. The *mujawars* of today fulfil the same needs by mediating the power of the Pir. In this manner they meet the requirements of their clients/visitors. They guide them to the tomb, assist their offerings and prayers, issue blessings on written *ta'widhs*, which the pilgrim may take home and have eventually re-issued and sent by mail by his particular *mujawar*. When a pilgrim gets down at the railway station or when he enters the *dargah*, several *mujawars* offer their services. If he has no special recommendation for a particular *mujawar*, he may choose any one of them. In most cases, he has little choice, since the *mujawars* are quite competitive and more or less force a visitor to accept their service. The *mujawar* then enquires about the visitor's problem or mission and suggests the appropriate procedure. The first four problems as enumerated above can be tackled in most *dargahs*. If, however, the visitor/patient complains of a psychic disturbance which is recognized as a psychiatric illness (the last two types of problems), he is sent to the Mira Datar Dargah. This *dargah* has a widely recognized reputation among Muslims for the successful treatment of psychiatric illnesses (see India, 1975:240). Since Ajmer occupies a pre-eminent position among Muslims in India, most of the psychiatric cases go first to this shrine. There they receive a *huqm* in a dream or by the guiding *mujawar*. This message, which is issued by an authority like the Pir or his *mujawar*, is a recommendation which the patient must follow. In fact, most of the patients we saw at Unava[6] had come from Ajmer, where they had received

[6] The psychiatric diagnoses at the Mira Datar Dargah were administered by Dr. A. Degen, Psychiatrische Klinik der Universitaet Heidelberg, during our joint fieldwork in September 1977. The results of our ethnopsychiatric study will be published elsewhere. The fieldwork on which this paper is based took place in March 1977, December 1978 and January 1979 and included visits to the *dargahs* at Ajmer and Delhi.

this *huqm*. The rituals which these patients have to undergo and the mechanism of their therapy will be discussed later in this paper.

6. *Medical care*

As pointed out above, psychiatric illnesses and social and psychic troubles or diseases are taken care of by the *mujawars* who mediate the power of the Pir. Physical illnesses, however, are transferred to a medical institution or to the Unani dispensary which is attached to most of the bigger *dargahs*. A *mujawar* might take certain steps like writing a *ta'widh* against a physical disease, but he does not get involved in treatment or diagnosis. In the dispensary, Unani doctors or healers[7] diagnose the patient according to the principles of Unani medicine, which is based on the ancient Greek theory of humours. In the Unani dispensary at Nizamuddin, diagnoses are based on an examination of colour of the thumbnails, which is supposed to give evidence of the balance of the humours. The appropriate medicine is concocted accordingly. Some Muslim healers, who are not connected to *dargahs*, write *ta'widhs* and give medicine. Concerning medical care we find the following division of labour within the *dargah*: in the Unani dispensary only physical diseases are taken care of; the *mujawars*, however, deal only with psychiatric and sociogenic diseases.

Mira Datar Dargah

The Mira Datar Dargha belongs to that category of Muslim shrines which derive their power and fame from a martyr who died for the Islamic cause. Mira Datar is said to have been a saint who became a martyr in a Muslim-Rajput war in the fifteenth century. The sanctuary which was built around his tomb is

[7] The difference between doctors and healers in Unani and Ayurvedic medicine is basically a difference of education. Whereas doctors passed through medical schools, healers might learn their 'skill' with a 'guru' and depend mainly on their 'charisma' and 'talent' (see Pfleiderer-Becker, 1978).

situated at Unava, about hundred kilometres north of Ahmedabad, near the district town of Mehsana. It belongs to the bigger variety of *dargahs* based on the number of pilgrims who visit it. Strangely enough, while it has an enormously widespread reputation among pilgrims, there is hardly any reference to it in the literature. Its reputation seems to have spread by word of mouth only.

The little bit of evidence available on the saint's lifetime is a footnote in an account of 'saints who settled and died in the towns and villages of the provinces of Ahmedabad' where mention is made of the 'striking omission' of a 'Sayed Ali known as Miran Datar, whose tomb at Unava Mehsana is visited by many thousands of pilgrims (Nawali and Seddon, 1928:75). His grandfather Sayed Ilm-ud-din came from Unchh [8] and settled at Ahmedabad in 830 AH (=1427AD). Sayed Ali's father was Dosan Miyan who married into the family of Sham-i-Burhani and settled at Unava in 867 AH' (=1463AD) (Nawali and Seddon, 1928:91.) In the legend which will be cited below, S. Ilm-ud-din is said to have been commander-in-chief under Ahmad I (founder of Ahmedabad) who reigned from 1411 to 1442 AD (814-846 AH). According to the above-mentioned evidence, however, he settled at Unava only in 867 AH (=1463AD). Other evidence seems to connect Mira Datar's life and death to Muzzafar II's attack on Mandu on Safar 2, 924 AH (=23 February 1518 AD), when 19,000 Rajputs are said to have died during the conquest (Commissariat, 1938:126).

The facts about Mira Datar's life and death seem to be shrouded in darkness, but we need not concern ourselves with this aspect. The *dargah*, which is situated on the Ahmedabad-Abu Road, is very similar to other sanctuaries of its kind. On both sides of the passage to the main entrance we find the usual line of flower shops, gift shops, tea stalls and wayside 'restaurants' for pilgrims and visitors (see Map below). Competing voices catch the visitor's ear as he approaches the main door. The shops are located even inside the *dargah*, most of them selling cheap jewellery and souvenirs. The tomb itself is situated in the centre of a fairly large courtyard which is surrounded—and

[8] In this fact the legends coincide.

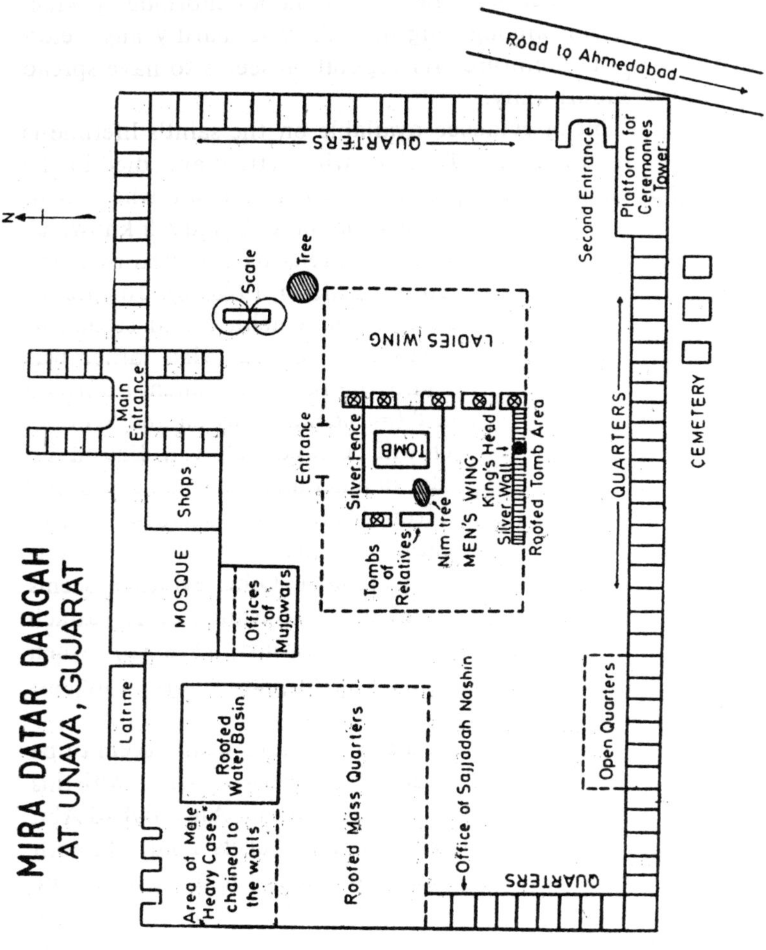
MIRA DATAR DARGAH
AT UNAVA, GUJARAT
N
Road to Ahmedabad
QUARTERS
Second Entrance
Platform for Ceremonies Tower
Scale
Tree
LADIES WING
Main Entrance
Entrance
Silver Fence
TOMB
King's Head
Silver Wall
Roofed Tomb Area
MEN'S WING
Nim tree
Tombs of Relatives
Shops
MOSQUE
Offices of Mujawars
QUARTERS
CEMETERY
Open Quarters
Office of Sajjadah Nashin
Latrine
Roofed Water Basin
Roofed Mass Quarters
Area of Male "Heavy Cases" chained to the walls
QUARTERS

at the same time secluded from the outer world—by accommodation for the pilgrims. There are about fifty cell-like rooms inside the *dargah*. Outside the *dargah* several *ashram*-like facilities are available for (long-term) visitors, patients and pilgrims. The tomb is secluded from the courtyard by a fenced, roofed area. Inside it is again secluded by a silver-fenced marble wall and a textile-clad roof. The tomb's cell is very small and cannot compare in size with *dargahs* like Ajmer. The roofed area around the tomb is divided into a women's and a men's wing, the latter being on the holy, Mecca-oriented side. The *dargah* has no facilities for public mass cooking as we find in Ajmer, nor is there an Unani dispensary or a Koranic school. Moreover, there is no *qawwali* singing on Thursday nights. The *dargah's* courtyard only provides for the needs of the pilgrims/patients who need to stay there for a longer time. Besides, the secluded cell-like quarters also serve as mass quarters for the poorer patients. Several *mujawars*' offices and the *sajjadanashin's* office are in the north-west corner of the *dargah*, with the washbasin situated next to them. Behind the washbasin and in the very north-west corner of the courtyard, aggressive and virulent male patients, mostly newcomers, are chained to iron rings, which protrude from the secluding wall.

So much for the physical setting of the Mira Datar Dargah. Of the six usual functions of Muslim *dargahs* described above, only one is represented here; namely religious guidance and healing in cases of social and psychic disorders, psychic disturbances and psychiatric diseases. The other functions of a *dargah* may have been dropped after some time or may never have developed at all. This specialization is, of course, reflected in the physical setting of the shrine and in its daily routine. The *dargah* is by no means a resort only for the poor, and is also visited by people who, from a financial point of view, could easily afford western treatment.

Legend

The *dargah* is run by the descendants of Mira Datar's father, Dosan Miyan. The descendants employ several methods to prove the legitimacy of their right to the management and income of the shrine. For this reason, they also try to prove their legitimate position in mediating and administering the pir's supernatural power. The first method is the legend, which we are given by the *mujawars* and by the *Sajjadanashin* in several, differing versions.[9] Since the family of Mira Sayed Ali Datar traces its descent back to Ali, the prophet's son-in-law, they are entitled to use 'Sayed' before their name.

Version I

During the reign of Muzzafar Shah of Gujarat and Prithvi Raj of Mewa (1473-1508), Mira Datar' father, Sayed Muhammad, was commander-in-chief in Ahmedabad. After a series of reverses in the Sultan of Ahmedabad's attempts to subdue attacking Rajput rulers from Mandu, astrologers predicted that the youngest son of Sayed Muhammad, sixteen years old Sayed Mira Ali at Unava, would be able to bring victory. So the Sultan called Muhammad and asked him whether he could ask his son for help, since he appeared to be the only one who would be able to win the battle against the rulers from Mandu. At this time, however, Mira Sayed Ali's marriage was being arranged. He received the message three days before the date fixed for his marriage. His mother received the letter and decided to withhold it until the wedding was over. When his father learned that he had not received the letter, he sent a messenger and instructed him to go directly to his son. Mira Sayed Ali received the letter while cleaning his teeth with a twig from the *nim* tree. He dropped the twig, which grew into a tree under which his tomb is now situated. He followed the call of Islam, left for Ahmedabad to lead the army against Mandu and won the battle. Mira Sayed Ali pursued the fleeing king of Mandu and, when he found him, he asked him whether he was prepared to surrender to Islam or ready for the fight. Thereupon

[9] The legends were recorded in March and September-October, 1977, and again two years later in January 1979. The first two versions were directly translated by V. Dharamsey in March 1977. Version 3 is a literally transcribed version of the Urdu text. It was recorded in January, 1979. N. Chopra transcribed and translated the text. The contents of these versions are basically the same but a few deviations are of interest.

the king beheaded Mira Sayed Ali, whose body continued to fight until the king was slain. That night he appeared to his father in a dream and told him that he had become a martyr. He asked to be buried at Unava beside the *nim* tree which is still to be seen there. The head of the king, he said, should be buried at his feet close to his tomb, so that every visitor would have to stand on the king's head.

Version 2

There was constant war between the kings of Gujarat and the Mandu kings. (The 'Islamic cause' is not stressed in this version). Councillors told the king of Gujarat that there was only one man who could help him to win the fort of Mandu, and this was the son of his commander-in-chief, who lived in a nearby village. A messenger came to the village asking who Mira Sayed Ali was. Mira Sayed Ali, while cleaning his teeth with a *nim* tree twig, said it was him. He opened the letter which the messenger had brought with him and saw at once that he would never return. He dug a hole and buried the twig and said: 'This twig will become a tree when I am killed in the battle' (his mother is not mentioned in this version). Mira Sayed Ali went directly to Mandu. Upon his arrival a powerful storm arose. The king of Mandu, who was frightened of the storm, saw a lamp burning in one of the Gujarati tents. He sent his spies out who reported that it was the tent of Mira Sayed Ali, where a lamp was burning unaffected. The king realized that a miraculous power had arrived. He decided to surrender and sent his messengers to the enemy's camp to convey the news that the fort would be surrendered the next morning in order to avoid unnecessary bloodshed. When Mira Sayed Ali entered the fort early next morning, he found that the king had escaped by a secret path. Mira Sayed Ali followed him and caught up with him after a few miles. The king said that he was prepared to fight to regain his kingdom, but for the time being he would be without a kingdom. So both decided to fight and succeeded in beheading each other. As they lay dying, the king said: 'You are a great saint, wherever you are buried, please bury my hair close to your feet'.[10] When his son did not return, Mira Sayed Ali's father started looking for him. Palace officials showed him the way that the two had left and they found the two bodies. The king was buried in the royal tomb. Mira Datar's body was to be taken to Ahmedabad. When they came through Unava, the camel which was carrying the body would not move on; and in this way they recognized Mira Datar's last will, which was to be buried under his *nim* tree. During all this Mira Datar's hand had remained tightly closed. His father addressed him and asked him to open his hand; and they found the king's hair in his hand. In the night Mira Datar appeared to his father in a dream and told him: 'This hair of the king's head should be buried close to my feet. Whoever comes to my tomb shall have his wishes fulfilled and his *illnesses cured.*'

Version 3

This, the last and longest version, was given by the *Sajjadanashin*, Sayed Mohammadhusun Valimiya. At present, he has the highest position in the shrine's hierarchy, which means that he is in charge of all important documentation.

'Mira Sayed Ali Datar used to stay in Unava village. When he was six months old his father, Dosan Miyan, left the house and roamed from village to village and it was from there that the king gave him the palanquin in which he brought his new (second) wife to the village. Mira Sayed Ali's mother, however, became annoyed that he had taken a second wife and so she left the place. The newly married young girl, who was about seventeen or eighteen years old, took Mira Sayed Ali Datar in her lap and was miraculously able to feed him on her own

[10] Here the question of the king's surrender to Islam is omitted and only the supernatural power of the saint is emphasized. This version is kept ready for non-Muslim clients.

milk. She then nursed Mira Sayed Ali Datar. This is the first important part of the history.

'Mira Sayed Ali Datar's father had become Commander-in-Chief of king Ahmed Shah's army. Ahmed Shah[11] could not manage to conquer Mandu (1420 and 1422); he was told by someone that Mandu could be conquered only through the hands of Mira Sayed Ali Datar, the son of Dosan Miyan, and asked him whether Mira Sayed Ali Datar was his son. He said "yes" and told that at present he was in the village Unava and was now seventeen years old. After that the father wrote letters on behalf of the king to his family in the village. His wife and wife's brother had in the meantime fixed the date of Mira Sayed Ali Datar's marriage and so they also had written a letter to Dosan Miyan in this matter. When Mira Sayed Ali Datar read his father's letter, he said that if his going to Mandu could save the lives of thousands of Muslims who would otherwise die in the battlefield, he would go and do this good work. So he left his village for Mandu. It was summertime when he left.

'There Mira Sayed Ali Datar was camping and while he was reading the Koran after the evening *namaz* (prayer) a storm all of a sudden came in the sky and houses and bushes started to fly. The king of Mandu wondered how all this was happening and said there was some mystery behind it; he sent his secret agents to investigate as to what the matter was in the enemy's camp. This was at evening time. They reported that an earthen lamp was burning in one of the tents and inside was a boy who was reading the Koran, and bushes and everything were flying. The king said that this is a miracle and so he will not fight. In the morning the doors of Mandu were opened and Mira Sayed Ali Datar was offered the kingdom. When Mira Sayed Ali Datar came back inside the village where their camp was located, he told his army that they should not fight or commit any excesses, and should treat everyone with love. Then he reached the palace and asked the wives of the king and the women as to where the king was; he was told that the king had already left through a secret passage. Then Mira Sayed Ali Datar also went through the secret passage and on meeting the king in a

[11] This is obviously Ahmad I, who reigned from 1422 to 1445 (see Haig, 1965:300 & 710).

cave he told him that he did not want his kingdom, only that he should surrender. . . . .

'Then the king said that he had given the kingdom of his own will and would therefore not take it back. "If want the kingdom you will have to fight with me", the king said, "only then I will give you the kingdom." Mira Sayed Ali Datar said that he was willing to do as the king wished. The king, however, did not have any sword. In those days a brave man usually carried two swords. So Mira Sayed Ali Datar gave one of his swords to the king. The king took the sword and at once cut off Mira Sayed Ali Datar's head. Mira Sayed Ali Datar was, however, a saint by birth, so when his head fell to the ground, it said smiling : "You have deceived me." Whereupon the king replied, "Whatever God wanted, I have done." After this, Mira Sayed Ali Datar's body cut off the king's head and his corpse fell to the ground. Where the saint's head fell heavenly flowers covered the cave. When Mira Datar's father came to find out about his son's whereabouts after meditation, he was told that the king had gone towards the cave. Mandu cave is famous even today. The father went there, meditated and saw that Mira Datar had died; he then brought his body here and then wrote to the king about the recent events and that victory had been achieved and that they were taking the body of Hazrat Mira Sayed Ali Datar and they brought the body here to Unava village. So the body said, "bury me here with my living miracle, under the tree. I have planted, 'a *miswak* bush'. And you will see that bush will be evergreen. And anyone who does not have children will have them. And people with all types of incurable diseases (which hakims and doctors cannot cure), will be cured by rubbing it on the affected part." He was then buried there and till now the bush is evergreen. Those people who cannot have children must take the fruit from here and they will have children.'

The Family

The second item of legitimation is the genealogy of the family, which is kept in the office of the *Sajjadnashin*, Sayed Mohammadhusun Valimiya. It is written in Arabic script (not Urdu) and gives the full names of all male descendants of Sayed Dosan Miyan. All living *mujawars* who are connected to the shrine or who claim connection to the shrine have to be listed in this genealogy. We could not find evidence of the origins of the genealogical tree. Sayed Ilm-ud-din, who came from Unchh to Ahmedadad, must have brought a list of ancestors with him. We find their names on top of the genealogical tree, without being systematically included. The tree itself starts with Sayed Dosan (Dosu) Miyan, who settled at Unava at 867 AH (=1463 AD) and who was Mira Datar's father. Mira Datar's date of birth is given in the genealogy as 879 AH (=1474 AD) and the date of his death as 898 AH (=1492 AD).[12]

The names at the top of the genealogy are preceded by 'Hazrat' and later change to 'Sayed' in the seventh generation of the genealogy:

1. Hazrat Abdul Mutalib
2. ,, Hasan Abu Talib
3. ,, Amir-ul Muaminin Ali
4. ,, Imam Hasan
5. ,, Imam Sainullabadin
6. ,, Jafir Jalilullah
7. Sayed Idris
8. ,, Al Kazim 'ulad Kawanin Gunind
9. ,, Abdul Rahman 'ulad
10. ,, Dastar Rabur Muwajar Gunind
11. ,, Al Mutazar
12. ,, Doyad
13. ,, Al Fasl
14. ,, Arshad
15. ,, Ali Baki
16. ,, Aljabin
17. ,, Ali
18. ,, Muhammad Kazim dar Mashahid Arabiya
19. ,, Safrul Kazim Muhammad
20. ,, Muhammad

[12] Since the dates of birth and death of Mira Sayed Ali Datar diverge in genealogy and legend, we felt we should not try to enquire about his historic lifetime.

21. Sayed Hasan
22. ,, Jafir
23. ,, Abdullah
24. ,, Ibrahim
25. ,, Shahkuddin milkat-ul Unava
26. Ilm-ud-din Hamid (settled 830 AH at Ahmedabad).

The last name in the list is, as we have seen, that of Mira Datar's grandfather. The genealogy proper starts with the name of Mira Datar's father, Sayed Muhammad Urf Dosu, who is said to have settled at Unava in 867 AH. The family is of course widespread by now and only a small proportion is still living at the village of Unava.

The physical connection of the family to the holiness of the *dargah* is further represented by the presence of ten family graves around the saint's tomb, all of them belonging to close family members. The closest one is that of Dosan Miyan, the father. The second closest grave is that of Ilm-ud-din the grandfather. The third grave—by degree of closeness—is Bura, his brother's second son. The fourth grave, which is actually closer than the other three but separated by a little gangway, is his older brother Abu Muhammad's tomb. The fifth grave is that of his stepmother who—according to the legend (version 3)—had nursed him at an early age. (His real mother's grave is situated some kilometres away from the *dargah*; obviously she did not deserve a tomb in the holy area). The sixth 'pseudo'-grave is the marked place where the *nim* twig is buried; the trunk of the tree is still there. The seventh tomb is the older brother's wife's grave, and lies among the group of graves which are about four metres away from the saint's tomb. Also in this group we find the graves of Murtaza and Usman, his nephews, and Fatma, a niece, who, being a female descendant, cannot appear in the genealogical tree.

This legitimation conferred by the proximity of family tombs is also found at Ramdeora *dargah* where Ramdeo Pir is venerated. The Mira Datar Dargah cannot compare with Ajmer and Nizamuddin in this respect, since there disciples also share the saint's burial ground. The only non-relative who is buried in the Mira Datar Dargah is the Mandu king. This will be relevant in the discussion of the therapeutic ritual, where closeness as opposed to distance plays an important role.

The proximity of the tombs of family members to the holy tomb is another means by which descendants reinforce their claim to sole representation and mediation of the saint's supernatural power.

Administration

This section will show how defined holiness may be exploited economically. The genealogy and the grave sites provide the bases for claims to an inherited right to share the *dargah's* income and the saint's supernatural power or for the life of a 'full-time' *mujawar*. Obviously, the complicated mechanisms of proving closeness to the saint serve mainly an economic purpose: a small group specializes in selling healing powers in order to make a living out of it. There are several sources of income:

(*i*) the *golakh*, a medium-sized metal donation box which is situated close to the entrance to the tomb in most *dargahs* receives the official contribution of the visitors to the *dargah*. This contribution is not easily accessible to the *mujawars* as will be shown below.

(*ii*) the *dargah* in Unava owns about one hundred small rooms which are situated inside and outside the *dargah* premises. For the rooms inside the *dargah*, pilgrims are charged Rs. 45.00 per month; for those outside Rs. 35.00. This rent belongs to the *mujawars*; it has to be shared among them, after a deduction of five per cent which goes to the *dargah's* reserve fund. Gifts like gold and diamonds cannot be accepted by the *mujawars*; they have to be sold, invested in stocks and finally they have to go into the shrine's reserve fund. The number of family members has reached almost five hundred by now; they belong to almost seventy families headed by nine lineage patriarchs.[13] All nine family members are also included in the Trust Committee discussed below. It seems that the persons really involved in the *dargah* are less than fifty (we were given the

[13] Except one, all the lineage heads were shown on the genealogical tree of Mira Datar.

number as 25-30). Also we were given a number of names of family members working outside the *dargah* as teachers, lawyers or perhaps simply as clerks and agriculturalists (Mohammadhusun's brother Iqbal is, for example, a Lecturer in Persian in a college in Surat). These persons are unlikely to fight over an irregular and small income which they could claim as a birthright. But there are still a fairly large number of 'full-time' *mujawars* who have to compete for their share.

There are a few activities which enable them to avoid the *dargah* economy:

(*i*) In case they attend personally on pilgrims/patients they are paid directly by their clients. They are allowed to charge Rs. 2.50 for each ritual they administer.

(*ii*) Visitors to the tomb have to be 'guided'[14] by a *mujawar*. They normally place flowers and money on the tomb. This money may be collected by the attending *mujawar*.

(*iii*) When a patient regards himself as cured, he puts goods, in most cases sugar and coconut equivalent to his weight, on the scale in the courtyard. Fifty per cent of these goods go to the *dargah* directly, the other half may be given to the attending *mujawar* or it may be given to the poor people in the shrine. It seems that the personality of the particular *mujawar* plays an important role in this context.

(*iv*) The *mujawars* may 'transfer' the power of the tomb to some other site. For this purpose they purchase small earthen lamps from local potters. They keep these lamps close to the tomb over several nights. An unlit lamp is then given to the visitor who wants to 'start' a minor holy site of his own, probably in his home. The lamp, when lit, is supposed to exude the power of the tomb. For each cure that the lamp is supposed to have effected, the *mujawar* who 'transferred' the power to the lamp receives a small amount of money.

(*v*) A similar procedure is applied when a new shrine is to be established in the name of Mira Datar. In this case a brick is kept on the tomb for seven days while the *mujawars* pray

[14] S. Mohammadhusun Valimiya, *Sajjadanashin* and present chairman of the Trust Committee, told us that he considers himself as a 'guide' to the spiritual powers of Mira Datar. He used the English term for this purpose.

continuously. This brick is then used for the foundation of a new shrine. The Mira Datar Chillah at Bombay (a branch of the shrine at Unava) was founded with such a brick from Unava. When the new shrine has achieved the status of a trust, it becomes economically independent and is no longer liable to pay for each cure to the *mujawar* at the original shrine. This custom has, however, been given up recently.

(*vi*) The *mujawar* may give or send *ta'widhs* to his pilgrims/patients, by using the water from the *dargah's* well, which is situated inside the shrine. The water, which is pumped to the surface by an electric pump, is mixed with tub water and put into a tank. The *mujawar* writes a *ta'widh* and carries the water three, five or seven times around the tomb. Then he puts the *ta'widh* into the water for a short while. After this the *ta'widh* is supposed to have the healing power of the tomb and may be given away. The *mujawar* receives personal payment for a *ta'widh*.

Assuming the number of visitors at twenty to forty persons daily, hundred to hundred and fifty on Thursday nights, and fifteen thousand to sixty thousand persons[15] for the annual *urs*, there should be a sufficient and constant income available for the *mujawar* working in the *dargah*.

What remains is the problem of sharing the income. Originally the shrine was the private property of the Valimiya family. They argued that Mira Datar gave his life for a pious cause and that their ancestor, Dosan Miyan, buried his body at Unava and that due to his saintly nature the tomb started attracting people in the course of the previous few centuries. Since this saint was a member of the family, they considered themselves to possess a certain right to be the proprietors of the beneficiary effects of the tomb. However, the government thought otherwise. When the accumulation of wealth became too obvious towards the end of last century (the *dargah's* income had been used mainly to increase the property of the institution), the *mujawars* were told that, since the tomb was an

[15] *The Gazetteer of India* (India, 1975) gives the number as 15,000, which might be outdated. The *mujawars* indicated that they had 60,000 visitors during the *urs*. The truth might be somewhere in the middle. The *Gazetteer* is also not correct in mentioning only Muslim visitors.

attraction not only for Muslims but for members of all religions, it should be considered a religious institution of public interest and no longer as private property. Therefore, under the pretext of misuse and mismanagement, the Baroda District Government pleaded in 1889[16] that the *dargah* be declared a religious institution under the Religious Endowment Act of 1863 (see Rashid, 1978:vii and 128).

The state government won the case and promptly attached all private property to the shrine. In 1892 the *mujawars* claimed their right to the private properties of the *dargah*, which was granted to them in 1904. In 1908 superintendance was withdrawn in favour of the *mujawars*,[17] who carried on managing the *dargah* until 1944, when the *dargah* was declared Waqf. A series of civil suits were initiated by the *mujawars* (1945-46, 1947-48), who were still fighting to regain control of the *dargah* as a private property. In 1948 it was decided that the Waqf officials had rules and regulations sanctioned by the state government, whereupon a managing committee was appointed to run the institution. Again the *mujawars* rebelled. In 1949 they again lost their case in the Bombay High Court and had to accept the *dargah* as being a public, charitable, religious institution. In 1953 the Bombay High Court handed down a judgement which was analogous to the scheme framed in 1889. Finally, in 1958, after several more civil law suits, the Mira Datar Dargah was constituted as a Public Trust. This was not so bad for the *mujawars* as they were granted the permanent and hereditary right of management, and a right to a share in the balance of the income after meeting all the legitimate and customary charges and expenses of the *dargah*. In 1960, however, they were forced to give up the share in the surplus of the *dargah's* income, since it was no longer private property. In a revision of 1968, the present form of administration was decided upon. The *dargah* is now managed by a Trust Committee of nine *mujawars* and two *non-mujawars*, who are non-Muslims. The non-*mujawars* are not entitled to share the surplus of the shrine's income. Their function is to protect the devotees' rights.

[16] S. Mohammadhusun generously allowed us access to all the documents concerning the property rights of his family to the *dargah*.

[17] See Rashid (1978;iii) for a similar development at Ajmer.

At present, S.Mohammadhusun Valimiya is chairman of the Trust Committee. One of the functions of the non-*mujawar* members is to be present when the *golakh* is opened. They have to ensure that the donations in it go to the shrine as framed in the scheme. Only a small percentage (about five per cent) goes directly to the *mujawars*. A District Officer also has to be present when the *golakh* is opened. In the various law suits that have taken place between the Charity Commissioner and the *mujawars*, not only were the personal rights of the *mujawars* discussed, but the financial and hygienic aspects of the shrine management were also considered; and this included matters such as investment of gold and silver donations, stock investments, and the improvement of the *dargah* premises. For example, the Charity Commissioner wrote on the occasion of the 1961 revision: 'I visited the shrine and I am constrained to say that hygienic conditions were very poor. . . . There is possibility of epidemics especially during the fair. . . . It is, therefore, necessary that one or two persons of the committee should be other than those (!) who are to share the surplus income . . . (who) are likely to save as much as possible . . . that (the) needs of pilgrims may not be properly attended.'

Law suits are still going on, but it seems that the general scene is set; there is not much change to be expected for the time being. There will be some change, however, when Mohammadhusun's office (*Sajjadanashini*) is taken over by another *mujawar*. Mohammadhusun is a very idealistic person, who certainly has played a positive part in bringing about the atmosphere of tolerance in the shrine.

The Cure

The setting is clear: the Mira Datar Dargah has specialized in helping people who are afflicted with 'madness'. The *dargah* dropped—or never developed—all other functions which are usually associated with Muslim shrines. Its only function is the religious guidance of pilgrims who are seeking social and physical well-being; and the religious healing of those afflicted with some kind of 'psychosis' or 'neurosis'. More precisely, it has a reputation for healing those striken by a *bhut*. Already in the last century Mira Datar Dargah was listed in the *District Gazetteer* as an institution being 'visited by many suffering from epilepsy' (India, 1883:128). We must assume that this was the most known mental disease for many centuries. Therefore, a certain lack of differentiation is forgivable in an old *District Gazetteer*.

The *dargah* attracts 'mad' people from all over India, including Indians from East and South Africa and England. It has the reputation of being a powerful *bhut*-casting institution, the saint's spirit being one of the most powerful exorcists in the country. Mira Datar is a name well-known to the people of the poor quarters of cities like Bombay, Delhi, Ahmedabad, etc. Mira Datar has a widespread reputation as healer of all kinds of 'undefinable' diseases. (It should have a similar reputation among medical anthropologists!) In our interviews we were often struck by the matter-of-factness with which people referred to Mira Datar's widespread reputation. It is completely natural for many of them to cast their western doctors aside and vest the saint with the responsibility for a cure of their illness. It seems that most of the patients are transferred to the *dargah* by a *huqm* from Ajmer or from the Mira Datar Dargah in Bombay.[18] The Bombay *dargah* is more or less a 'walk-in' place, where people cannot stay and nor are they encouraged to do so. Quite different is the *dargah* at Unava. It is a very busy place all day and all the quarters are inhabited. Often we find large families occupying the little quarters where they have

[18] There is another Mira Datar Dargah in Poona (now Pune) which is related to the main *dargah* at Unava in a very interesting manner. The father of B.G. Kachi, who is a furniture contractor at Poona, went some 50 years ago to Unava to have his personal problems solved. He returned to Poona with five cotton horses as relics of the saint. He established a *dargah* in his private courtyard and, though a Hindu, he administered the healing power of Mira Datar as *mujawar* to patients who were afflicted by a *bhut*. Now his grandsons, three elderly men, are in charge of the shrine as *mujawars*. They do not charge anything for treatment since they are well-off financially. The shrine is open to the public from 5 A.M. to 10 P.M. Daily five *nagara* ceremonies are held where drums are beaten and incense is burnt. Most patients react with screams and trances to the rhythmic sound of the drums. The shrine is heavily frequented by both Hindus and Muslims from Poona and its environs.

to do all their hausehold chores. There may be only one family member possessed by a *bhut*, but all of them feel involved and all of them stay on; some for weeks, some for months, and some for years. Those who do not live in the *dargah* or in the *ashram* outside, may live in private quarters in the village.

A Theory of Illness

People who come to the *dargah* as patients must have been faced with the problem that something was wrong with them. They may have stopped functioning properly or might even have been unable to follow their every day routine. Their families might have decided that a healer or doctor be consulted. They might be quite helpless, since their culture does not provide a label for the difficulties they are facing. There is no behaviour pattern they know of to respond to the trouble. In most cases a long search starts for the origin of the unease. Doctors might give names for their disease, but to no avail. Medical terminology might be untranslatable for them, might not fit into their cognitive system. Caught within so much psychic insecurity and dissatisfaction with courses of treatment, the patient might be taken to a *dargah* or another faith healing institution by his relatives who act as a therapy managing group. Since the Mira Datar Dargah's special capacity for healing mental illnesses is recognized by all other *dargahs* in northwestern India, the patient may be sent to Mira Datar's *dargah* by an official from some other *dargah.*

If a young boy in a rural family all of a sudden starts rolling on the ground (see patients: case no. 8) and is no longer able to walk due to fits of hysteria or to an acute stage of psychosis, the whole family is horrified. An intense search for the reasons of this sudden (psychic) accident starts. In the beginning nothing more than an explanation is needed for this happening. The parents of the boy described in case no.8 got some help from constructing their own legend, which remineds us of biblical miracles. When a family suffering from these kinds of symptoms of undefined disease enters the courtyard of the *dargah*, they are offered a *theory of illness.* This theory is based on the concept of magic. This means that some patients have to change their belief system. We experienced this very drastically with a Christian, 'Anglo-Indian' family from Bombay, which has spent most of the last eight years at the *dargah*. The father of the family, who is an allopathic doctor explained the nature of his son's disease (who is severely mentally handicapped) in terms of this (magical) illness theory, which he must have adopted in the *dargah*. He explained to us that his children were given chocolate by his neighbour when both of them were very small. This chocolate was poisoned by magic which resulted in the premature cessation of their mental development. His neighbours had become angry with him because he and his wife did not allow them to use their bathroom in their flat in Bombay. As a revenge these neighbours 'made, what you call a *jatak*. . . . They had sent me one scorpion *jadu*, so I went out of my head', the doctor's wife complained, 'and I felt the trance, because the africa *jadu* was sent on me'. The doctor explained that his neighbours had made a contract with a group of *bhuts* for a period of fifty years during which time they will torture all members of his family in turns. It is interesting to note in this context that the word *jadu*, which in Hindi means 'miracle', is used for 'evil spirit' by the patients in the *dargah*. The doctor and his wife, whose fate it is to have two mentally retarded children (probably due to an organic brain damage), solve their problem by escaping into a magic belief system.

This does not mean that all patients have to change their belief system when they enter the *dargah*. At the time when the psychotic behaviour starts, most of them believe that they noticed some bewitching or malevolent items in their food (black threads, knots, dog's blood) and later on in their stool or blood. Since the magical theory of illness has to be based on a *social conflict theory*, it is believed that a malevolent person of their own social group has mixed the charm into the food. By eating this charm, the body is unprotected and therefore open to lingering spirits (*bhuts*). *Bhuts* are believed to be the roaming souls of unpeacefully deceased persons (suicide, violent death). The symptoms which result from this latent possession are somatic ailments combined with mental disturbance. It is not so much the symptoms themselves which determine the therapy, but the *illness theory* which makes the patients go to some *bhut* exorcist. Nearly everybody inhabiting the courtyard of the Mira Datar Dargah appears to subscribe to the same illness theory no matter what their previous belief system might have been. Patients seem, therefore, to have a curative influence on one another, which is reinforced by the spiritual, semi-conscious interaction between the saint's holy, benevolent spirit and the patient. By the time the saint's spirit has revealed to the patient during trance the cause and social origin of his illness, the patient has reached the final stage of the therapy. The *bhut* has been named and labelled and can therefore be driven out.

The Ritual

After entering the *dargah* the patient is received by the *mujawar*, who will attend on him during his stay in the shrine. For the patient he is the mediator of the healing capacity attributed to Mira Datar. The *mujawar* asks the patient first to tell him something about the nature of his disease. Patients who tend to be aggressive are put into chains. Men are taken to the west side of the *dargah* and their chains are tied to the wall (as described above). Women are left in the courtyard, chains being tied around their feet. For the ritual, men are taken inside the roofed tomb area, where they sit down beside the tomb. Patient and *mujawar* sit opposite each other. The *mujawar* places a red thread into the hand of the patient and recites the following verse:

> *O Datar Baba*
> *O giving father*
> *O look at me*
> *in this assembly*
> *as I am tying this thread*
> *against all of them*
> bhut, palit, cudel, jinnat, jhapadi,
> *who made their seat within me*
> *burn them o father*
> *turn them to ashes*
> *clean my body*

and forever
remove all my difficulties
and suffering

Then the patient is asked to repeat this invocation all by himself. When he has recited the verse, the red thread is taken from his hand and tied to the tomb's fence. All the 'pending' cases of the *dargah* are represented by red threads at the tomb, which amount to quite a large number at a time. After having tied the thread to the tomb, the *mujawar* touches the patient's head three times with a peacock feather. The *mujawar* places the utensils he is using for the ritual between himself and the patient. These utensils are kept in a little box which the *mujawars* always carry with them. There are, besides the peacock feathers, little pieces of papers to write *ta'widhs* on, threads, the Koran and twenty-five small horses made of material and cotton. After the invocation the twenty-five horses are crossed over the head of the patient five times. The *mujawars* told us that the horses symbolize the hundred-and-twenty-five horses of Mira Datar's army and are supposed to fight the evil spirits which are residing inside the patients. There seems to be a shamanistic residue in the ritual which might have some connection with vernacular rites. The ritual effects that the hundred-and-twenty-five horses are sent out to persecute the *bhut*, to fight it and eventually prevent it from going back into the patient's body.

The red thread remains tied to the fence for three days. Then it is removed and the ritual repeated. This may be done again after five or seven days. If the patient does not get better, he is given a *ta'widh* which is taken around the tomb seven times before it is applied. This may be done in the morning and in the evening. The same rituals are used for women. They are, however, not admitted into the interior of the tomb. Therefore, the rituals for women, children and families are performed at any place in the courtyard. The ritual of reciting the verse is applied only to single persons, also the horse ritual, whereas the triple touch of the peacock feathers is also used in group rituals. These may include whole families who accompany a sick relative, or larger groups of pilgrims who gather around the tomb to receive the blessings of the *mujawars*. Group rituals are regularly administered on Thursday evenings, when incense is burnt on the platform of the tower in the south-east corner of the *dargah* (see map). On this occasion, all patients—women and men alike—gather at five o'clock to listen to the *mantras* which are recited by the *mujawars*. After the recital, the whole congregation is blessed and touched three times by the feathers. During this ceremony several patient might fall into a trance or start singing. The whole affair is very noisy and even tumultuous.

The Therapeutic Meaning of the Ritual

The rituals described above are only the initial steps in the patient's therapy. The *mujawars* told us that by means of these rituals they hand the case over to Mira Datar who takes charge of the patient from thereon. The rituals, therefore, initiate the patient's interaction with the saint or, more precisely, the interaction between the saint and the possessing *bhut*. In the beginning of the cure, patients believe that the *bhut* rebels against the saint's influence over them. *Bhuts* sense, they say, that they are going to be expelled and, therefore, they become quite obstinate. 'It often happens that a spirit, in spite of the frequent punishments and castings out, does not leave, or departs but for a moment to at once return. . . the man possessed by one of these stubborn spirits is seen dragged by unwillingly as if by an unseen agent to a post where without any visible cord his hands seem to be bound and he to writhe and rave as if under severe corporal punishment. . . .' (see Bombay, 1883:128 & 1889:610).

On the mental level this 'obstinacy' may reflect the patient's reluctance to undergo the cure—a well known phenomenon in western psychotherapy. This reluctance is manifested ritually by the patient's *inability to approach the interior of the tomb* in the first stage of his therapy. He rationalizes this occurrence by saying that the *bhut* is not allowing him to approach the saint's tomb. Whenever he approaches the tomb he is attacked by his *bhut*, which results in a fit of trance. This means that the closer a patient comes to the tomb, the more likely he is to fall into a trance. Since the case is handed over to the saint by the *mujawar*, it is an unwritten law in the *dargah* that the patients are expected in a way to fall into fits of trance while approaching the tomb, since the trance is an important part of the therapy. The trance represents the interaction of the saint with the *bhut*. If there is to be any progress in the cure, these two have to meet quite often.

The social function of the trance, however, is that it allows the relatives of the patient to listen to all his utterances during a semi-conscious state. So, all of the patients mentioned the 'revelation' they were waiting for. The *bhut*, who takes over the body of the patient might start speaking during the trance; and in this way the identity of the *bhut* might be revealed. But the name of a roaming soul is not enough for a patient who is searching for the social origin of his disease. If he is fortunate, he might also learn about the party which ordered the *bhut* to move into his body. In the case of the doctor which we mentioned above, he heard the name of his neighbours when his wife was in trance and therefore credited them with all his misfortunes.

Patients who feel that a *bhut* moved into their body are in a stage of latent possession. Whenever they fall into trance, their possession becomes manifest. Manifest possession is characterized by a change of the victim's personality: his voice changes, his gestures and his movement are different than before. He is supposed to represent the personality of the possessing *bhut* physically and is simply used as a vessel by the *bhut*. While the patient is acting out his social conflicts in a motoric and psychic excess, he delegates the task of solving the conflict to the *bhut* and the saint. They are in charge of the battlefield. The 'evil' is separated from the patient's person. 'It' is a conflict between the *bhut* and the saint. 'It' has nothing to do with the patient. The relief that the patient thus gets from the realization that he is not to blame for the illness is an important part of the therapy. Thus the courtyard of the *dargah* becomes the psychic battlefield of the patient. The trance provides an opportunity for a scrutiny of the past so as to identify mistakes in the patient's social relationships and enables repressed conflicts to come to the surface of his consciousness. Again, we may note the analogy to western psychotherapy. There is another interesting 'therapeutic trick' provided by the *dargah*. A look at the map of the *dargah* helps us to recall that the king's head is buried a few metres away from Mira Datar's feet. We also recall that the men's wing is situated on the west side of the tomb. When male patients fall into a trance they move back and forth constantly between the saint's grave and the king's head, on which they step violently. While they approach the tomb, they are increasingly molested by the *bhut*; stepping back they feel relief; stepping on the king's (!) head they feel satisfaction.

Women are not admitted to the men's wing. They fall into trance wherever they happen to be, in the courtyard or in their wing. Women may touch one of the relative's graves while being in trance. They are oriented towards the main tomb. Their trance behaviour is different: they kneel, sit or stand while moving back and forth in rhythmic motions. Witnesses agreed that they repeat the movements of sexual intercourse.

We may conclude the description of this psychic battlefield by remarking that even in trance men and women are reduced to their sex-specific social roles.

The Patients: Nine Cases of 'Madness'

Case I

Mr. G.R. is fifty-eight years old. Being a manager in Bombay, he belongs to an upper middle class family. He is Hindu like many patients in the *dargah*. He is married and has thirteen children. He started feeling weak, depressed and hopeless and had a painful burning sensation in the chest twenty-five years ago. He went to see several doctors, but they could not find a somatic disease. Therefore, he visited the Mira Datar Dargah in Bombay. While staying there, his condition improved considerably. For years he had no more somatic complaints except some minor colds or infections. In 1970, his disease started again with the same symptoms. He then took to alcohol and prostitutes which resulted in strong guilt feeling. Doctors again could not find any disease; so he finally decided to visit the Unava *dargah*. For the last seventeen months he has been staying here. Whenever his condition deteriorates, he feels that a *bhut* is entering his body. Then he sits in the *dargah* which makes him feel much better. Even his sleeplessness started bothering him since he started living at the shrine. In his dreams, Mira Datar appears as a doctor or a police inspector, promising him the restoration of his health.

Case 2

Rehmat F. is twenty-eight years old. She is married and has one child. She lives together with her brother who supports her. She has been separated from her husband for the last nine years. Five years ago she began to feel pains and a heavy uneasiness in her body. Suffering from sleeplessness, she went to see a doctor, who did not find any somatic symptoms. At that time she started to loose weight. She is very thin now. Two-and-a-half months ago she came to Mira Datar. Here it was revealed to her that magic was put into her food and that this was responsible for her disturbances. When she approaches the interior of the *dargah* she feels that a strange force is pulling her away from it. For this, a certain magic is responsible which was put into her food. She believes that her in-law's family has given her the magic. She found a black thread in her stool which proves to her that the magic has started to move out of her body.

Case 3

Mohamed H. is sixty-five years old and is a labourer from Bombay. He feels depressed and hopeless. He gave up his job as a coolie two years ago and takes only occasional jobs. This was at the time when his daughter, Naaz, started to show unacceptable traits of behaviour. She mentioned one day that somebody had put magic into her milk. Since then she is not interested in anything and unable to continue to go to school. He has another healthy daughter, who is twenty-three years old and married.

Case 4

Naaz H. is seven years old. She has no somatic complaints. However, she is restless, cannot concentrate and is socially retarded. She had been to hospital two years ago for a period of nine months. The doctors told the parents that due to an organic brain damage she would feel weak and full of anxiety. After she had left the hospital the father took her to the Bombay branch of Mira Datar. For the last six months they have been staying at the *dargah* at Unava. We watched Naaz several times a day when she was in trance.

Case 5

Viswambhar K. is about thirty years old and was a policeman in Aurangabad. He started visiting the *dargah* regularly about five years ago. He had received psychiatric treatment in a hospital in Pune and later on in Bombay. The doctor told him he was possessed by some kind of evil. He heard about the Mira Datar Dargah from a relative and has been staying there for the last four months. He says he was a responsible family member and a reliable worker before his disease broke out two years ago, when he started to beat up people with his gun and to act madly. He believes that magic was put into his *papad*. Now he is waiting for the disclosure (revelation) of his case. He is not married—he said his madness had prevented him from doing so. He has no family to support him, which means he has to depend on begging. He feels a burning sensation in his head, stomach and chest, especially in the later part of the day. When he approaches the shrine he feels that he is being pulled away by a magical force.

Case 6

Muhammed M. is an unmarried young man from Madras. He began to feel a heavy painful pressure on his chest and permanent sleeplessness six years ago when he was working as a taxi driver. He went to see a doctor who did not find bodily symptoms. He went to Ajmer, where he received the *huqm* to go to the Mira Datar Dargah at Unava. He feels possessed by a *bhut* which looks like a human skeleton constantly pulling out his tongue at him. He believes that this *bhut* makes him unable to work; whenever he tries to do so he afflicts him with pain. His family lives in Madras and he has a good relationship with all of them.

Case 7

Ismail A. is thirty-seven years old, is married and comes from Bombay. We find him chained to the entrance pole of the *dargah*. He started visiting Mira Datar ten years ago to offer prayers when he was still in good health. Now he has been here for the last six months. Three years ago he started having headache and fever. Before this he was able to support himself and his wife. He was earning up to Rs. 200.00 a month. It was difficult for him to maintain a conversation. He was taken to the shrine by his brothers; now his cousin is with him.

Case 8

L. is thirteen years old and comes from a village near Udaipur in Rajasthan. Several months ago the boy started showing abnormal behaviour. After an attack of hiccups in the morning, he lost his speech and his ability to walk. He started rolling on the ground and, so said his parents, eventually rolled under his bed. There he knocked four times on the wall and when he opened his hand a little round ball, covered with threads, appeared. Since he had lost his speech, he made signs that the little ball should be ignited. The parents did what he wanted them to do and after setting fire to the ball it is said to have exploded, accompanied by a loud bang, and burnt to ashes. After the explosion the boy rolled out of the house and dug a pit about eight inches deep in front of the house in which he put the ashes of the ball. He remained in this condition for two months. Then the family took him to the shrine. Seven days after his arrival he started, according to his parents, to recover from his loss of speech and asked for tea. After a further eight days he was able to walk. It was revealed to the family that an uncle was responsible for the magic which had done harm to the boy. At the time of the interview the boy did not show any signs of disturbed behaviour.

Case 9

Padma P. is thirteen years old. Her parents work in a cotton mill near Bombay. She is the fifth of six children and is accompanied by her mother. She is the one of the only patients mentioned here who did not see an allopathic doctor before coming to the shrine. When we saw her first she was in trance and we were able to record the following text which she screamed out loudly, while tossing her head to the ground and shaking in a rhythmic pattern:

(The original text is in Gujarati).
"*O master today my death of complete dying has approached*
O master my whole life is ruined
O Mira today my age of 45 is ruined
O master I haven't given the blood of sinner to drink
O master today I got blood from the crematorium to drink
O Mira today I got to drink the black blood of a dog
O Mira what remains today are the skulls from the crematorium
O master 18 humans I was feeding along
O king of kings the world of the 6 humans is destroyed
O Mira life of 18 humans is ruined
O master you made me useless for my life
today you have ruined the life of your questioner
today you have ruined me completely
O master
O Mira the destroyer of the questioner's life
O Mira you have ruined today so much
(the same five times)

O master emperor
O master Mira
O Allah of Medina
O Mira, if you say so, I swear on Qu'ran Sharif
O master Ali, this is your main conspiracy
O Mira the whole life is ruined

O Mira, the whole life is ruined
O Mira my age is 35 years
O Mira my name is Malta Yashwant Dargarkar
O master Ali, my room number is three
Ulhas Nagar is my village
O Mira, I am a resident of Goa
O Mira, she is for 24 hours either to wander or to stay with
O Mira, for 22 years goes this profession of prostitution
O Mira, today each and every girl was for sale up to 50,000 rupees
(the same . . .)

O master Ali, this account of prostitution is running since 22 years
O Mira your conspiracy is too much
O Master the son of destruction has caught me
O Mira this son of a Marwari has got me caught
O Mira, now you have recognized the son of the questioner
O Mira now you have seen me
O Mira you have recognized the account of my prostitution
O Master, this 22-year old account of prostitution of mine
O Mira, each girl is to be sold up to 50,000 rupees
O master, so is the girl, so is the money
my thousands of lakhs of rupees are burnt up on a fire
O Mira, you have brought my death of full dying
O master emperor, today you brought the day of my full dying brought the time of my ruin
O Mira, today I had to drink your dirty water again and again today I should be doomed, o master.

She repeatedly recited this text for about one hour in a shrieking and hoarse voice while moving her body in the rhythmic pattern of the verse.

Padma's mother told us that the shrine had appeared to her in a dream whereupon she took her daughter to the Mira Datar Dargah. Now they have stayed here for the last twelve months. Only from her 'song' they have learned that the magic, to which they ascribe the illness of the girl, was given by an individual named Malta Yashwant Dargarkar. The illness of the girl started with aggressive fits so that she had to be tied with chains to a pole in the shrine when she first arrived. In the first few weeks she sometimes went into as many as four trances in a day. Now it is down to one or two trances in the evening. She feels that her health has improved during her stay at Mira Datar's. Only stomachaches and headaches are left.

Diseases, Miracles and Bhuts

It is interesting to note that all the patients, except one, had seen an allopathic doctor, and even a psychiatrist in some cases, before they had come to the *dargah*. Obviously most of them suffered from a disease which would be treated in a psychiatric hospital had they been living in a western country. If one applies the International Classification of Diseases (ICD) devised by the WHO, these patients would be classic psychiatric cases. In this context, one may ask how a western psychiatrist would judge the healing capacity of the shrine.

As I mentioned above, there are two mechanisms to which the therapeutic effect of the shrine may be attributed. In severe cases, like a psychotic fit, which affects the structure of a whole family, people turn to miracles and build up legends which fit into their cognitive system. This helps them to adapt to the new situation and gives them a feeling of psychic security. Especially for chronic diseases, it is true that the *dargah* has a palliative effect. For smaller disturbances like neuroses and hysterical cases, however, the curing effect is achieved by the culture-specific illness theory: the possession by a *bhut*.

Bibliography

Bombay, Government of (1883), *Gazetteer of the Bombay Presidency*, Vol. VII, Baroda, Superintendent of Government Printing.

———, (1889), *Gazetteer of the Bombay Presidency*, Vol. IX, part II, Gujarat Population Musalmans and Parsis, Baroda, Superintendent of Government Printing.

Commissariat, M.S. (1938), *A History of Gujarat*, Vol. 1, Bombay, Longmans.

Haig, W. (1965), *The Cambridge History of India*, Vol. 3, New Delhi, S. Chand & Co.

India, Government of (1975), *Gazetteer of India: Mehsana District, Gujarat State,* Ahmedabad.

Mujeeb, M. (1967), *The Indian Muslims,* London, George Allen and Unwin.

Nawali, S.A. and C.N. Seddon (1928), *Mirat-i-Ahmadi,* Supplement, Baroda, Oriental Institute.

Pfleiderer-Becker, B. and V. Dharamsey (1978), *Materialien zur Ethnomedizin,* Bensheim, Kiibelstiftung.

Pfleiderer-Becker, B., and B. Ludwig (1978), Merkmale traditionellen Heilens in Gujarat, *Internationales Asienforum, 1.*

Rashid, S.K. (1978), *Waqf Administration in India,* Delhi, Vikas Publishihg House.

Shah, Z.H.S.G. (1977), *The Life and Teachings of Khwaja Moinuddin Hasan Chisti,* Ajmer, Asma Publications.

Schwerin, Kerrin Grafin V. (1978), 'Functions and Sources of Income of Muslim Dargahs in India', Paper presented at the VIth European conference on Modern South Asian Studies held at Paris, June 10-16, 1978.

Glossary

acar, rule or custom.

adat, custom, usage, customary law.

alam, standard.

asthana, a sacred structure, a shrine or grave of one or more saints but without the bodies of the saints being buried there.

azan, call to prayers.

Bakar Id, festival to commemorate Abraham's (Ibrahim's) offering to sacrifice his son Isaac (Ismail).

Bara Wafat, literally twelve days of sickness leading to death, hence also the name of the festival marking the sickness and death of Prophet Muhammad.

basant, spring season, so-called because of the predominance of mustard blooms in the fields.

basanti, bright yellow.

Bhagwan, Hindu word for God.

bhasa, language.

bhut, wandering spirit, restless soul of a murdered person.

bisram, rest.

burqa, loose garment covering the entire body and having veiled openings for the eyes, worn by Muslim women.

chaddar, covering, including shawl, mantle or sheet.

chillum, tobacco-cum-fire bowl, earthen pot used for smoking tobacco.

dargah, shrine.

derwesh, Sufi teacher, Muslim mendicant.

desh, country, region or locality.

dharma, the proper way of life, righteousness; duty prescribed by the sacred literature.

dhoti, loin cloth.

din, faith, religion (usually only with reference to Islam; *mazhab* is the more general word meaning religion.
doli, palanquin.
dua, private prayer.
duldul, clay horse commemorating Imam Hussain's horse.
fatiha, an offering to God, the Prophet or a Muslim saint, so-called because the first chapter of the Koran called surah fatiha is usually read as part of the ritual.
golakh, donation box.
gotra, a Hindu clan tracing descent from a common ancestor, usually a saint or sage.
hadith, report of a statement the Prophet is alleged to have made.
hafiz, one who can recite the Koran by heart.
hajj, pilgrimage, one of the religious duties of Muslims.
hakim, a practitioner of Graeco-Arab medicine.
haram, forbidden in Islam.
haveli, mansion.
hijara, eunuch.
hookah, water-pipe or 'hubble bubble', a popular form of smoking in rural areas.
hujra. cell.
Id, festival, holy day ; there are several Ids, for instance *Id-ul-fitr* and *Id-ul-Zuha*, or *bakar-Id*.
Idgah, place where *Id* prayers are held.
Id-ul-fitr, festival marking the end of Ramadan.
Itar, perfume.
jadu, black magic.
jagir, landed estate.
jati, the effective endogamous unit in the caste system.
jibbah, garment.
jizya, capitation tax.
jummah, Friday, a day considered auspicious by Muslims.
kafir, misbeliever.
kalima, Muslim attestation of faith.
kar, work or occupation.
karkun, civil servant.
Karma, the law of action and causality.
kasb, skill.
khadim, literally a servant, hence also the keeper of a shrine.

khandan, a group of families bearing a common name and enjoying more or less similar social status ; a non-exogamous kin group of four to five generation's depth.
khanqah, Muslim hospice.
kola gor, family priest.
kurs, Tamil Muslim word foi *urs*.
kurta, long shirt.
lathi, bamboo stick.
leylatu-i-miraj, the day the Prophet was invited to heaven.
lingam, phallic symbol.
lungi, sarong-like garment worn by men.
maatam, mourning.
madarsah, Islamic school.
maduli, amulet.
maktab, karanic school, usually attached to a mosque.
mannat, vow.
mansabdar, noble.
mantra, incantation.
masjid, mosque, Muslim house of prayer.
maulood, religious discourse, usually by recitation, held to commemorate the birth anniversary of the Prophet as well as on other social occasions.
mela, fair.
mercia, a poem of mourning, especially lamenting the massacre of Hussain and his companions.
milad-e-nabi, Prophet's birthday.
milap, meeting, reunion.
mlechcha, lowly, an outsider.
moharram, the festival to commemorate the tragedy of Kerbala.
moulut, book commemorating the Prophet, hence also a recitation in praise of the Prophet.
moulvi, Koranic college degree-holder, usually a priest.
mufti, a person learned in the Koran and Hadith and in Muslim works of law.
mujawar, keeper of a shrine.
mumin, believer.
murid, disciple or devotee.
mushaira, recitation of poetry.
namaskar, Hindu greeting.

namaz, prayer, the Islamic form of worship supposed to be performed five times daily.

nupak, impure.

naqara, large drum.

nari, umblical cord, nerve.

nazrana, offering.

para, neighbourhood.

pawati, mother-to-be.

pesh imam, one who leads at prayers in a mosque.

pir, saint.

pirzada, lit. a descendant of a Pir; hence also a custodian of a shrine.

preta, wandering spirits.

purdah, veiling of women.

qadam-e-sharif, Prophet's footprints.

qawwali, devotional singing.

quom, lit. nation, in colloquial Urdu the effective endogamous units in the Muslim social system.

Ramadan, the ninth month of the Islamic calendar: the daily fast from dusk until sunset that is rigidly enjoined during the month.

roti, hard-baked cakes made from cream of wheat.

roza, fast.

sajjadanashin, a spiritual superior at a mosque or religious endowment such as a shrine.

salam, greeting.

samaj, society.

sawar, rider.

shab-e-barat, a kind of All Soul's Day.

shahid, a martyr.

shastra, Hindu litturgical literature.

shirk, idolatory or the sin of establishing associates to God.

silsilah, a Sufi order.

stri-acars, married women's rituals.

tabarruk, blessed food.

tasha, a flat drum with a metallic base.

tacwidh, amulet.

tazziya, a representation or model of the tomb of Hassan and Hussain.

thali, metal tray.

topi, cap.
umma, universal Muslim brotherhood.
upanayana, sacred thread.
urs, marriage, hence also the anniversary of a saint's death which is regarded as his union with God.
ustad, teacher.
varna, classification of Hindu society which places all castes into four major categories, viz., Brahman, Kshatriya, Vaishya and Sudra.
wali, protector.
yajaman, patron.
zakat, the compulsory tithe, which is one of the five pillars of Islam.
zat, Urdu equivalent of *jati*.
ziyarat, pilgrimage.

Index